To
Mary and Hal Ottaway
with best wishes and many
fond memories of happy
days we shared in
the land down under —
Sincerely
Anne Clark

April 2ⁿᵈ, 1970.

Australian Adventure
LETTERS FROM AN AMBASSADOR'S WIFE

Ambassador and Mrs. Edward Clark

Australian Adventure

LETTERS FROM AN AMBASSADOR'S WIFE

by Anne Clark

FOREWORD BY DAME ZARA HOLT

UNIVERSITY OF TEXAS PRESS, AUSTIN & LONDON

Standard Book Number 292-70001-6
Library of Congress Catalog Card Number 73-97905
© 1969 by Anne Clark

Printed by The University of Texas Printing Division, Austin
Bound by Universal Bookbindery, Inc., San Antonio

To my own H.E. who took me along for company

FOREWORD

When Anne Clark asked me to write a foreword for her book I was delighted for many reasons.

Firstly, because I feel that her letters from Australia will make my country more "real" to many people who have never had the opportunity to visit us, and also because I feel that the bonds of affection between Anne and myself have now been strengthened, when time and distance might have faded them a little.

I think, also, that Anne's warm and feminine approach to life and her strong love for her friends and family will shine through and illuminate her letters, which because of her position as the wife of one of America's most beloved Ambassadors to Australia must grow in interest as time goes by.

I would like to congratulate Anne on keeping alive a little piece of history.

DAME ZARA HOLT, D.B.E.

October, 1968

CONTENTS

ILLUSTRATIONS

Australian Adventure

LETTERS FROM AN AMBASSADOR'S WIFE

INTRODUCTION

June days in Texas are always warm. Certainly, June 10, 1965, was typical. We drove back from East Texas to Austin, a distance of 250 miles, with our granddaughter Margaret Wynn. She was eight years old. I'd just finished an interesting project, remodeling and furnishing my white cottage on Straddlefork Farm, ten miles from my husband's birthplace in San Augustine, Texas. It is a dear little saddlebag cottage, first built in 1835, rebuilt with the old timbers in 1875, and lately completely restored by ourselves. The first running water was put into the house and, thanks to the Rural Electrification Authority, it gained heating and air conditioning. Two days before, more than two hundred friends had gathered to see the unveiling of the Medallion that had been placed on the cottage by the Texas State Historical Association in recognition of its historical interest. We had speeches, fried chicken, and watermelon, and as we closed the house that day we expected to return often for leisurely visits when we would complete the decoration and the garden. It was the realization of a dream we had long cherished.

But things didn't work out quite that way. As we opened the door of our house in Austin the phone rang loud and harshly. It was my husband's secretary, the same Mrs. O'Donnell who faithfully typed and mailed the letters that follow. Her message was, "The White House has been calling urgently all day." Soon Edward was in touch with a Presidential aide who said that President Johnson wished him to take the next plane to Washington and to bring his wife. It took a bit of arranging to store little Maggie with friends, cancel appointments, pack, and get off.

When we reached The President's House (I call it that because the table silver is marked so), we received word that Sir Robert Menzies,

Prime Minister of Australia, was in the Capital. After conferring with Mr. Johnson, his words were, "Mr. President, we have been too long without an Ambassador. Send us an old friend, send us a Texan." To which the President said he replied, "Sir Robert, I'll have a man here tonight for you. If you like him, he's yours." At first sight, the Prime Minister fancied the future envoy, and the deal was made. Edward was immensely impressed with Sir Robert, and thus began a lasting, rewarding friendship. Much pro-and-con discussion took place the next evening at a gay party aboard the Presidential yacht on the Potomac River.

All was not completely simple. We didn't depart in ten days, as the President had first suggested. It was two months before the hearings of the Foreign Relations Committee of the United States Senate and the vote of confirmation took place. Much rearranging had to be done in our private lives, also. The house we'd lived in for twenty years was sold. It was there our daughter had grown up; down its stairs she had walked as a bride. There the lawn and the ivy and the iris had been my preoccupation for nearly half my life. The furnishings were divided between my daughter, my nieces, Straddlefork, and storage. Suddenly, the newspapers wanted to interview me, as well as the Ambassador Designate, even by long-distance telephone from Australia. A wardrobe for winter in the Southern Hemisphere had to be assembled. This took a bit of managing in Texas in midsummer.

But somehow we made it to Washington by August 10. At the State Department we had immunizations and briefings. A hundred friends came from Texas to our farewell party. It was a barbecue catered by the President's favorite, Walter Jetton, given by the Texas State Society, and attended by a thousand persons.

Then suddenly we were on our way, and my pleasure and amazement began to cool somewhat. I realized it was 10,000 miles that I was putting between myself and my child, my mother, and the friends of a lifetime. I was on the roller coaster and there was no getting off. The letters that follow tell the story of my Australian adventure. My fond and interested friends and relatives at home knew lots of distinguished and famous people, but an Ambassador was something new in their lives. Australia was a sort of mythological land with its kanga-

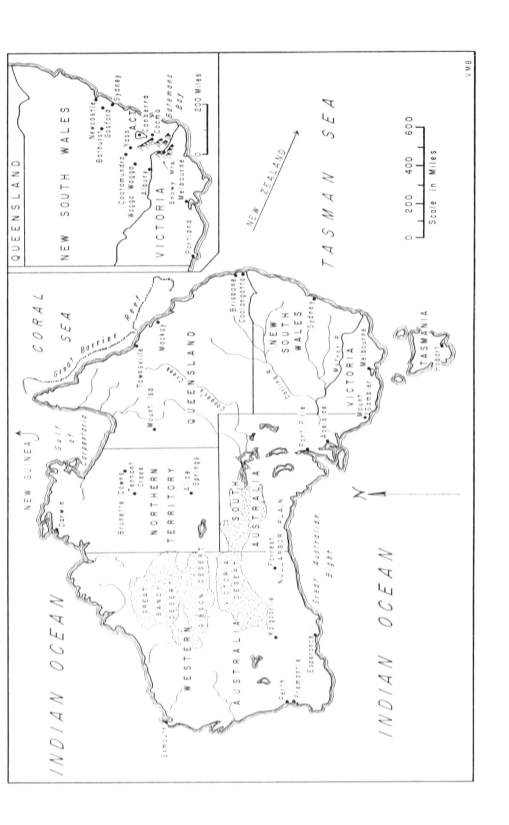

VMB

roos, aborigines, and diggers. I soon found it impossible to write everyone separately in the elaborate detail they'd wish. Besides answering
their desire for information, I myself had a compulsive need for a con-
fidante. I had not a single friend. Edward was far too busy in his new
work to listen to me marvel at my experiences. Thus, out of my need
to share these new interests and the most flattering curiosity of friends
at home, this collection of letters came into being. In them you may
read the story of how I changed my pace and found an exciting new
world in the sky, land, and water "down under."

Addresses and remarks are included because they reflect the interest
that the Australians had in us as Americans. Several schedules of official visits are also included to show the many details governed by
protocol.

We served from August 15, 1965, to February 1, 1968. Edward
traveled over 400,000 miles in and near Australia. He is such a robust,
eager traveler. Though I did not go with him every mile, I feel as if I
had. Meeting and entertaining Australians were our two biggest as-
signments. The guest book at the Residence held two thousand names
when we farewelled the continent.

My grateful appreciation goes to many people, the first of whom is
President Lyndon Johnson, who gave to us the rare privilege of serving
our country in that happy southern land. Bless him now and forever
for his perceptive matching of two Texans to a country that understood them. My gratitude goes also to my friends back home, who read
the missives and wrote pertinent replies, inspiring me to keep at the
project of recording my experiences. My friends Dorothy and Paul
Bolton gave me the benefit of their professional skills in the revision of
the letters for publication. Lastly, I am humbly grateful for the pa-
tience, skill, and drudgery that dear Mrs. O'Donnell, my husband's
secretary in Austin, contributed. It was she who typed and multiplied
the letters in the first place from hastily scrawled scripts, and who re-
typed them several times again when I reviewed them. Without her,
they could never have seen light.

A.M.C.
Austin, Texas

THE LETTERS

The Residence
Canberra, Australia
August 17, 1965

Mrs. D. C. Wynn
1130 Arnold Avenue
Greenville, Mississippi

Dear Leila:

We arrived in Australia early on Sunday morning, after spending two nights in Admiral Sharp's guesthouse in Hawaii. Admiral U. S. G. Sharp, Commander in Chief in the Pacific, is a direct descendant of General U. S. Grant. We also spent one night in Nadi, Fiji. The time changes took a terrible toll of me. We lost a whole day; luckily it was Friday the thirteenth. I was not as overwhelmed by the beauty of Hawaii as I had expected to be. The Rio Grande Valley has almost the same flowers and tropical verdure; it just lacks the blue Pacific and the mountains.

When I stepped off the plane in Sydney, it was a cold day in August. This is normal for the Southern Hemisphere. A nice lady pushed into my hands a nosegay of Australian orchids and daphne. All day I clung to them, bewitched, bothered, and bewildered. Much later, I learned that her name was Anne Clark, too. I had changed into a wool suit between Nadi and Sydney. In Sydney we were met by the Deputy Chief of Mission, Jack Lydman (known in State Department parlance as the D.C.M.), and his lovely wife, Jodie.*

At Canberra all the Embassy people were at the airport to greet us. Remembering the recent heat of Washington, I was startled at the sight of the children in red hoods and mittens. At the Residence we were welcomed by the household staff, Huang, Foo, Ming, and Ching. Huang is the impeccable major-domo, a charming Cantonese whose

---

*Jack Lydman was named Ambassador to Malaysia in July 1969.

name is pronounced "Wong." The house was filled with early spring flowers, especially long sprays of orchids from Dame Mabel Brookes, the President's friend in Melbourne, and lovely spring blooms, daffodils and tulips, from Wendy and Sant Perry of San Augustine.

The Residence is a handsome, white-columned, red-brick Georgian building, situated on a grassy hillside. It has five bedrooms, a black-and-white marble foyer, a drawing room, a dining room, paneled library, central heat, and five fireplaces. *Gone with the Wind* could have been filmed right here. A fine winding staircase leads to the upstairs rooms. For ourselves, we appropriated one large bedroom with a smaller connecting one. The big master bedroom has twin beds, three bedside tables, two highboys, one dresser, one high chest, a sofa, two overstuffed chairs with a low table in between, two desks, and a seven-light chandelier. This house seems to have every piece of furniture that is listed in the Williamsburg Craft House Catalogue, including twenty-four dining-room chairs, and a $1,200 desk in my bedroom. Mrs. Lydman brought her Chinese maid, Ah Foo, to unpack me. She's only four feet tall and wears a little suit of black pants and white blouse. Ah Foo arranged my lingerie in the drawers and made a bouquet by colors of my hose. All of our six footlockers were here save one. In its place was substituted a pasteboard box addressed to someone in Tokyo. I first thought perhaps it was my name in Japanese. The only crucial thing in the missing trunk is the Ambassador's cutaway, which he must wear when he presents his credentials.

A series of coffees and teas was arranged for me by Jodie Lydman so that I might meet the staff. About twenty-five came to each gathering. They were all warned not to stay over forty minutes. This morning the gardeners, drivers, and maintenance personnel came. All were shined and polished and in white shirts, coats, and ties. I think I may have achieved my life-long ambition, that is, to have a personal plumber.

Monday your father had me walk over to the Embassy (Chancery) with him to meet the staff. I think my presence gave him some support, like carrying a fan that occupies the nervous hands, or as Jack Benny

has Rochester to be the straight man. At eleven, we had photographers
and pressmen at the Residence. Finally, I had a few minutes to fuss
with the house, arranging flowers and deploying the granddaughters'
pictures and objects I had brought in my trunk. I felt rewarded when
Jodie Lydman came in saying, "Your signature is already on the
house." She is so competent that she quite intimidates me. They won't
be here for long. Soon they will go to a new assignment in Jakarta.
I shall miss them both.

Your father won't ring the bells himself. He still shouts, "Honey!!"
and I have to run about this huge house looking for him until Huang
appears to say, "Ambassador upstairs." Huang really tries to please me
and has done up a small table for our meals *à deux* in a corner of the
dining room. We have candles and finger bowls even when we are
alone. The Ambassador comes home to lunch.

By the way, those bedspreads are as tacky as they appeared in the
photographs. They are too short and faded as well.

Love,
Mother

The Residence
Canberra, Australia
August 18, 1965

Mrs. John D. Clark
San Augustine
Texas

Dear Mamma,

I trust you have already had some news of us through Leila.
The trip out was ghastly because we were so exhausted from our
festive departure in Washington. This is a new world, a new climate,
even a new language, for, though it's still English, it's not the deep

East Texas kind. There are new flowers and birds, animals, and even new stars. The food prepared by our Chinese chef, Ching, is delicious. Last night we had a wonderful clear soup with the thinnest slivers of vegetables, a marvelous cheese soufflé, and a green salad. His salad dressings are too bland for our taste.

We had a very pleasant visit in New York with Exa Bell Sublette Gray, whose husband, Harold, is president of Pan American Airlines. Then we learned in Hawaii, as we arrived, that their son had been killed in Vietnam. It was the first death there of a young American with whom I had any connection. Now I feel that the war really is here.

I will try to tell about our life here, but, honestly, I am stretched just to keep going, and I fear that long letters will be the first thing I have to X out of my life.

Fondly,
Anne

The Residence
Canberra, Australia
August 20, 1965

Mrs. Kay Graham, President
The Washington Post
1515 L Street, N.W.
Washington, D.C.

Dear Kay:

Just ten days ago, we departed Washington City and ten hours later deplaned in Honolulu, where we were met by our own Navy brass and all the traditional Hawaiian flower welcome. Our stay there provided just the kind of relaxation we needed after a busy week in New York with the so-called financial community and whatever you call the people in Washington, including the State Department.

At the Department, Ed had two days of official briefings by Navy, Air Force, and Army officials. Each lasted several hours and he says nowhere was there repetition or redundancy—absolutely the most efficient, concise, and useful presentations he has ever seen. Frankly, there have been times, he says, when, as a self-assumed, overburdened taxpayer (in his own thinking), he has felt a bit cynical about misuse of our funds and doubtful of the capacity of our armed services personnel. They have, however, won him over and now he finds himself singing their praises far, wide, and often.

The Embassy is beautiful colonial Williamsburg in design, set on ten acres, with just a few steps between the Residence and the Chancery. The staffs, both domestic and official, are marvels of efficiency and are most eager to be helpful to us in getting started on the right path.

The Ambassador will not officially present his credentials until August 23, so we are using this week to make and receive some unofficial calls and visit about the Chancery offices with the personnel. While they have not been counted, there must be approximately one hundred members on the staff. Yesterday the Ambassador called on the Minister for External Affairs and on Wednesday received the Malaysian High Commissioner. This gentleman actually lives in Singapore, but no longer represents that government. Singapore and Malaysia recently dissociated their governments, and will soon have separate High Commissioners.

We had TV for breakfast the other day, and I did an unrehearsed and unplanned tour of the Residence. The official Australian Broadcasting people came this morning and did Ed over in his office. We have an understanding with them that none of this will be used until after the Ambassador has presented his credentials.

I am quite overwhelmed with the curiosity and really friendly interest the Australians show in us. I hope we can make it carry over into matters of more importance than our personal lives. There is a great opportunity here, which Ed hopes to make the most of. We are deeply moved by this totally new look at wider horizons. Ed says he perceives problems he had never dreamed of and we both love our country more sincerely—all of its corners from Maine to Texas—than ever before.

All of this is only a prelude to extending to you an invitation to visit "your home away from home" in Canberra. It is a wonderful country and I know you would take home a keen perception of our mission here, as well as help carry the word.

With all good wishes and the high hope that we will soon hear from you that you are on your way to Canberra, I remain

Sincerely,
Anne Clark

The Residence
Canberra, Australia
August 21, 1965

Mrs. George Bolton*
Seton Hospital
Austin, Texas, U.S.A.

Dear Mrs. Bolton, Paul, and Dolly,

I address this letter to all of you because time and arm muscles don't permit me to write separate letters to everyone to whom I would like to pour out my impressions and thoughts. My consolation is that since I don't have to see this whole continent in four weeks, as Dolly and I did Europe, I don't have to knock myself out this week.

The trip here by United Airlines, Pan Am, Qantas, and the final lap on the Embassy's own Convair, was an experience in itself. Going out to Honolulu, we were served two lunches on United (exactly the same —lamb chops). The rapid passage from one time zone to another

---

* Mrs. Bolton, Paul's mother, died on September 6, 1965.

plays havoc with both my sleep pattern and my appestat. Pearl Harbor and the memorial over the battleship *Arizona* made my heart throb. Everyone wears muumuus, beginning with the stewardesses on the airlines. They are so bright and so easy fitting, though some are quite intricately cut, that I'd like to transplant the costume. Then, with small effort, we could be fashionable, comfortable, pretty, and economical.

Ed thought the briefings he received in Hawaii on defense matters were superb. They generated in him new respect for the armed services and their officers.

The arrival in Australia was made exciting by so many photographers, reporters, and "just people" who met us. It's hard to believe *that* many people care! Even the glamorous French Alphands couldn't generate this much interest in Austin, Texas. I have been so eager to oblige that I let myself be trapped into doing an unrehearsed, unplanned (I hadn't even been to the hairdresser) TV tour of the Residence, just like Jackie Kennedy. In fact, twice, once for a Sydney station and once for ABC (*A* for Australia). I miss my board of advisors, as I call my long-time Austin friends who take all my problems to their hearts. Here I have only Mrs. Lydman, the wife of Ed's deputy. She is lovely, capable, and very correct. She addresses me as "Ma'am" in front of people and tells me that I must always refer to "The Ambassador" to Huang, Foo, Ming, Ching, and Miss Fleming. I am afraid the old boy may get ideas of glory. They call me "The Madam." The most ubiquitous bird in the garden is the magpie, same as the European blackbird. I wake to his or her cooing each morning, a melodious sound.

Fondly,
Anne

The Chancery
United States Embassy
Canberra, Australia
August 21, 1965

Mr. W. W. Lynch*
Texas Power & Light Company
P. O. Box 6331
Dallas, Texas

Dear Bill:

You will never know how pleased we were to have your darling Marty with us in Washington. We readily understood that you were overwhelmed by an accumulation of your work while you had been in Europe. I also know that your public relations absolutely required you to come to Washington with the Trinity River Improvement Group.

First, I want to thank you for your letter, which arrived just at the right time to keep me from feeling a little bit lonely and neglected, longing for news from home. I give the electric industry "A" grade because in the same mail I had a letter from Beeman Fisher, in which he sent me a "whole passel" of Texas clippings concerning my appointment and our leave-taking from the United States. I got both of the letters very quickly at the Residence, since the Chancery is closed on Saturdays. Anne and I had a real feast looking at the pictures of our country house and reading the clippings. I must give both you and Beeman an "A+" for being my best correspondents.

Seven days in Canberra find me rather eager to share some of my small experiences with friends like you back home. Frankly, I guess I am a little homesick, not being able to do those things to which I had become so accustomed during the past quarter of a century; I mean simply to pick up the telephone, call one of my good friends, and talk about whatever seemed to be very interesting and important at the moment. I remember some most pleasant and inspiring chats that I

* This letter, on which the Ambassador and I collaborated, contains interesting information and reactions not recorded elsewhere.

have had with you over the telephone, for a half-hour many times.

As Marty told you, we left Washington at 10:30 A.M. on Tuesday, August 10. Many of our Texas friends saw us off from the Carlton Hotel. At the airport, to wish us Godspeed, were Federal Judge and Mrs. Eugene Worley, formerly of Shamrock, Texas. We were both surprised and pleased that the Australian Ambassador to the United States and Mrs. Waller were there. We changed planes in Los Angeles and arrived in Honolulu at 3:00 P.M. that same day, but the elapsed flight time had been ten hours.

We were met in Honolulu by Admiral U. S. G. Sharp and other Navy and Army brass and given the traditional flower-lei and music welcome. We spent two days in Honolulu and were entertained in Admiral Sharp's guesthouse. My briefings from the military in Honolulu were superb. They gave me new respect for our armed services. One day we lunched at the Royal Hawaiian Hotel with the Sheraton manager, Mr. Richard Holtzman, who served in the Army not only at Paris, Texas, but also at San Angelo, where he took unto himself a beautiful Texas girl for his bride. I did not see any Hula dancers, but I did see some mighty pretty American girls. I hasten to say that I only took a fleeting glance, but I can report they were well covered by muumuus, not grass skirts!

After two days, we went on to Nadi, Fiji Islands, for an overnight stop. It is primitive but interesting. For some reason, unknown to me, all the plane arrivals and departures there are between midnight and dawn. We departed at 4:30 A.M. and the airport was teeming with people, just like Love Field in Dallas at high noon. At Nadi, we changed to Qantas Empire Airways and flew to Sydney, where we were met by our Counselor and Deputy Chief of Mission, Mr. Jack Lydman, and his wife; we then boarded our own Air Force plane, a Convair piloted by Colonel Tex Burns, a graduate of Texas A & M University and a native of Port Arthur, Texas. His wife, Phyllis, is a Fort Worth girl. Tex is the CINCPAC representative here.

The flight from Sydney to Canberra was only forty minutes. We arrived in a cold winter rain and found practically all the Embassy staff, wives, and children out there to meet us. It was hard to believe that not only the press, radio, and television, but also the Australian people were so intensely interested in our arrival. Beginning with the moment our plane set down, we have been overwhelmed by reporters, photographers, and TV cameras—all seeming extremely interested and friendly. Because I regard cooperation as my job, we have submitted to it all in the best humor possible. I only hope the Australians will not tire of reading about us, because if all the material is printed that has been written it will fill a Sunday supplement.

Canberra is the kind of beautiful city that Washington must have been when it was young—before old Andy Jackson built the Treasury Building where he stuck his stick into the ground, thus ruining the perfect plan. The Embassy is magnificient. The United States provides well for its representatives. The Embassy grounds comprise ten acres and contain the Residence, the Chancery, and a second house for another staff family; presently, the Political Counselor occupies it. I am enjoying the luxury of going home to lunch for the first time in my life, for it is only a few steps from the Chancery to the Residence. The service and food provided by our Chinese domestic staff are un-excelled. In fact, our life is so good that I am eager to show off for our old friends who knew us when! When do you think you and Marty can arrange to come? Soon it will be spring and I will by then be prepared to discourse on the country's unusual flora and fauna.

I am really serious about the invitation I extend. Somehow, I think that you two are among the few of those close friends who would have a real interest in being with us for quite a little spell. I here and now promise you soft beds, good food, excellent service, and, above all, I will make the price right for you at the expense of the United States official taxpayer!

Anne joins me in sending our affectionate regards to you and Marty.

Your friend,
Edward Clark

The Residence
Canberra, Australia
August 28, 1965

Dear Leila:

Saturday is the day of rest here. The office and everything else closes. I think about my favorite comment by Satchel Paige, "The social ramble ain't restful."

Last night we hosted our first black-tie dinner for the P.M., the Minister for External Affairs, the Minister of Defense, and our faithful supporters, Jack and Jodie—a total of ten people. In spite of Elizabeth Hutchinson's quick short course in diplomatic etiquette, I still find myself painfully unsure, and often blunder. However, I don't think Sir Robert and Dame Pattie care a flip. Sir Robert's greeting to me was, "Your husband has told me of your *brilliant* comment on the mountebank, Smith." You know, your father does often put words in my mouth. What he said I said was that the man in question had lots of useless information.

I really feel that I am beginning to make headway with the house. For awhile I thought the ladies' powder room was the only room small enough for me to conquer. It's like a small parlor with the plumbing hidden in another small room. Jodie introduced me to the Chelsea Antique Shop and I have bought some badly chipped but effective Crown Derby plates for the dining-room mantelpiece and a nice brass fender for only twenty dollars. My slogan is get the most effect for the least money. There are no nice flower containers or centerpieces for the table. We make shift with candles surrounded by small blooms in finger bowls. I used my Danish Christmas spoons for dessert last night and my own monogrammed napkins. Everyone loved the spoons. I'll be glad when the things I had shipped by surface come, especially my pictures. I can't abide the ones that are here.

Canberra is a clean, green, spread-out city. I can sit in my second-story bedroom window and look out at the surrounding hills, the Snowy Mountains foothills. It's like a cup rimmed with mountains;

the glow is pinkish, not the violet crown of Austin. The weather is like one of our dry, crisp winter days. Oddly enough, the oak trees have turned brown but the leaves do not fall.

I confess to being lonely and I feel isolated, but I plan to break the bonds some way. I don't like being set apart, or for my own contemporaries to stand when I come into the room and call me "Ma'am."

Love and kisses,
Mother

NOTE: Following is a letter from Anne Clark written to Mary and Pauline Goldmann and all others who might be interested in what's happening to the Clarks. She writes she doesn't get around to newsy letters for everybody individually.—Mrs. O'D.

The Residence
Canberra, Australia
August 30, 1965

Dear Ones All:

By way of beginning, I'll say that Madam is damn lonesome. I miss all my board of advisors, my loving detractors, Daisy Yett, Mr. Nelson of Checker Front, Susan Cullen, Mrs. Fulcher, Alma, Madam Watts, Billy Koen, the Hike and Bikers, the bird watchers, historians, cooks, packers, sewing club, and needlepointers. Miss Fleming is no substitute for Mrs. O'D. Huang, Foo, Ching, Ming, and Ernie Everly don't take the place of Daisy and David Tienda, and Frederick Hirsch and the Checker limousine are no substitute for Annie at the wheel of her own big Black Maria.

Last night, we went alone to Canberra House, residence of the British High Commissioner, Sir Charles, and Lady Johnston. They are here by only six weeks from Singapore. As far as I can find out, we are the only people here who are not career diplomats. I find myself over-

whelmed by the conventions, like who goes first—even to the bath-
room. Ed got on famously with His Excellency, the H.C.; in fact, they
were "Charles" and "Ed" by the time I rejoined Ed. Not that the
compliment is personal, but the American Ambassador really attracts
attention. In the morning paper there was only one picture—Ed and
Charles, yet. Tell Geneva Potter I wore the ivory cocktail dress and coat
and I thought it was by far the prettiest dress there. Most of the Australian women I have met are extremely petite. They seem to wear
somber colors, while the Easterners in their golden, vivid saris lend
color.

The flowers, I mean those from florists, are lovely and apparently
abundant and cheap. I have received several wagonloads, mixed spring
blooms—daffodils, stock, carnations, glads, delphinium—and, several
times, sprays of orchids. Some of the orchids have been in the house
almost three weeks now. I notice they undergo a change of deepening
color as they age, so some of the brown ones we get from the florist
in Texas may be just slightly stale.

This is especially for Sis Byram's interest in the house: The large
drawing room has a pale gray rug and pale gray walls, with a heavy,
denticulated cornice and dadoes. Moldings on the walls produce a
paneled effect. The walls are all masonry. Therefore, I have been slow
about hanging pictures (only the ones brought in my suitcase are
here) because I must have a man with a drill come to hang them. You
can't even use the moldings. There are three French doors, Palladian
type (like the window over my stairway at 2300 Woodlawn), ceiling
height, opening on the terrace. The fireplace is on the inside wall.
There are double doors at either end, one set opening into the dining
room and one into the library. The only color in the room is in the brocade, tied-back curtains and two velvet wing chairs of a dull pome-
granate red, or orange or peach tone. The curtains are not particularly
full or conspicuous, so the room is rather monotone.

Paintings would show to marvelous effect. Furnishings consist of
three (two-seat) sofas in gray and pink brocade; one sofa is slightly

larger. There are also four wing chairs, one very dull blue velvet barrel-back chair, four other chairs in ivory brocade, two Chippendale pull-up types, one grand piano, six white alabaster lamps with white shades, two gold mirrors, three tables, one tea table, six lamp tables, one large round piecrust table, one drop-leaf table under each gold mirror, one screen, and two inconspicuous ginger jars on the mantel. You can identify every piece in Kittinger's Williamsburg catalogue. I have placed a silver framed photo of the President on the piano; a large vase of peach blossoms and two vases of spray orchids were put in the drawing room today. When I say it still looks huge and barren, you have some idea of the scale of things.

Tonight we go to the Malaysian National Day Reception.* This afternoon I go to the hairdresser. Tomorrow I interview an upstairs maid, have the cast of *Any Wednesday* for drinks, and go to Captain Mooney's (Naval Attaché) black-tie dinner. Ed's fighting his hayfever and I, a cold.

Love and kisses,

Anne

* The mission of every country celebrates its own national day. Ours is, of course, July fourth. The entertainment is usually a large reception, sometimes stag, sometimes with wives. If the Ambassador himself is unable to attend, the next ranking officer of the Embassy attends to represent his country.

Canberra, Australian Capital Territory
August 30, 1965

Mr. Allen Duckworth*
Dallas Morning News
Dallas, Texas
My dear Duckworth:

I really want to oblige you about the letter, but, honestly, they have kept me so busy that I fall on the bed whenever I have a free moment and cannot discipline myself to stay awake long enough to catch up with correspondence. In fact, I was just having my tea from your and Helen's gift tea ball while reading your letter. I have been trying to write this one for a week in between engagements, and, therefore, if it rambles on, please understand.

Monday, August 23, was the big day when the Ambassador presented his credentials to the Administrator of the Commonwealth (also known as the Acting Governor General), Sir Henry Abel-Smith. Mr. Clark went to the ceremony in striped pants, accompanied by four more pairs of pants and three attachés—Air, Army, and Navy—in full panoply, including epaulets and three swords! (I was not allowed to go.) At 5:00 P.M. that day the Ambassador received the press, about thirty of them, for food, drink, and conversation, which included many penetrating questions. I might say that he carried on a considerable amount of conversation, and I do believe that he held the floor considerably more than all of the thirty people from the news media put together. At 6:30 that evening we had fourteen guests for dinner, theoretically a buffet, but we had four waiters besides the cook.

The staff consists of four Chinese people: Huang, the butler, who is tall and handsome; Foo, the steward, short and rat faced, who trots about in soft slippers and does most of the work; and Ching, the cook, who understands English but does not speak it. Clark, whom they call "Meester Ambassador" (and I am "The Madam"), says their only answer is "yes, yes, yes." Huang tyrannizes the other servants and allows no one else to open the front door. Ming, Huang's wife, is the laundress. Her only word is "wash."

Every night we eat by candlelight, and we have finger bowls even for breakfast. Kings and queens cannot live better. One of the Ambassador's few complaints is that the newspaper doesn't come early enough.

* The late Allen Duckworth, political writer for the *Dallas Morning News,* was a close personal friend. The letters to him answered his request for news that he could use as a feature story. The tongue-in-cheek tone reflects our close relationship.

I don't know how long it will be before H.E.† locates the Canberra equivalent of the Headliners Club or Harry Akin's Night Hawk restaurant. Meantime, the gentlemen from the Matson Lines are lunching with us here at the Residence.

Time passes.

I take up again. I have been photographed and interviewed and taped and recorded ad infinitum. I have been so eager to oblige that I hadn't the sense to refuse. Last night I heard myself on radio. A staffer's wife said that my voice was pitched right and I didn't "er-er," but in my heart I knew I sounded like "Mammy's little baby loves shortenin' bread."

Wednesday, August 25. This is the night we go to Government House to a black-tie dinner with the Acting Governor General. Government House is where I am supposed to curtsy, which always poses an enormous question because some Ambassadors feel strongly that the representative of the President of the United States of America should never bend his knee (or rather his wife's) to any man. Mrs. Battle, wife of our predecessor, told an amusing story about this. She put the question directly to President Kennedy. His answer to her was, "Curtsy you must, but keep a stiff upper knee." Personally, I don't care; I just fear that neither life on the old plantation nor handshaking at an East Texas political graveyard working equipped me for the gesture. Miss Freddie Craft, my dancing teacher in Greenville, Mississippi, didn't have that in her curriculum; not being a Roman Catholic, I don't even genuflect. I believe the motion corresponds roughly to the abbreviated curtsy known as the "bob." You did know, dear Allen, that the Ambassador—any Ambassador—represents the person of the Presidency and is accorded all the conventional courtesies due the President, mak-

---

† "H.E." means "His Excellency." The English use the abbreviation affectionately, and the phrase is appropriated by us, though, properly, in the American Service there is no such term. The correct form of address is "Mr. Ambassador."

ing me a sort of lower-echelon Lady Bird. This is not true of a minister; he only represents the government.

In all my interviews, I have been forced to pirate anybody's good lines that popped into my head. Also, the press has upgraded a lot of my accomplishments. As my friend Becky Debegorry Horton said: "In my effort to make a dull life more exciting, I must exaggerate some!"

Canberra did not grow like Topsy; it was planned by a competent architect, Walter Burley Griffin. Of course, he was from Frank Lloyd Wright's studio and shared his vision. The man-made structures are planned as enhancement of the God-made landscape. Like all the capital cities of the world that I have seen—Washington, Mexico City, Paris, Rome—it has the wide avenues, the plazas, the fountains—only newer and better. The structures are not baroque, nor superficially ornamented, but engineered. It will be a long time before they have a traffic problem here, except when I start driving. I know that when they turn me loose with a car and this left-hand driving, I will play havoc with all the plans of mice and men.

Yesterday I had the intellectuals for lunch: Dame Mabel Brookes, and her husband, Sir Norman Brookes, a great tennis star in 1907; Lady Ferguson, whose husband, Sir John, is the leading collector of Australiana; the director of the National Library; and the Chief Justice from Tasmania, Sir Stanley Burbury. I have also entertained for cocktails at the Residence, Congressman Young's nephew, Philip, and his wife; he is a nuclear physicist, who has recently completed his doctorate at the National University here. Also, Professor and Mrs. Risser of Rice University. She wrote me a welcome letter, so we promptly made contact asking them to come and see us. Mrs. Risser said that the Clarks provided the touch of home she was needing, and that she felt she had really put her feet on American soil. Then I knew we were doing the job we were hired to do by the President.

Friday, August 27. As you can see, I have been working on this letter for several days. Since the letter was started we have dined at Government House, the official residence of the Governor General.

They had dozens of aides who made it impossible to make a mistake.
Sir Henry's wife, the Lady May, is a great-granddaughter of Queen
Victoria. I thought them extremely charming. Sir Henry told me that
he was born in 1900 and his wife in 1906. The curtsy took place as the
Lady May and I left the dining room together. When we reached the
door, we turned and curtsied to Sir Henry. When the Australians toast,
they simply say, "The Queen," but we and other non-Britishers must
say, "To Her Majesty Queen Elizabeth the Second." Then everybody
jumps up and murmurs, "The Queen."

Friday night, August 27, was our dinner for the Prime Minister.
He is a great gourmet. As a result, we had to order special wines. You
can tell Frances Rafetto that the wines were Chateau Margeux (red)
and Berncastler Reisling (white). The cigars were Partagas from Cuba;
the gin was Gordon's (Beefeaters is not his favorite). The menu:
consommé, lobsters, fillet of beef, three or four vegetables, and straw-
berries in brandy. Pretty high on the hog for old Clark!

The furnishings are very handsome in the Residence but the personal
touch is lacking. For example, there is not a clock in the house. The
"Art in Embassies" program that you have perhaps read about is not
working out here. Some pictures were sent before I arrived, but they
are lost in this vast house.

Thursday, August 26, Ed's Deputy Chief of Mission introduced us
to Canberra at a reception with a wide range of guests: other Ambassadors (there are no African states represented here), the Anglican
Bishop, the Cabinet officers, and their "grazier" friends. Graziers are
like ranchers, and it is a proud term here, like landed gentry.

The Minister for External Affairs here corresponds to our Secretary
of State. The Secretary for External Affairs is a career man like DeWitt
Greer or Homer Garrison. Each department has both Minister and
Secretary. The Minister is a member of Parliament. Parliament sits at
night here, and the members are careful to be in attendance always.
Since the majority is very slim, the ruling party could lose an important
vote. Pretty sneaky, isn't that?

The weather here is like our winter, cool nights and bright sunny days. The Residence is centrally heated but not air conditioned. I get varying reports about whether or not we will suffer in summer. The wattle trees are in bloom. This is a form of acacia with showers of tiny yellow balls; it is a member of the same botanical family as our hui- sache, which it closely resembles. I think it causes hay fever, because Ed's eyes are beginning to smart. Another early spring blossom beloved by Australians is a species of laurel that they call daphne. It has an inconspicuous little pink cluster flower, very fragrant. Bits of the bloom often are worn by both men and women. If you comment, they im- mediately transfer the sprig to your lapel. Spray orchids are plentiful and must surely be reasonably priced, because I have received them three times as gifts.

About sending us things! If you use the APO, you can use ordinary United States postage. They say *everything* is flown out, so don't even bother to use air mail. The APO is slower because the mail leaves San Francisco once a week, and if you happen to reach San Francisco a day late, there is another week's delay. Anything—save red-hot news— would be fine sent this way. The address to use is: American Embassy, APO San Francisco 96209. I would like an occasional magazine (not *Time, Life,* or *Newsweek*), and, if you would get me on Neiman- Marcus' mailing list, I would like to receive all catalogues. In fact, I'd like Everts', Linz', Harris'—anybody's. I'd also like the book and theater page of the *Dallas Morning News.* Any nice gifts from Nei- man's will be appreciated.

I really hope this long and rambling letter is the kind of news that you asked for about our activities. Please don't make idiots of your old pals when you write a story about us, if you should decide to do so. Give my warm regards to Paula and to Mrs. R. This is fun, but we miss our friends and particularly you, Duckworth.

Sincerely,

Anne Clark

P.S. I sent some news clippings to an Austin friend and asked her to pass them on to Mrs. O'Donnell to reproduce and send a copy to you. Old Ed says that if you will get in touch with Mrs. O'D., she will send you everything she has, including pictures, mementos, and other junk mail we have sent home. However, you must promise to return them promptly to Mrs. O'D., as I am gathering them for my grandchildren, who are probably the only ones who will care one hoot about what I do. She also has a copy of the remarks made by the Ambassador on his arrival in Sydney and in Canberra, as well as his remarks made on the presentation of his credentials in Canberra. With all good wishes, I remain

Anne

Canberra, A.C.T., Australia
September 22, 1965

Mr. and Mrs. Sterling C. Evans
1601 South Shepherd
Houston, Texas

Dear Evanses and other friends:

Ed orders me to direct this to you, for it will largely concern our trip to a "property" near Wagga Wagga in New South Wales, about 150 miles from Canberra.

We left the Capital City at 8:00 A.M. Saturday morning, traveling in a converted Convair. Accompanying us were the United States Air Force and Army Attachés with their wives, General and Mrs. McKay (pronounced "McEye"—Australian Army), and the Jack Lydmans (D.C.M.). Even before 9:00 A.M., there were people out to meet us in Wagga. Group Captain (that's a full colonel in our services, and if you shorten the title say "Group," not "Captain") and Mrs. Lamb drove us out to the property called "Book-Book." That is supposed to be the call of the dainty, brown boobook owl, like our Texas owl's "who-who." The owner is Mr. Keith Dunn, a successful, self-assured grazier, who has only been "on the land" about fifteen years. Before that he was a prosperous grain merchant in Wagga. He is also president of the shire, comparable to a county in the United States, an unpaid job. Your Nine-Bar Ranch was never more polished and manicured for the largest South American buyer than Book-Book was for the United States Ambassador. Mrs. Dunn is a tall, neat woman with spectacularly unfashionable clothes. The house is a turn-of-the-century cottage, spotless but also unfashionable. The garden, a neatly fenced plot about the house, is lovely. That day one rosy pink camellia bush was ablaze with several hundred blooms on it. There were violets, pink, white, and blue; a grass tennis court in absolutely perfect condition; and a beautiful tree, which they called a silky oak, that has a ferny leaf and red blooms. I do not trust their terminology, because here chinaberry trees are called white cedars. The Dunns have only one child, a daughter married to a cousin of the same name. Son-in-law Robert is now "on the land" with them. He is an open-faced, redheaded young man. The Australian nickname for a redhead is "Blue." I asked if either father or son-in-law had training as agronomists. The answer was, "No, but they constantly attend short courses."

We drove a Mercedes around the property, and came upon a flock of three thousand sheep minded by a single stockman (their word for ranch hand), Alec Smith, and two dogs called Whisky and Spud. It was miraculous to see them work. Our host told us that Alec rode in to Book-Book as a boy fifty years ago and has stayed to raise a big family, all of whom he has been able to start in business from his own earnings. Part of every hand's wages is free meat, a considerable item.

With the discovery of subterranean clover a few years ago, and knowledge about top dressing everything with superphosphate, they have increased the productivity of the land 400 per cent in less than twenty years. Mr. Dunn kept speaking of a pasture crop that he called "loosun." As it turned out, he was pronouncing "lucerne," which is alfalfa to us.

Book-Book's main cattle type is a cross between a Hereford and a milking Shorthorn because the graziers produce "vealers" and need a mother cow who supplies plenty of milk. The cows have highly individual markings on their white faces. The Dunns also raise beautiful palominos, and you should see the stockmen crack those long whips! There are only three men working on this property, which also produces certified grass seed that sells for $75.00 a bag. I could go on forever because it was one of our most interesting experiences. We left about noon after being served an elaborate morning tea in an icy cold house. Have you heard about the "pneumonia holes" in Australian houses? Long-standing building codes require that houses be built with double walls with an airspace in between. Near the ceiling are ventilators about the size of a large waffle iron through which cold air pours —even bathrooms are thus permanently chilled.

We stopped for the night in Alice Springs, a Godforsaken little dump, not even picturesque. We saw our first aborigines there. The Administrator of the Northern Territory came down from Darwin to meet us, a distance of nearly a thousand miles. He had flown part way and driven an American Pontiac (with right drive) part way. The Pontiac is considered a high prestige car in Australia. When the Queen visited Alice three years ago the district officer's residence was completely remodeled for her accommodation. At that it was not too plush. The town was established as a relay station on the telegraph line. The telegraph and mails are both post-office realm. Alice Springs is also set apart in my mind by the fact that one has a time change of a half-hour there. Ever hear of that anywhere else? It is the geographical center of the country, Australia's "great red heart."

On to Perth the next day, an all-day flight, with the usual fanfare at the airport, even though it was Sunday afternoon. It's heart-warming to know that the United States is treated with such courtesy, interest, and enthusiasm. The wide, clear Swan River is the beauty of Perth.

Fremantle, the port, is a few miles away at the mouth of the river. The black swan is Perth's symbol everywhere. It is a distinctive piece of decoration, live or pictured.

Our reception at the City Hall couldn't have happened in the United States. I called on the Lady Mayoress, the Mayor's wife, who is literally called that. She even has an office in the Council House. Here the office of being wife to a public figure receives its due recognition.* There was also a functionary called the Town Crier. He wore morning clothes with a black gown around his shoulders and made all the introductions. His Worship, the Lord Mayor, wore the great silver chain and the medallion of office. He opened his speech by addressing the "Distinguished Guests; Your Grace, My Lord Bishop; Knights of the Realm." Don't tell us the Australians are informal.

Ed also had a meeting with a group called the Pastoralists and Graziers. He said they are easily the most interesting and attractive group he has met—tall, handsome, rugged types. You know I am surprised at the little people, that is, of small stature, whom I meet, both men and women. In fact, the financial wing of the government is referred to as the seven dwarfs! Sir Richard Roland and Sir Roland Wilson are each about five feet two inches.

Perth is perhaps the cleanest city I have ever seen with its broad avenues and beautiful parks. Even the old Victorian buildings are not smoked and oxidized. They are just as crisp and white as if built yesterday. King's Park and its wild flowers are nearly equal to the Swan River as points of pride. Our driver said, "We call these flowers the fifteen-pound-apiece blooms, because if caught pulling one, that is the fine." If Perth hadn't turned on its lights to make a giant volunteer tracking station, the astronauts would have had to wait quite awhile before seeing signs of life. It is the only large city for many thousands of miles—fifteen hundred miles to Adelaide, eight hundred miles to Jakarta in Indonesia, and after that the next nearest settlement is

* It caused me to consider as a title for these memoirs, "The Lady Ambassadoress."

Africa. In fact, Perth is just about as far as you can get from Straddle-fork. By the way, a man telephoned from Chireno, Texas, in Nacog-doches County (Ray Horton's town), and reported that it had rained two inches at Straddlefork yesterday.

We flew from Perth last night, refueled in Adelaide, and arrived in Canberra at 3:00 A.M. Made it to the installation of the new Governor General complete with striped pants at 11:00 A.M., but that will be another letter.

Anyone in the land market had better get out here before all this land is sold—it's going fast.

Love,
Anne Clark
(Mrs. Edward Clark)

℮ℐ ℴℭℐ ℴℭℐ ℴ

The Residence
Canberra, Australia
September 24, 1965

Dearly Beloved:

Your father wishes me to write long, descriptive letters about our trips to the various capitals, and I find it difficult to steal time to write at length to all the people who would like to hear. So, I am going to practice this letter on the dictaphone to you. It will be multiplied by Mrs. O'D. in Austin.

We are keeping up our usual hurried pace. I do not know when I will make peace with the schedule. I am a slave to the little black book that is my calendar. This morning I have Embassy wives' meeting.

I received Lady Johnston, wife of the British High Commissioner, at 11:45 here at the Residence. Lady Johnston is one of my favorites. She has asked me to call her Natasha. Ed makes it into "Nasturtium." She is a White Russian, one of the most attractive and smartly dressed women in the diplomatic set. We will dine with them tomorrow night. Their residence is called Canberra House. On Sunday evening we will be dining with the Prime Minister and the new Governor General at the Lodge. The Governor General never accepts private invitations. The Prime Minister is a special exception.

We had lunch today for an Australian couple named McMahon, who were recommended to us by Bob Anderson. It turns out that they are rather intimate friends of Forest Crockett, Dr. John's brother. You will remember Forest and Olive stayed a long time with Pat and John when we lived on Northwood Road and they had a very sick child.

This afternoon I will have another caller, the wife of the Belgian Ambassador, and another newspaper interview. The media and I have just about run out of newsy things to say about ourselves.

I could use quite a lot more spring clothes, as it is beginning to get warm here. It was almost impossible to buy summer clothes in Austin or Washington when I left, and I knew then I was going to need more things than I have. Please see if the stores have anything left.

On Monday we shall be going to Melbourne for our official visit of three full days. They have sent a book of directions about what we shall do there. After each engagement there is a notation, sometimes it says "SBC," which means short black coat for the Ambassador, or it might say "LS," which means lounge suit. Your father had to purchase a Homburg. Those light Texas Stetsons won't do with gray striped pants, and he must wear a hat, in order to remove it when he lays a wreath at the War Memorial. The directions are so specific that you can hardly make a mistake and I appreciate that. Dame Mabel will entertain us twice in Melbourne. I certainly hope she manages to get out the famous gold dessert service that I have heard so much about. I would say that Dame Mabel has all the drive of Eleanor Roosevelt, Rose Kennedy, and Oveta Hobby combined.

Your father sent you a bunch of little kangaroo pins that he had gotten from Qantas airlines. I suggest you send some to the children in San Augustine and some to Carrielu Christensen's children and the

Perlitz children in Austin. There seem to be plenty of tennis players here without my making any special effort about it. On Friday a regular group of Australian women play on the Embassy courts, and I believe some of the younger fellows from the Embassy play Saturday mornings. They make out very well without any lemonade.

So far I have heard no report of the things I sent from Austin by ship. It has been almost two months now since shipping, and I think they should be arriving soon. If they do not appear before the Red Cross Benefit Tour, we will have to make do with flowers. I have made a friend in Lady Huxley, who is borrowing two birds, "friends of hers," she calls them, that will sit in the sunroom and serve as decoration. I told her when she was offering them that you had said people were very "ticky" about their birds, and she said, "Well, I'll ask and see." She has now called to say that she will have them here for the tour.

The Johnstons will have as their guest of honor a famous Professor of Byzantine history. I don't know how much I will be able to fake about that. Byzantine history is pretty hard to fake.

Your father received his official autographed photograph of the President, to be hung in his office, yesterday. It was inscribed "To Ambassador Edward Clark and Mrs. Anne Clark, with the love and envy of their devoted friend—L.B.J." What do you make of that?

Did Doug ever tell us the name and address of his former roommate who lived in Perth? I wish I had known something about him while I was there—just something to make conversation about.

Since you are interested in everything, I will report on a quaint little custom that I have run into. I kept receiving little notes and cards with the letters "P.T.O." on them, which I puzzled over for a long time. Finally I asked what that meant and was told, "Please Turn Over."

I hope you read the letter I wrote to Aunt Martha about the installation of the Governor General. It was really very magnificent but did not seem to attract the enormous crowd that a similar ceremony would have in the United States. In fact, the parade watchers were very few. Of course, the Senate Chamber in which the ceremony was held was small,

so it was witnessed by comparatively few people. I guess you might say
Australians are a bit phlegmatic, for I have not seen them stand in the
rain to watch a hero pass by or cheer anything as yet. Your father continues to fret over his formal calls. He will be very glad when he has
finished with them and is able to get on with business he considers far
more important.

The fly season is about to start in Canberra. In fact, even though
our fireplaces are carefully and neatly screened, the flies come into the
fireplace, and make loud buzzing noises. In Alice Springs we got a
full dose. You know how your father hates insects of any kind. I don't
know whether he is going to take leave home for the duration of the
fly season or not. They are unbelievably numerous and tenacious. They
seek moisture, which means your eyes, nose, and mouth. I saw a man
keep his mouth open a second too long and in flew one of the little
pests.

Jack Valenti sent a cable asking the Ambassador's assistance in pro-
curing the services of Joan Sutherland for a United Nations concert in
Washington, of which Jack's wife, Mary Margaret, is the chairman.
So far Sutherland has made no reply to the telegram that was sent to
her from here. I think it would be great for her to go because, to most
Americans, I am sure, she is the best known name in Australia, and
that includes even the Prime Minister.

Do you remember when I told you in Asheville, North Carolina,
about the foot rulers that were made of different kinds of native wood?
I have bought several and will send them to you for the children's
Christmas stockings.

I hear now that Anne Fisher is going to be married, perhaps at
Thanksgiving. I bought a set of Marghab linen mats for her in Sydney,
which I plan to send for a wedding present. I understand duty is high,
so I will send them to you and, if they charge duty, please pay it and
send the mats on to Anne. I do not want to send a present on which
she has to pay duty. I wish I could find something genuinely Australian, but so far have found nothing worth sending.

I am planning to get myself a pair of throw rugs in pretty colors that are made of Australian wool for the foot of my bed. If I think they are attractive enough, I may send some of them home.

I have been steadily going to art exhibits wherever I hear of them. They are pretty crazy about art here. I went to one in a department store the other day. Visits to the local museums are always arranged when I go on official visits. However, I am not very sure that I am ever going to like Australian painters. Nearly everything is landscape, and even the abstracts are strongly influenced by the local landscape.

We have set aside a few hours to go shopping in Melbourne. It is my understanding that Melbourne has beautiful shops and antique stores, and I plan to look a little there. I have never considered myself the world's greatest comparative shopper, but there is something about not being able to do a thing that makes you wildly anxious to do it, and I am beginning to feel that way about shopping. Mrs. Lydman is determined to leave me in as good shape as possible. She even made me play bridge on the plane coming back from Perth so that she could decide whether I was capable of holding a hand with ladies for an afternoon of bridge. My only purpose in ever playing would be to use it as a vehicle—you know what I mean by that.

They have just delivered a television set to the Residence, and word has come of shipping a Chrysler Imperial for the use of the Ambassador. Your father was outraged about the Checker limousine. Personally, I thought it was sort of cute. I don't know when I shall rise up and demand a car of my own. So far I haven't missed it too much, but I know the time will come when I will simply have to have one, though I continue to be overwhelmed by the idea of driving on the left-hand side of the road. Whatever made the English think of left-hand driving when all the words like sinister and gauche, which mean left, imply an awkward way of doing things.

How is Anne Wynn's school paper on Australia coming along? Does she have sufficient material for it yet? If not, I can load her with a good deal more printed material. We get it on every trip we make.

Meantime, love and kisses to all my little Wynns, and, of course, to Bannie and Aunt Martha and to Margaret and Clint. I hope that dear Bob is getting better.

Devotedly,
Your Mother

P.S. This was typed in my absence. Considering the Australian typist's difficulty with my voice, the script fared pretty well. The package of cookbooks you sent from San Augustine with the wild rice and corn meal has arrived. Thank you. I'll write about Melbourne later.

The Residence
Canberra, Australia
September 29, 1965

Mrs. Lafayette B. Herring*
3023 Reba Drive
Houston, Texas, U.S.A.

Dear Fredeen, and all my little Herring friends:

By now I know you must be home, because Bubber has to be back in Mississippi to pick his cotton crop. I do hope you made a wonderful representation of capitalism to the Russians. Did you lose any weight? I can't imagine thriving very much on the Russian diet.

We have been in Canberra almost six weeks now, and I am, as the Australians say, "settling in at last." The Embassy is beautiful and very comfortable, though it is quite large, and I find the scale of the rooms forbidding. I have a wonderful staff of Chinese and a Viennese chauffeur, Frederick. Of course, I have been more than overwhelmed by the conventions of diplomatic life, but I suppose that even these I will find a way to overcome soon.

---

* Fredeen Beaird Herring, born in Yazoo City, Mississippi, was my college roommate. She assisted me in correcting the manuscript.

Did you know that our first guests were the Dillon Andersons and the Frank Michauxes from Houston? Jodie Lydman, the wife of Ed's Deputy, has been a wonderful help to me, but they are about to be transferred to Indonesia. I have needed and worn every piece of the wardrobe that you and Mary Carpenter pushed me into buying in Houston. The only problem that I am having is that it is now getting to be spring and summer, and I do not have enough clothes for those seasons. My only hope is that the social life will slow down soon.

We have now started on our round of official visits to the six state capitals in Australia. We have already been to Sydney, state of New South Wales, and to Perth, and next week we will go to Melbourne. After that to Hobart in Tasmania, and at Thanksgiving we will go to Brisbane.

Every capital is different, and I am enjoying that part of it very much. Our Consul in each place makes all the arrangements and sends most elaborate schedules, which tell me when to wear short dress, long dress, hat, gloves, or what have you. This schedule also tells when the Ambassador should wear a blue shirt for television. Because of so much news coverage, they have about run out of anything to say about me, and you know I never was a very exciting subject to begin with. I wonder if Mrs. O'Donnell, Ed's secretary in Austin, has put you on the mailing list. I know I asked her to send you at least one letter. She sends out regular round robins and sometimes I am reduced to writing my letters to her, asking that she reproduce and forward them to the list of friends who want to follow our activities.

Today I was photographed and interviewed by an Australian woman who has a commission to do a story for the *Houston Post*. It is very heart-warming to know how many people are interested in us as the representatives of America in Australia.

It is really something when I have so many new things to learn— not only new faces, new people, and almost a new language, but also new flowers, new animals, and new stars. Did you know that the new moon is upside down in Australia? The forsythia and the pansies are blooming now in September, as is the little lavender thrift.

Everyone is tremendously interested in gardening here. In fact, this "planned" city has a scheme to give every new house builder a number of shrubs and trees for free. One plant they seem to have never heard of in Australia is the caladium. I do not see how they keep a summer garden without it. The birds are superb in color and the thing I really like about them is that they are mostly big slow birds, so I can see them. There are flocks of beautiful parakeets called rosellas flying across our garden, and also white cockatoos with yellow crests. They are quite tame, and I am told that birds here do not have many natural enemies. That nationally beloved fellow, the kookaburra, roosts on top of our bedroom chimney and hollers down at us, Ed says.

In the past week, a new Governor General was installed here in Canberra. He is an Australian. His name is Lord Casey and he is the first native-born son in a long, long time. He was the first Australian Ambassador to the United States, and a very popular Ambassador there. The swearing in was a splendid occasion with plenty of knee breeches, white-wigged judges, and gold braid everywhere. The red carpets were out, literally, and I don't mean just short strips. There was plenty of red carpet and you know who was walking right down the middle of it all. The Ambassador has had a number of occasions to wear his morning coat but none yet to use his white tie and tails.

We have already dined once at Government House with Sir Henry Abel-Smith and the Lady May, when he was Acting Governor General, or Administrator, as he was called. I have never met two more charming people. It was a splendid occasion itself with a gold-braided footman behind every chair, and the most beautiful table service with literally dozens of gleaming tapers in the candelabra.

Even the morning prayer service at church is ceremonial when the Governor General and his wife attend. They enter before the service starts. Everyone rises as though they were bringing out the Eucharist, and the organ peals out with "God Save the Queen." After the service is over, it is just like a wedding: everyone remains in his pew until the Governor General makes his exit and his wife is escorted out on the arm of an usher.

People on the Embassy staff keep apologizing for the fast pace at which we are moving, but it is not so bad to old hands like us who are used to carrying our own suitcases, buying our own tickets, hailing our own taxicabs. Will you ever forget that woman at the station in New York who almost set her dog on us when we got into her cab? This pace does not seem so fast to us, because there are many helpful people available at the Embassy.

Learning to understand all the various accents with which we must cope is amusing, but sometimes difficult. Our Huang, the Chinese butler, accents words one way, while Frederick, the Viennese chauffeur, accents the same words in another way. The end result is that we are all three saying the same thing and no one says it alike.

Canberra is a small town of about sixty thousand population, and so there are a good many things that are unavailable here, but, when I give it some thought, I remember that the same situation would probably prevail in any small American town, even Lufkin, Texas, or Greenville, Mississippi.

Things I sent by surface have not yet appeared, and I don't know when they will. On October 9 the Residence will be open for the Red Cross Benefit Tour. Last year, about a thousand people came. I wish that my possessions would come before that time, but by the time they do come, everything will have been done. We will have been photographed so much, the Prime Minister will have been to dinner, and I really won't care whether I have those things by then or not.

You would certainly like at least one phase of this life because I literally have been in the kitchen only twice since our arrival. There is at least one virtue—in the fact that I am not tempted to eat out of the icebox between meals. I am afraid I will have to end this career by even playing bridge. Someone said it was a nice way to while away a dull afternoon. If I do take up bridge, that will not be my reason. I do not have enough dull afternoons to myself yet. I only regard bridge as a vehicle to get to know people with whom I otherwise do not have much in common. While the Asians are very nice people, small talk is often difficult, since we do not always laugh at the same jokes.

Art is as much a craze in Australia as it is everywhere else. For instance, here in Canberra there are four art galleries with pictures for sale. I find that unusual because in Austin, with four times the population, we do not have one sales gallery as such.

It seems to me that I have spent the better part of my life here going back and forth to the hairdresser. I have been photographed so much and have gone out so much in the evening that I am constantly working with my hair. I really do not consider that I have accomplished much.

Since Ed comes home to lunch every day, I see more of him than I have in a long time. Tonight, for the first time, he is going out to play cards with some of the men from his office. As soon as he finishes with all of the formalities, like calls, I think he will enjoy this work, finding it far less strenuous than were his "five-and-dime" businesses in Austin, Texas.

Did I explain to you about the use of the APO address? If you address us through the APO, you use just plain United States postage; you do not need to bother with air mail, since everything is flown out anyway. We love to get mail, and, even though I can't read much of your handwriting, I can decipher enough to make it worth your while to write sometimes.

I have been reduced to ordering some things from the Sears Roebuck catalogue. For example, a bird feeder, which is an unknown object of merchandise in Australia.

I have worn your elegant black dress many times, and it really looked rather becoming, I thought. If you see any summer things at Esther Wolf's that you think would be appropriate and cheap, my friend, send them to me. I can envision running out before the summer is over, which will be about March 1. Don't send me anything smaller than a size 14. I can always have them taken up, but letting them out is sometimes impossible.

Since there is no air conditioning in Australia, I suggest that you put off your visit until next fall, which will be about spring in Texas.

If this letter seems a bit disjointed, I will explain it by the fact that I am trying to learn to use a dictaphone.† As my correspondence simply will not get itself in hand, I am trying this method. I have practiced on you and Leila—forgive the structure and love the spirit.

As ever,
Anne Clark
(Mrs. Edward)

† This dictaphone plan fell through, as I could never find an office typist with leisure. Back to Mrs. O'D. in Texas.

Canberra, Australia
October 16, 1965

Dear Friends:

I can't remember when I wrote my last round-robin letter for reproduction and dispersal. This week has been relatively calm. We had one large party for about ninety people at the Residence to introduce our new Counselor for Economic Affairs, Walter Smith. He has served several places in Southeast Asia, and also in Scotland, Paris, and Spain. I tried a new plan and had food on the table—roast beef and chicken legs. Canapés, which are called savories here, are usually passed and we have eaten so many I pale at the sight. Anyway, the Australians liked my food and we completely gave out. Chicken and ham are both expensive and rather scarce items here. They are considered the greatest delicacy to serve. When I have a party, besides my Chinese help, there

The A.D.C. in Waiting is desired by
Their Excellencies
The Governor-General and Lady Casey
to invite

His Excellency the Ambassador of the U.S.A. and Mrs. Clark
to Dinner on Saturday the 9th
of October at 7.15 p.m. for 7.30 o'clock

Government House,
Canberra   BLACK TIE

An answer is requested
to the A.D.C. in Waiting

is Mrs. Peter Fleet and Frederick, the chauffeur (who opens the door),
and I still have to hire four extra waiters.

We have had Mr. and Mrs. Gene Howard here. He came with
letters from J. C. Kellam, so be sure and call Mr. K. They came up to
the Residence for a drink and we gave them the full tour. He, being
in the nursery business, was interested in the garden. Two big dogwoods are in bloom, and that oak that didn't shed its brown leaves has
finally discarded the old brown for new green. The Parks and Gardens
Department gives away flowering trees to new householders, and there
are pots of other flowers on the public greens. Iris is coming into bloom
now. However, the gardens haven't much style. I wanted a bird feeder
to attract the birds nearer the windows but couldn't locate one at all, nor
a bath. Finally, I ordered two from Sears Roebuck; one is for Dame
Pattie, who also wanted one. A friend of hers who saw it asked me,
"What is that little gadget?"

Last week we had the John Harpers here overnight. Ed had a stag
luncheon, which the Prime Minister, Sir Robert, attended and I had

a ladies' luncheon at the hotel. I was so pleased that at last there were ten women I could invite and know their names and faces. I feel that's making progress.

We had the Residence on tour for the Red Cross. More than eight hundred callers walked through between 2:00 P.M. and 4:30 P.M. However, the Embassy wives fixed all the flowers and acted as hostesses. They said I didn't even have to show up, but both Ed and I did. He stayed downstairs and signed autographs and I visited with the people.

We dined at Government House that night. Lady Casey presented me with a hat to wear to the Melbourne Cup. Tell Charmaine Denius I am going to wear that beige suit she bought at the last moment for me. Ed will wear his gray topper and his cutaway. My hat is made of all-over green leaves with a big red silk rose over the ear. Stunning hats are a must at these fashionable races.

Thursday we went to Cooma, a small town about seventy miles from here. The Ambassador addressed the combined Rotary, Lions, and Apex clubs. I had tea and dinner with a group of ladies. Their idea of tea is about six kinds of sandwiches—pinwheels, ribbon, meat, cheese —and an equal number of sweets—iced cakes, tarts, shortbreads, snowballs, *et cetera*. Cooma is the site of the Snowy Mountain Scheme, in a small way like our Tennessee Valley Authority. It is a town of about 7,500 people. There are lots of motels because the sightseers and skiers stay there on their way to what is known as "the snows." My hostess was a Mrs. Liebman—mid-forties, a plump and pretty brunette. Her husband is a wool buyer. Their home was in Brooklyn, New York. Their twenty-year-old son works for the radio station in Canberra and wants to come to the United States. Their daughter, Wendy, is thirteen. Her hair and eyes are black and she is bright as a new penny—mad about Barbie dolls. In Cooma live many of the "New Australians," twenty-three nationalities. These people were all brought in to work on the Snowy Mountain dams. Now there is a question about whether enough industry will come there after the dams are completed to keep the workers. The government is urging immigration to Australia but they want especially North Europeans. First choice would be those from the British Isles. Nothing is written into the law about "all-white" Australians, but applicants who aren't white appear to be screened out.

Friday, Ed went with a group of men, including the Air Minister, Peter Howson, and the New Zealand High Commissioner, Luke Hazlett, to see the air exercises at Evans Head, on the northeast coast of New South Wales. I made diplomatic calls on the wife of the Minister for External Affairs (same as our Secretary of State), the wife of the Peruvian Minister, whose name is Gallagher, and the wife of the Indonesian Ambassador. I felt rather sorry for the Indonesian lady. She spoke sadly of the time when "things will be better in our country." The heavily spiced cookies she served made me ill. I came home violently nauseated, an unusual state for healthy me. I even had to go to bed.

No one hits a tap here on Saturday, so both Ed and I have been in bed all day. Had our meals on a tray upstairs. It's misty, foggy, and rainy outside. Even the stores all close by noon. We have to make special arrangements for the chauffeur to come on Saturday.

A newcomer said Australia was like living in a gymnasium. You can't look up without seeing someone practicing a sport of some kind, such as running in the park, rowing on the lake, bowling on the green, and those millions of tennis players! Even quite older people play tennis and ski, surf, and swim.

Our new D.C.M. has come. He and his attractive wife, Dottie, came from Bonn, Germany, to us. I can't see how they can be very helpful with my problems, however, since they don't know Australia.

Fondly,
Anne

The Residence
Canberra, Australia
October 17, 1965

Mr. Allen Duckworth
Dallas Morning News
Dallas, Texas, U.S.A.

Dear Duckworth:

I have been reliably informed that you have been referring to His Excellency as "Captain Kangaroo." For such impertinence, I should cut you off without a jot of international news. If, after due warning, I hear that you continue in this outrageous insolence, I shall make the crime fit the punishment, or vice versa.

Because I confine my information to things social, I do not want you to think the Ambassador concerns himself only with such things. In fact, he keeps quite busy conferring on matters of defense and investments that are of interest to the United States government and to individual citizens. Friday he took an all-day trip to Evans Head on the northeast coast of New South Wales with the New Zealand High Commissioner, Mr. Luke Hazlett; the Australian Air Minister, Mr. Peter Howson, who is one of the youngest members of the Ministry; our own Air Attaché, Colonel Hal Ottoway; and other officials. They watched the aerial defense exercises. The Ambassador said the United States showed up well. The shadow of Asia hangs darkly over everything here. I have heard the remark frequently quoted that the Far East is the Near North here. Australia is twice as far from England as South Africa and Australians know they can defend themselves only with the help of the United States. The neutralists can be neutral only while the umbrella of United States protection is held over them. There are thirty-nine missions here. I count twelve of them as Asian; that includes the Philippines. There are eight High Commissioners from Commonwealth nations. I am now on a first-name basis with Sir Charles and Lady Johnston (Natasha) of the British High Commission. The dean of the diplomatic corps is **Mr. Mariano Ezpeleta** of the Philippines. His wife, Gloria, is a warm friend of the United States. Their Embassy is just across the road from us. We were invited there last Saturday to meet Madam Macapagal, the wife of their President. Thence, we went on to Government House to dinner with Lord and Lady Casey. Lord Casey is the newly installed Governor General. The Governor General is a Queen's appointee but he is chosen with the advice and consent (really mandatory) of the Prime Minister of Australia. As Mr. R. G. Casey, he was Australia's first Ambassador in Washington in 1939. Later he was Minister of State and sat on the War Council with Churchill. Following that he was Governor of Bengal. Lady Casey, Maie to all her friends, is a person of great talent, too. She flies a plane, writes, paints, and composes music. Both of them belong to the old Australian establishment. They are an elegant matched pair.*

Afterward, we stopped briefly at the Peruvian Legation where a merry dinner dance was in progress as a farewell party to Jack and Jodie Lydman, the departing Deputy Chief of Mission. He was a very popular chargé for a whole year between Bill Battle and Ed Clark, so he and Jodie are being widely entertained with farewell parties. The "Latinos," that is what we call the envoys from the Latin American countries, are the gayest people here. The reason is that they don't really have any work to do.

Before all this, on Saturday afternoon, our Residence was open for the Red Cross Benefit tour. More than eight hundred people walked through. H.E. stayed around and signed autographs, and everybody thought that was wonderful. One of my callers last week was a Mrs. Jackson, whose husband is with Hunt Oil Company. She is from Dallas and will be going home in December. An Australian friend of hers whom I met told me that Mrs. Jackson had never been in the American Embassy before, so I hastened to invite her. Ed and I think this place

---

* Lord Casey was made the first Australian Knight of the Garter in 1969.

belongs to all Americans; since they are paying for it, they should at least be able to look at it. Perhaps when Mrs. Jackson returns, you can interview her and find out how we are doing here.

We have just gotten a new Deputy Chief of Mission. The name is Edwin Cronk. He comes directly from Bonn, Germany, where he had been Economic Counselor for George McGhee. The Cronks are quite nice but the rapid change in personnel makes problems. We are also getting a new Air Attaché, a new Economic Counselor, and at least one more replacement, the Administrative Officer who does the buying and cares for the Residence maintenance. Most of these people are switched around in Southeast Asia, for example, between Japan, Korea, Indonesia, Laos, Vietnam, or Taiwan. Two years, at most, three, is the normal term.

Did anyone tell you that John Harper of Pittsburgh, formerly of Rockdale, Texas, president of Alcoa, was here last week? Ed honored him with a stag luncheon for eight to which the Prime Minister, Sir Robert Menzies, came. My staff really go into orbit when they hear he is coming. Everything changes. The wine, the soup, the flowers, the cigars are all upgraded. Sir Robert really is quite a fellow. Tall, portly, white-haired, deep-voiced, and eloquent, he loves good food, fine wine, England, his daughter Heather, dry Martinis that he makes himself, Dickens novels, double-breasted suits, Mary Martin, and his title, which is Knight of the Thistle. The papers are always speculating on his retirement. It does not seem imminent to us. Personally, I think Australians need him as they need the Queen—for a rallying point. You know, Australia has a singularly unpicturesque history. No war of independence, no invasions, and no national heroes. It is sort of interesting to talk about the convict settlements, but that stops pretty abruptly because no one will willingly admit descent.†

We had only one large party last week. I tried an American-style buffet with roast beef and chicken drumsticks and gave out of food.

† Later I met a friend who told me of her ancestress, a convict girl who was transported when she was only eight years old.

Ed and I are so tired of hors d'oeuvres that we could scream; Jack and Jodie call them "small chow." I wish I had some Virginia ham or hot tamales, hot okra, or something. When you have a cocktail party here, all the drinks are passed—no bar. The liquor is served in rather small glasses with stems, like a whisky sour glass. Therefore, they must go round often. On the tray must be whisky (Scotch)-water, whisky-soda (no bourbon except in the American Embassy), gin and tonic, beer in small glasses, Martinis, tomato juice, and several soft drinks. Bitter lemon is a favorite.

The Australians' favorite dessert is a "Pavlova." It is like a meringue with fruit and whipped cream. The lamb and beef is good but it is not cut as we do it. For instance, I can't seem to get loin lamb chops double thick, the kind we think are so good. They talk a lot about "grills," which is anything broiled. Shrimp are always called "prawns," and the lobster is "crayfish." Formal dinners usually have soup or fish, often both, with an entree of beef, lamb, or fowl (chicken is the most expensive thing, therefore considered the greatest delicacy). Salad is served as a separate course; sometimes there is a savory, then dessert, followed by fruit accompanied by cheese, and, finally, mints and bonbons. Ed has learned to peel and eat a banana with a knife and fork. The toasts are referred to as the "loyal toasts," first to the Queen, then to the President of the United States. They are drunk sometimes in champagne, sometimes in port. There is no smoking at the table until after the toasts. I've certainly had a lot to learn.

Last Thursday we went to Cooma, a small town about seventy miles from here, scene of the Snowy Mountain Scheme (like our Tennessee Valley Authority). We were accompanied by Mr. LeVan Roberts, head of the Public Information Section, and Maxine, his wife. He served in the Army with Dorsey Hardeman. The men were taken to visit a property, a big sheep and cattle ranch, while I had tea with about thirty ladies. The Ambassador addressed the combined service clubs that night—Rotary, Lions, and Apex. Cooma is full of "New Australians" (that's what they call immigrants), who are skilled workmen brought in to work on the dams, numbering about twenty-three nationalities. The town square is decorated with flags of all those countries. The United States flag is pretty ragged and I think H.E. will have to get a new one for them. The Yugoslavs regularly tear theirs down because they say that the Communist flag does not represent them. Cooma is also the gateway to the ski country. "Going to the snows" means a ski holiday.

Dogwood and lilacs are flowering in the Embassy gardens now and about a million rosebuds are about to pop open. We want to plant a pecan tree here to memorialize ourselves. See if you can find one of those Jim Hogg pecans. They say we might have better luck starting from a seed nut.

I am enclosing two silver sixpence for your daughter, Paula. I hear it is the traditional thing for a bride to wear in her shoe. Australia is about to go on the decimal system, so I assume there won't be any more Australian sixpence.

You know, I was a little mad at the *Dallas Morning News* before I left because of its far right leanings, but now I am so homesick for a bulky American Sunday newspaper that I have recanted everything I said. The only paper we receive is the *San Augustine Tribune*. Write and tell me a little confidential news. When you have read this, please send it on to Mrs. O'D. so that she can circulate it among our friends.

Fondly,
Anne Clark

P.S. Friend Allen:

May I add a postscript to Anne's description of our life in the Embassy? I'd like to say that the Prime Minister, Governor General, *et al.,* see more of us than all the other Ambassadors combined. That's the way it ought to be. I have my staff 100 per cent with me and they all like me and give me perfect cooperation. My Texas way is not their State Department way but I think they like my informality and making them work five times more than they did before my time. Half of the staff had never been to the Embassy Residence. We have had all to receptions and all to supper. My key men and women have all been to dinner and lunch five times. I make everyone say "our Embassy Residence," instead of "the Ambassador's." Formerly, no American citizens were permitted to come beyond the Chancery. Since I have been here, every American has been escorted to the Residence by me or a senior officer and shown the Residence and our garden, which is the largest and most lovely in Canberra. We try to have all Americans for coffee, tea, lunch, or dinner. They all love it and some say they have been all over the world and our way is most like America and they will not forget it. We personally greet local groups and I receive or go to talk to all university groups.

Oh, yes, they had signs everywhere saying Private Property—Ambassador's Private Residence—Keep Out—No Visitors, and such. I took them all down and got the staff together and told them that I had removed them myself, that this Chancery and Residence belong to the taxpayers of the United States and I want them to see all of it and be welcome.

Canberra, Australia
November 12, 1965

Dear You All:

Do you wonder what the Clarks have been occupied with the last few weeks? Well, we haven't been resting; the schedule has been full of everything from balls to funerals, interspersed by our steady stream of callers. Ed makes it a rule to bring all Americans to the Residence on the ground that it belongs to the taxpayers of the United States. He says they shouldn't go home without seeing their property and receiving a souvenir of at least a match clip with "American Embassy, Canberra" on it. Unfortunately, they also say "Made in Austin, Texas." Matches are scarce and hard to get here, at least dainty ones.

Last week, visitors came in more than the usual numbers. Ed spoke to a group of advertising people and opened by saying, "Now, I would like to surprise my wife. Everybody come to our Residence between 4:00 and 5:30 for tea." I didn't blink, because I knew I was going to the hairdresser at just that time, but luckily I can call on some staff members' wives to help out. That day, the wives of the Navy and Army Attachés and of the Political Counselor were my saviors. Earlier in the week, Ed had asked people to lunch without consulting me. I was committed to the Australian-American Association Women's Group as guest of honor. Mrs. Rodman, wife of the Agricultural Attaché fell into the breach, bringing along Lady Bunting, who had been her previous luncheon hostess. The American guests were enchanted because Peg Bunting is young and beautiful. She looks like Norma Shearer.

I opened a fete last week; Ed made two speeches; and we had a reception for two hundred to "farewell" the Lydmans (our departing D.C.M.) and to welcome the new D.C.M., Ed Cronk, who has been with George McGhee in Germany. "Farewell" as a verb is part of my new vocabulary. I adored Jack and Jodie Lydman. Their appearance, manners, and education would have qualified them to be lady and gentleman in waiting to the Queen, but I know I shall like the Cronks as well. Dottie C. comes only to my shoulder and looks as Nelwyn Howard did when we were that age—about forty. We also lost Mary and Colonel Hal Ottoway, who go to Akron, Ohio. Both men are so talented that I expect to see Hal as Chief of Staff and Jack as Secretary of State before I am gathered to my reward, sometime after the year 2000.

All this is prelude before I try to paint a word picture of the indescribable Melbourne Cup Week, an engrossing Australian institution. A school holiday, nation-wide, is proclaimed and, during the running, it is as though the world had stopped turning. A constant excuse heard is, "You see, I was at the track." Everybody has a wager of some kind. It's tagged "having a flutter." Went to a hospital auxiliary luncheon the day before, and they had a pool even there—five shillings a share or three for ten shillings. They divided the pot three ways: one-half to the holder of the winning horse, one-fourth to second place, and one-fourth to the hospital. That's a typical episode. Ed attended two stag dinners with Premier Bolte (he would be the same as Governor of our state) of Victoria, at the Australian Club and the Athenaeum Club. There the pool is a Calcutta, just like the Labor Day golf tournament at the Austin Country Club. So they bought Matlock, the favorite, for a pretty penny. Do you know what, Matlock fell down and brought down two other horses with him. However, Old Lucky Boy Clark had a one-eighth interest in a four-thousand-pound pool on Light Fingers, the actual winner. I am waiting to hear how he finally comes out with the one thousand dollars he thinks he won. You know, Ed likes to gamble, but he also likes to win, and he was sweating because he didn't really understand the system. Mr. Bolte is one of the few big gamblers I have met. He's on the VRC (Victoria Racing Commission). Many men are horse lovers and breeders but some go just to socialize, not to bet.

Saturday, October 30, was called Derby Day. As our plane was late, we arrived just in time to allow His Excellency to change into striped pants, full cutaway (no short black coat for this), and gray topper. I wore my yellow silk and a small blue cornflower hat—not half elaborate enough. I was saved only by the cornflowers. Mrs. Sam Wood (Sheila) was pinning cornflowers on all her group and the diplomats, removing Mr. Bolte's yellow carnation wherever possible. Sheila Wood was cited as the best-dressed woman at the races. After the races, we hurried into our cars. In ours rode Dame Mabel and Sir Norman Brookes. The rest of the diplomats had to ride alone unless, like Sir Charles and Lady Johnston (British High Commissioner), they had brought an aide and a lady secretary. Our Consul and Consul General met us at the gate, so I felt pretty safe with Dame Mabel and Fran Smith at my side. Having Dame Mabel for your sponsor is like having Alice Longworth, Perle Mesta, and Mrs. Rose Kennedy all rolled into one body. She has fame, money, wit, old family, and *strength* at seventy-two. Darling Sir Norman is eighty-eight years old and he sometimes slows her up a bit. Under Dame Mabel's sponsorship, His Excellency, the Ambassador of the United States, and Mrs. Clark sat at table No. 1 at every function. As we promenaded into the grandstand, with the bands playing and the flags flying and the cameras popping, my thoughts kept turning to a line that dear Herman Brown quoted from his old friend, Hook McCullough, "I don't see how po' folks live." God rest their souls. I am still here to carry on.

Luncheon was served in the Committee Rooms of the Club House. Mr. Grey-Smith, president of the VRC, was the host. Champagne, beer, and whisky flowed like water, but I never saw anyone even slightly inebriated. Between the fourth and fifth races tea is served in the Committee Rooms. A woman in uniform carrying what I would describe as a valise comes to the stands to take bets. Five shillings is the minimum, that is, about fifty cents. I went all out and bet five to win and five to place each time. The bookies were down on the ground level under big striped umbrellas, but I got lost once and never left the stands again. Saturday night I went to the Italian Consul General's party and Ed went to a stag dinner.

Sunday we had drinks at Sir Leo and Lady Curtis'. She has children from thirteen to thirty, admits to fifty-two, has a beautiful house with a pool and tennis courts but no visible servants, and is considered one of the prettiest and best-dressed women in Melbourne. There we picked up the Irish Ambassador, Dr. MacWhite, and wife, Kathleen. They are youngish and he reads Russian—intellectual type. They drove with us to Sir Rupert Clarke's place, an hour out of the city at Clarke-field. He's a partner in the King Ranch in Australia. His grandfather was the first Australian baronet, he is the third. It is a hereditary title, the only one in Australia. Dame Mabel said Sir Rupert I was a true Edwardian rake and promenaded Collin Street with a train of beautiful actresses. The present Sir R. is a solid citizen. They had luncheon for 150 under a lovely blue marquee. We sat at table No. 1. Sir Henry Abel-Smith and wife, Lady May (Sir H. is Governor of Queensland), Lady Delacombe (wife of the Governor of Victoria), the Premier and

Mrs. Bolte, Sir Rupert, H.E. the Ambassador, and me. They had a pool on the race there, too.

That night we dined at Dame Mabel's. It seemed like Rome before the fall. A tent draped in billows of gold satin, long swags and garlands of gold flowers, twelve tables, each seating ten, enough candles to light Times Square, every table with candelabra, silver bonbon baskets, silver dredgers, and *gold dessert* plates. Four wines, six courses. I sat with Dame Mabel, the Prime Minister, Sir Henry, the Ambassador of the Philippines (who is dean of the diplomatic corps), a scientist with a goatee, Lady Lloyd-Jones, Lady Johnston (who is the wife of the British H.C.), and Sir Rohan Delacombe. Ed sat with Sir Norman and the corresponding husbands and/or wives and the Premier and Mrs. Bolte. The P.M. and Sir Henry had a heated argument about Rhodesia. I, across the table, couldn't hear a word. I was frantic. Sir Rohan kept the attention of Dame Pattie with a story about his wife's inheriting a wine cellar, and how you must have an expert brought in to decide which bottles must be recorked.

Monday, no races. I went to a meeting of the American Women's Auxiliary to the Royal Children's Hospital for lunch, bought a hat, and attended *The Sound of Music*. Ed made diplomatic calls, visited manufacturing plants (U.S.), and went to another stag with the Premier. Tuesday was Cup Day. By this time, I was an old hand. I bet ten shillings on three different horses—total one pound, ten. Had a ticket on the winner and got back four pounds, ten and six.

That night at six, to cocktails at the Harold Holts'. He is Federal Treasurer. His wife, who never comes to Canberra, owns two *couturière* dress shops, one in Melbourne and another in Sydney, and looks like Kay Leary. On to a ball at the Hotel Menzies given by Messrs. J. & F. Livingston, yachtsmen. They participate in the America Cup Races, belong to the New York Yacht Club, and are bachelors, though Frank Livingston does escort a nice lady to whom he has been engaged for thirty years. He always introduces her as "my fiancee"—only Theo and

Nita Davis can match that. The hosts wore kilts and they had an act in which they played bagpipes for four dancers who did the Highland fling. I wish I had the menu. The last course was "haggis." I looked it up in the dictionary. Mr. Webster gives the following definition: "A pudding made of the heart, liver, lights, etc., of a sheep or a calf, minced with suet, onions, oatmeal, etc., seasoned, and boiled in the stomach of the animal." [I don't blame Mrs. Clark for leaving before it was served.—Mrs. O'D.] I left before they served it. I sat a long time by a gentleman named Armstrong. He's Dame Nellie Melba's own son, age ninety, an arrogant old coot.

Next day, I shopped with my friends Fran Smith, Lee Weiland, and Jocelyn Caldwell, wives of Embassy staff. We went to antique shops, Chinese stores, and the Royal Botanical Gardens. That night, we went to a benefit of the American Women's Auxiliary—dinner dance aboard a ship anchored at the pier, P & O Line, the *Francis Drake*. I had never been on any ship except the *Queen Mary*. This was exactly the same, just smaller. Sat at the Captain's table.

Next morning, we left early. Ed had to attend a state funeral. He said, "This is my first funeral where I never met the departed. If they open the casket, I sure want to look." The only piece of useful information I had from the State Department was that every lady should have a black dress and every gent a black four-in-hand for funerals. I was ready, but no ladies attended. The church was too small.

After the funeral, there was a stag lunch for eight at the Residence and today there is lunch for twelve. We went to a university lecture last night, and tonight at eight, dinner at the Italian chargé's. Tomorrow I have dinner for ten; Sunday the Argentinians have mid-day barbecue. Monday I receive three Ambassadors' wives, Swiss, Greek, and Swedish, in the A.M.; have stag lunch for Charles Lloyd-Jones. They own the biggest chain of department stores in Australia. Ed is trying to promote an Australian Fortnight at Neiman-Marcus. Next visitor will be Benno Schmidt, and, at the last of the week, the Christensens, who seem to have gotten *us* invited to Government House. They will be houseguests. I got them invited to a dinner dance by Walter Phillips of Esso and to Canberra House with Sir Charles and Lady J. I open a doll exhibit Friday for the Pan Pacific Association, and leave for Adelaide on Monday.

Anybody want the job?

Love and kisses,
Anne

Canberra, Australia
November 22, 1965

Greetings:

The days are never long enough to do all I want or to record all the interesting things that happen to me. Ed's posting as Ambassador to Australia should be labeled "the re-education of Anne Clark." I forget where I left off. Just before the Christensens came, I believe.

Benno Schmidt spent a night with us and we had a dinner party for him. Ed went with him to the airport and the two of them stood talking in the terminal while the plane to Sydney departed without Benno. So you can see that the Clark brand of confusion is beginning to take over. Wednesday we lunched at Parliament House with the President of the Malagasy Republic—Madagascar in our old geographies—black as ink and spoke only French. He is the first head of state who has ever come to Australia. On Thursday, November 11, we had a coffee for forty wives of the Institute of Management—mostly Australian women whose husbands are quite high-powered businessmen. Ed has now discovered that parties can go on here without my presence. There are at least twenty wives who can hostess as well or better than I. This was one of the times. Betty Smith, wife of the Economic Counselor, and three others took over. I went with Ed to the wreath-laying at the War Memorial. The rain came down in sheets. I was glad I went, though, especially when, at eleven o'clock sharp, a cavalcade drove up and Sir

Robert, Dame Pattie, and Lord and Lady Casey emerged from their cars, stood silent, unblinking, bareheaded in the rain to pay their tribute. Mind you, they are all past seventy. Boy, if you can do that at the same age, then you are a man.

Friday afternoon, I opened a fete. The Australians pronounce it "fight." These affairs aren't nearly as big or as lavish as, say, the Good Shepherd Bazaar, but they are ubiquitous. I had to name the bride doll for the guessing lottery. I named her Pattie. The Japanese doll I called "Yum Yum" from recollections of *The Mikado*. The procedure is to stand and say a few words regarding the history of the organization and the purpose to which the money will be put and to conclude by saying, "I declare this fete officially open." Then the newspaper photographs you and the organization makes a presentation to you. Once it was a basket of flowers, this time, a box of homemade candies.

The Christensens arrived by car. A charming Australian couple named Riggs, of International Harvester, was accompanying them. We dined that night at the Management Group's dinner dance at the Rex Hotel. Walter Phillips, American manager of Esso, has a beautiful Australian wife named Betsy. He married her here since his first wife's death. He advised me to write my "impressions" quickly, else they would not impress me any more. Soon all customs, words, and natural phenomena would be usual and unimpressive, he said. Next day, we lunched at Government House. The Christensens had entertained the Caseys when he was Ambassador to the United States while Chris was Dean at Wisconsin. Lady Casey even remembered the first name of a dinner guest whom Cora had forgotten.

That night we dined at Canberra House with the Johnstons. I consider Natasha (Lady J.) my best friend, even though she's a Russian princess and often tells funny stories of which I miss the whole point because of her heavily accented English. I am now also friends with their Egyptian butler, whose name is "Mo" (real name Mohamid). The No. 1 boy, head man, butler, whatever title you give him, is always standing outside on the stoop to greet you on arrival. When you depart, the hosts come out and stand on the steps and wave as you depart. You look out the window of the car and wave back.

Sunday we had Chinese lunch for ten. I now have a lazy Susan for
the center because the correct service requires putting all the bowls on
the table (family style at Lung's Chinese Kitchen). Huang wants us to
eat everything out of small rice bowls. You should put a little of each
concoction atop the rice and also use chop sticks. I insist on a plate and
a fork. We had a grazier couple, the C.'s, the Riggses, and a departing
staff member, John Call and wife, Katie. He's off to Vietnam and
Katie, who can't go, will set up a home in Hong Kong to be as near as
possible. John Call said he'd been in the foreign service eighteen years
and this was the first time he'd been invited to an Embassy for anything save large receptions. You see why we feel so keenly that all
Americans, including any staff members' visiting aunts and cousins
should have a chance to be a guest at the Residence. After lunch, the
Hyles took the Christensens to see their property. The 'roos weren't
out, but unusual water birds were on their ponds and we saw their
foals. Alison Hyle is a dedicated horsewoman. She goes away to equestrian schools, and breeds and trains her own horses. Packed the Christensens off, including Cora's sixty snapshots of the Embassy, at 5:00
P.M. Before the door closed on them, Colonel Carlson, our new Air
Attaché, entered with his friends, the Christian Science lecturer from
the Mother Church and his party. More tea and cookies, tour of the
rose garden, and explanation of the photographs of the President and
family. After that, I fell in bed, and died, until Huang knocked at 6:00
A.M. The following day we were off to Adelaide, the Boston of Australia, capital of the state of South Australia. While changing planes in
Melbourne, I attempted to make two phone calls. Neither Ed Cronk,
new D.C.M. out from Bonn, nor I, could use the Australian pay phone.
You press buttons as we do on car telephones. Finally talked to Dame
Mabel, but I nearly missed the plane. Met in Adelaide by usual greeting party with bouquets. Always, there is the warm welcome from the
officials of the Australian-American Association. The members are al-

most never citizens of the United States. On our departure, the president of A.A.A. and the chairman of the Women's Group were at the airport again. They must be the heritage that the American troops of 1942–1945 left to us, and it's *all good*. Departed from the airport via the Governor's Rolls with his aide, Captain Morrison, twenty-five years old, six feet, five inches of blonde, proper Englishness. Received at Government House, which is a huge Regency building of yellow stucco, shutters, antique cannons, gorgeous garden—right in the heart of the city. Lady Bastyan says the location is a "great advantage," since they have a staff of sixteen, eleven of whom live in. Sir Edric says the house is "quite well arranged," because when Her Majesty comes they can move into a small back wing and turn the residence over to her staff.

The British inevitably have pets. There are always stylish dog baskets around the house. And some old lumbering animal waddles in and Lady Who-ever says, "He is rather sweet, you know," and Sir Veddy English says, "Ho, ho, he's rather one of us, you know."

This house was full of those huge portraits, most prominent, of course, Queen Adelaide and King William IV. Also, Victoria, and usually George V and Queen Mary. Money seems to have run out, because they now have dinky little put-together things of Queen Elizabeth as compared to the fourteen-foot-high representations of bygone monarchs. George VI isn't there at all, save maybe in a silver frame on the library table.

Girls, I want to tell you that you haven't lived until you've had the services of an English maid and valet. Everything to the last bottle of pills is unpacked, so you must be careful to have nothing scroungy in your bag. The valet immediately noted he was unable to locate "His Excellency's" white tie, which had been slightly hidden by me. I broke a strap on a slip and when I next saw the slip, the strap had been sewed on again. Lady B. saw me to my room and discussed breakfast: upstairs or down? cooked eggs and bacon, or cold biscuits and tea? porridge or corn flakes? fruit or juice? early cup of tea to wake on or wait for break-

fast? tray or table? tray with legs or flat tray? I thought of the Roths-
childs asking whether the milk should be Jersey, Guernsey, or Hol-
stein. We did the usual things, including a reception at the Consul's
residence. Jack and Jan Linahan are New Englanders (she's Radcliffe) and tote their grandfather clock around the world. Visit to a
charity for me, Meals on Wheels, a remarkable service run by a remarkable woman who is more than chairbound. She has a sort of half-
reclining bed on wheels. Ladies' lunch at the Consulate with Premier's
wife, and the Lady Mayoress, and, unfailingly, the wife of the leader
of the Opposition. The Opposition has real status. The Bishop always
comes to the Consul's reception. Without even a gulp, I can say now,
"Good Evening, Your Grace. I bring you greetings from my friend,
the Presiding Bishop of the Episcopal Church in the United States."

Monday night, Australian-American dinner dance—toasts, speeches,
receiving lines, three bands, English, Australian, and New Zealand.
Ed and I waltzed alone to the "Yellow Rose of Texas." They had a
loud, gay, and, I thought, amusing floor show done by Maoris from
New Zealand in grass skirts like Hawaiians. The Maoris, unlike Australian aborigines, are Polynesian. Then to bed and dead!

Up early next day to view opals and the Consulate itself. Everybody
in Australia has a favorite opal dealer and is determined that you be
shown. I finally saw that I'd better buy some now, else I was going to
have to look every place I went. I bought some small unset ones to
have mounted in a Southern Cross pin. I plan to have it done on 47th
Street in New York. A drive in the Adelaide hills and lunch with the
dean of the consular corps' wife, Mrs. Nelson of Austria, with only
half-a-dozen ladies, her neighbors. It was one of the most enjoyable
days I've had. Mrs. Nelson reminds me of our Austin German ladies
like Freda Bohn. Their place is called "Redwoods" because they actually have California sequoias growing there. They are about eighty
years old, pygmies in size compared to the Muir Woods, but big
enough! The flora of the hills is quite different from the town due to
the difference in altitude. A beautiful little mountain sedum with a

purple blossom twice the size of a dollar is called "Pig Face," and a blue weed that covers whole meadows is called "Salvation Jane," or sometimes "Patterson's Curse."

That afternoon, we visited a winery. Penfolds is one of Australia's oldest. The plant there makes only champagne. The pressed grape juice is brought in from many vineyards in stainless steel tankers. Then the processing is done in Adelaide. There is no "trampling in the vineyards." Everything is very scientific and sanitary. They do have a few thousand bottles resting in the old caves that the monks built, but that is just for show. Did you know that besides being bottled in magnums and Jeroboams, champagne also comes in Rehoboams (6 bottles), Methuselahs (8), Salmanazars (12), Balthazars (16), and Nebuchadnezzars (20). I am not at all sure I spelled those names correctly. I'll bet nobody in the world has a piece of useless information that can top that!

We skipped tea with Sir E. and Lady B. for a nap after liberally tasting the champagne. That night they had a white-tie dinner, our first. There were twenty-two guests, eight waiters, and four wines. One of the unusual parts of their service is that the place mats are removed and the table crumbed before dessert. The bonbons (which were on the table already) are passed around between the meat and the sweet, and the fruit comes last. I am completely at ease with the fish knife and fork, and can peel and eat a banana with knife and fork. At the conclusion of the meal, Lady B. catches my eye, and she and I rise and leave the table together, followed by the other ladies. Gentlemen remain in the dining room. Lady B. said, "You Americans all leave together, don't you?" The aides and girl secretaries arrange and rearrange your seating in the drawing room, a fruit-basket-turnover sort of thing.

Next morning before our eleven o'clock departure we visited with the Bastyans. They are old friends of Huang, our butler, who served them in Hong Kong. He sent them a present of Chinese tea and Lady B. sent gifts back to his children. There is an enormous oak on the grounds like our live oak called a Turkish Oak. Silver gulls flew in and marched about the lawn. I saw the willie-wagtail for the first time. He is an Australia-wide, fluttering, wren-size bird. Sir E. paints good, conventional landscapes.

We lunched between planes in Melbourne. Dame Mabel came out to visit, also Consul General and Mrs. Weiland. We arrived at the Residence in Canberra just in time to receive Governor Otto Kerner of Illinois, who had been entertained here for lunch in our absence. Ed had a stag dinner away from the Residence that night. I sorted mail and planned the next day, when we would be giving another stag luncheon, and Ed would be attending another dinner. Saturday morning we received Mr. and Mrs. Nial Jackson. He is a banker from Melbourne and a friend of the A. G. McNeeses from Houston. At eleven Ed's tailor came, name of "Chorley," and at twelve we departed for the country to lunch with the Bedford Osbornes, an old grazier family. Mr. Osborne's American mother was an actress named Maude Jeffreys from Memphis. I am trying hard to claim kin, they are so charming. He's sixty and a second-generation owner of that property. The house is simple, but also simply elegant. We drove out and saw his 'roos, including a mother with twin joeys. Mr. O. believes in the balance of nature, and allows no animal on the property to be killed. Their property has been declared an official reserve.

Ed's portrait painter came at 8:30 Sunday. Her name is Valerie O'Neill. The picture is about finished and fairly good, I think. We went to church and ran into Sir Stanley Burbury, the Chief Justice of Tasmania, who had been our host in Hobart. Invited him and his hosts, Sir Reginald and Lady Sholl, to come for a drink and meet two American gentlemen whom we had never met ourselves, but had invited for lunch: Mr. Lewis Graber of Mississippi and Mr. George Younger of Alexandria, Louisiana. Mr. G. is grandfather of our Maggie's soulmate, Ethel Graber, and Mr. Younger is her other grandfather and the father of Leila's friend, Georgia Fisher (Mrs. Rob Roy). Both of them are Southern gentlemen. Mr. G. is stone deaf. They were glad to see us and we them, a touch of home for both of us. Then all hell broke loose. The Junior Chambers of Commerce from Liberty and Odessa, Texas, phoned from Sydney, twenty-two of them, expecting lunch at the Residence on Monday. We had them scheduled for cocktails from 3:30 to 5:30. A dinner that night and a wives' meeting that morning made it impossible for me to change. I wished for Ralph Moreland or a Randy's Circle R or a Mary Koock, who could have sent box lunches to be eaten on the terrace. I am afraid it's the Commonwealth Club or the Rex Hotel for them, though. Ed still thinks I could have managed if I'd wanted to. But even though my China boys would have to go back to Hong Kong if they quit, I am afraid they would have rebelled on that one.

This has been far too long. I wouldn't read it unless I was a daughter or a mother. I guess I just wrote it for the exercise. All I need now is time and strength. I want to rearrange my bedrooms, rehang one of the Kefauver Art in Embassies pictures in the gentlemen's powder room, have the crewel-work cushions made for the library, and make a pot-pourri of the rose leaves.

I should end this like an Uncle Wiggily.* If the President doesn't recall us too soon, next time I'll tell you about my new dog, my parrot, my studies of Gallipoli, and our projected trip to Brisbane.

A hug for all from

Anne

* *Uncle Wiggily,* by Howard R. Garis, was about a well-loved character in children's stories during my childhood.

Canberra, Australia

December 1, 1965

Dear Everybody:

We have just returned from our state visit to Brisbane. Though we felt we had been kindly received in all the capitals of Australia, nothing compared to the warmth of our reception in Brisbane. If you do not already know it, there is what is known in Australia as the "Brisbane Line"—the line above which it was planned to abandon the continent to the Japanese, who were already landing in Port Moresby, and to defend only the southern part below the line. Then came Mac-Arthur with the announcement that the United States would defend all the island. The Battle of the Coral Sea followed, making its anniversary the greatest day of celebration in Australia.

Brisbane is not so lovely a city, not so tidy nor so English as the other capitals, but its display of unabashed love for Americans makes it my favorite. It is "way up north" in the tropics, the capital of Queensland. The vegetation is more like our own southern vegetation. The colors are bright, the ferns and petunias sprawl and spread. There is more wooden construction and the houses are built higher off the ground, like beach houses, giving the same appearance as our city of Galveston. There are many handsome oleanders, but the glory of the town is the gorgeous royal poinciana now in full scarlet bloom.

I had only a short visit in the Zoological Gardens of Brisbane. There was not a great deal of bloom, only tropical greenery, much like that in Texas' Rio Grande Valley, but I did watch the famous black swans. Have you ever seen swans walking on dry land? Those gliding, grace-ful creatures seen floating on the water are the most awkward, the clumsiest, the ugliest things possible when walking.

In Brisbane, we had the added pleasure of being entertained at Government House with Sir Henry and Lady May Abel-Smith as our hosts. The Abel-Smiths are the only real royalty that we have known in Australia, and undoubtedly the most relaxed of the Governors of any of the several states. Even Government House reminds me of a beach house. It has wide verandas and louvered doors and transoms. My bath-room was on a balcony and I had to step outside in order to reach it.

We found the usual little mimeographed schedules on our desks, but minus much formality and detail present in other Government Houses.

There was not a screen on the place, and every bed was equipped with a mosquito bar. My little Scottish maid tried her best to make me sleep under the mosquito bar, but I absolutely refused.

Lady May's mother is the Princess Alice, still alive and active in her late eighties, and her father was Earl of Athlone. Perhaps you remember that he was Governor General of Canada during World War II years; Lady May spent some time there with her children when the blitz was on in England. The house was decorated with family portraits. There was a pair of Queen Victoria and Prince Albert in their early youth. Sir Henry explained to me that he had found Government House sadly lacking in portraits and, knowing that there were extras (by the hundred) stored at Buckingham Palace, he simply requested the Queen to lend him those two, which she did; she has now placed them on permanent loan. They also had their own family portraits: Sir Henry's mother like a Gibson Girl of 1906, Lady May in a "hat *pour le sport*" looking herself like Iris March, Sir Henry's grandmother in a nice little lace cap and ruffles. Another portrait was of an English woman, Frances Stuart. It was she who modeled for the Britannia whose face appears on the English penny. Every table was absolutely loaded with photographs in silver frames with such inscriptions as "To Henry and May from Bertie." Bertie was the familiar name by which George VI was known while Duke of York before his succession to the throne after the abdication of Edward VIII.

Large, handsome flower arrangements are always a charming feature of Australian and English houses. I felt really at home when I saw on the table, just as I entered, a huge vase of plain old-fashioned southern magnolias.

There was an enormous collection of very grand Victorian silver in the house. The part I was able to examine most carefully consisted of the appointments on the desk in my sitting room. Most of this seemed to have been Sir Henry's personal silver inscribed with his crest, the head of an elephant. There was even a silver rack for the pipe. Also, a lovely old-fashioned desk clock, which had been presented to him on his twenty-first birthday. By the way, he was twenty-one in 1921, making him sixty-five now. At the base of the clock was the following inscription: "To Henry Abel-Smith on his 21st Birthday from the old servants, inside and outside staff, Coburn Hall."

A simply magnificent cigar-cigarette box, complete with spirit lamp and a little knife for cutting the end off the cigar, was inscribed with the crest of his regiment, the 7th Hussars. In my sitting room hung a collection of Gould birds, unfortunately not Australian, but South American ones. They, too, were Sir Henry's own. The family book-mark shows two coats of arms halved and says "Henry Abel-Smith—May, his wife."

My desk was equipped with a stick of sealing wax, which in my opinion is the height of something or other. The inkwell had a small clock inside the top. Breakfast was served every morning on the balcony by a butler and a footman. On my tray was every possible kind of fruit—peaches, mangoes, pawpaws, cantaloupe, grapefruit—and delicious English bitter marmalade.

The Scottish maid who looked after me had once lived in the eastern part of the United States. She offered to, and did, rinse out what she referred to as my "smalls."

Every Government House staff has a private secretary for the Governor, often a retired army officer of great elegance and poise. Also, an aide de camp, usually a young officer with the rank of captain. Frequently, he is an old friend of the family out from England for just this purpose. Then there's always a lady in waiting. Here, she was an older person named Mrs. Sewell, who lives in Australia. Lady May said she was the last of a long line and that, since they were going home in March at the end of their five-year term, she had not replaced the last one with a young English girl, as had been her custom.

Visiting the Abel-Smiths was their daughter, Anne, and their son-in-law, whose name was Liddell-Grainger. They were out from Scotland for about six weeks, having left their four children at home with the Nannie.

On our first day in Brisbane, we had our formal luncheon with the Premier and the official family of the state government of Queensland. Then in the afternoon a reception by city officials, the Lord Mayor, and the Lady Mayoress. In the evening our own Consul entertained us with a reception, followed by an elaborate smorgasbord-type supper.

We had been invited by the Abel-Smiths to look in on the dance they were giving for their young friends, but by that time we were so completely worn out that even my strong curiosity was not able to carry me through. We stayed only long enough to see that they were having supper and did not wait for the dancing. I would love to have had at least one waltz with Sir Henry.

Next morning I was forced to cancel part of our busy schedule, which was to have included a trip to the Koala Bear Sanctuary. However, we did join Sir Henry at the cricket matches. I thought they were interesting. It looked a good deal like baseball to me. You either like cricket or you hate it. Some persons, even Australians and Englishmen, declare it the dullest possible form of entertainment.

From the cricket matches, we went straight to the races with Sir Henry, riding in a Daimler car. Sir Henry explained that this car was purchased new in 1947. When he arrived in Australia in 1960, he considered that Government House had no suitable official car, and so, hearing that the Queen was changing cars from Daimlers to Rolls Royces, he wrote and asked Her Majesty to send her old car out to him, and she complied. The top rolls back for parades and I *had* to ask to have a little ride with it rolled back. Can you imagine just asking the Queen for her old car!

We lunched in the clubhouse with the president of the Racing Committee. His name is Dr. Clive Ure. He and Mrs. Ure devoted much time to making us have a pleasant time, and to enjoying the races generally. Betting is made terribly convenient in the members' stands, and it is not crowded. I did not hear of anyone being what I would call a heavy gambler. Though Lady May appears a devoted follower of the races and was very knowledgeable about the horses, "very keen," as they say, her bets were always small. Ed had a relatively successful day with his bets. Of course, the first three or four races he was making me place all the bets because, as you know, if he is unsure the least bit, he doesn't like to participate until he knows exactly what he is doing.

That night we had our big evening at the Australian-American Association dinner dance. As I have said, it was the most rewarding state visit we have had. A goodly crowd turned out. The repast was what they conceived to be an American Thanksgiving Dinner with the Ambassador carving the turkey. More of the crowd were Americans than I have seen anywhere previously. Much of the Australian oil development is up in the Queensland area. This attracts Americans. Dozens of United States oil companies are drilling.

We ended up singing "The Eyes of Texas," clapping our hands to "Deep in the Heart of Texas," and dancing merrily to the strains of "When the Saints Go Marching In." The replies for the Australian-American Association were done by Sir Douglas Forbes. He is not a statesman, but a banker, apparently not well known in Canberra or in government circles. I thought him one of the most eloquent men I have ever heard. He spoke apparently off the cuff, and one of his most memorable remarks was, "But for you Americans and the Grace of God, we'd all be pulling rickshaws now." The affair was held in the Lennon's Hotel, the same place and, I believe, the same room in which General MacArthur had his headquarters during the war. To the Australians, this is almost holy ground.

The next day was Sunday, which we spent all of with the Abel-Smiths. We attended the early church service in the Cathedral, which, like many cathedrals, is still in the process of building after more than fifty years. Without returning to Government House, we drove straight to a place in the country owned by friends. Sir Henry did the driving himself, this time in a Rolls Royce. Our destination was one unit of several properties owned by the Wally King family. At this particular place they prepare young bulls for sale, largely Herefords, but here also are some fine specimens of a breed called Afrikanders imported from

South Africa. Afrikanders are a beautiful cherry red and look a good deal like our Santa Gertrudis cattle. Mr. King was absent that day, but on hand were his wife, three daughters, one son, and a young Scottish friend who was out in Australia "jackarooing"—a term for an apprentice cowboy. Apparently young Englishmen frequently do this before they return home to "go on the land." The Australians sound the second *e* when they say "Hereford."

A simple but delicious lunch was served buffet style. It was what Australians call a "salad lunch," but included several kinds of cold meat. Finally, a cart was rolled in carrying every possible variety of beautiful tropical fruit, all grown in the Queensland area, including watermelon. After lunch we drove over the property and looked at the animals. Even the girls knew a great deal about the creatures, their physical points, and their possible selling price. One of the daughters, Robin, had a small baby just learning to crawl. She had come home to her mother in order to leave the baby for a two-week stay while she went out to the West to cook for the sheep shearers. The shearers are highly unionized and every meal has to be served exactly on time, including "smoko," which is tea in mid-morning and mid-afternoon. The term, like our coffee break, means time for a smoke as well as tea. Tea includes sandwiches and sweets in plenty. There is a complicated system whereby the shearers pay so much for their meals and, in turn, the owner of the property sells them back the meat, lamb and beef. Robin says she comes cheap as a cook. One other outstanding and attractive feature about this place was that, although their home was a simple country house, akin to a Mississippi plantation house, there was a large ballroom smack in the middle. That day it was being put to use as the baby's crawling ground.

Before departing we signed the guest book, a rite never omitted in Australian homes. In this guest book, besides Princess Alice and the Duke of Gloucester, there were many other distinguished names. I am sure most of the famous were brought there by Lady May and Sir Henry. We tooled back to Brisbane, Sir Henry driving at high speed with Lady May remonstrating with him constantly, after the manner of all wives, suggesting a wait for the other car in which their daughter and son-in-law were following. We paused briefly at Government House, just long enough to change clothes—Lady May put on slacks and Sir Henry a sport shirt—and off we sped to Mount Glorious. By that time, it was drizzling rain and sundown. The roads were steep and dark, but Sir Henry was master of the situation. When we arrived at the appointed rendezvous, it was black as ink and pouring rain. Cars were getting stuck and Lady May was advising Sir Henry about his driving. Sir Henry, unlike an American husband who would have said, "You shut up," countered with, "Keep quite quiet, keep quite quiet." At last we were forced to turn about to a spot two miles down the road, where we took over what Lady May called the "tea kiosk." Tables were set up for us, and the proprietors, Lady May termed it, "cooked those miserable chops," and we had a nice barbecue supper under shelter. Our party was joined by some nice intelligent friends of theirs, all graziers, so the conversation turned naturally to the drought (pronounced "drout"), and how the next drought could be better handled by property owners. One woman praised her husband for having one of the few credit balances in a bank. She said they had tried to teach their children never to try to outlast or outwit a drought. Sell your stock and wait for the rains and then rebuy, she said. We returned to Government House late with plans for an early morning takeoff. Sir Henry was up at seven to say "Goodbye" to us. At that hour, he was his usual gallant and debonair self.

We flew back to Canberra via Navy plane, a DC-3, arriving there about noon to find guests streaming in the front door for lunch. Our guest of honor for luncheon was Mr. John Lawrence of Dallas. We had tons of lovely APO mail to go through, a task that took me nearly a whole afternoon. I sort out the things that have to be answered, the clippings, the American things, the newspapers, and the packages.

On Tuesday I had lunch with Mrs. Hasluck. The other guests were Mrs. Henrietta Drake-Brockman, a West Australian friend of Mrs.

Hasluck's; Mrs. Ritter, wife of the German Ambassador; Mme Brière, wife of the French Ambassador; and my dearly loved Natasha, whom Ed insists on referring to as Nasturtium. I believe Mrs. D-B, an author of note, did an article for *The Texas Quarterly* on Australia. Mrs. Hasluck is the wife of Paul Hasluck, Minister for External Affairs, who has the duties of our Secretary of State.*

Last night, for the first time in a long while, Ed and I dined off a tray, alone, and enjoyed it thoroughly. Then we waited for the arrival at eight o'clock of Ralph Hall, a member of the Texas Senate, who is traveling with two associates in the aluminum business. I stayed long enough to greet them before retiring for an early bedtime. Ed took off this morning at daybreak for a return visit to Adelaide, where he will talk on the subject of trade, specifically trade in bourbon whiskey. He titles his speech "Keeping Trade Liquid."

I have a comparatively free day, broken only by a conference with the Administrative Officer concerning some of the refurbishing I would like to do in the Residence. This afternoon I will have a small tour and tea for seniors of the Girls' Grammar School. There will be thirteen girls and three mistresses.

Saturday we are having a wedding reception for an Embassy staff officer. His little bride is coming in from Karachi to be married here. I believe her home in America is Mobile, Alabama.

Next week a trip to Sydney is planned. This time not official, so I hope to have some few hours for shopping and just looking around.

Goodbye and good luck to everybody. I miss you all more than I can say and I wish especially I had a friend with whom to talk over all my interesting experiences.

Devotedly your friend,
Anne Clark

* Sir Paul Hasluck is now Governor General.

Canberra, Australia
December 14, 1965

Holiday Greetings to all my friends:

I don't keep copies of the letters I write, but someone has written that my last was dated November 30. After today I am sure that if I write another letter, it will be on the plane when I return to the United States some time a few days after Christmas, because, from now on, it looks as if my life is very full.

On December 1 I had tea for the Church of England Girls' Grammar School graduating class of thirteen. They were darling and wore little school uniforms of brown jumpers and the required hat. I think they enjoyed the dog and the parrot more than they did the Residence. Children are not impressed easily.

Ed was out of town on the following day, so I went to see his finished portrait at Miss O'Neill's house and to choose a frame for it. Like many things in Australia, picture framing is a generation behind the times. There are only long strips of molding in the rough that later are finished in natural, gold, or silver, but you have no way of knowing how the frame will turn out before ordering.

That afternoon I called on Mrs. Menzies, whose husband is the new High Commissioner of Canada. Of course, they are beset with the question, "What is your relation to the Prime Minister?" Answer, "None that we know of save that we belong to the same Scottish clan." That night I went to Duntroon to a benefit with Mrs. Gerard, wife of our Army Attaché. It was called a "late afternoon." Duntroon is the military academy, like our West Point, for Australia. It is certainly small by comparison with West Point. The New Zealand cadets train there, also. A lovely old Victorian Gothic house survives on the grounds. It was one of the original Campbell homes of Canberra Station before it became the Capital Territory.

Next I called on the wife of the Argentinian Ambassador. She says she speaks no English (though she does speak some), so she called in her nine-year-old daughter, Josephine, to be her interpreter. The Señora is a beautiful woman and quite young. The Argentinian Embassy, though a small one-story house, is beautifully appointed with things they own personally. Some of the Latinos, or South American diplomats, do not have a great deal of business here. I am under the impression some are paying their own expenses and come only for the honor of the position. "Madame Argentina" told me that her husband is the owner of a large ranch in the Argentine where they lived before coming "down under."

On Saturday the Ambassador gave the bride away at a wedding. The groom is a member of our Embassy staff, newly posted to Canberra. He and his bride, also a foreign service employee, met in Karachi. She came to Canberra directly instead of going home to be married in Mobile, Alabama. The wedding in St. Christopher's Church (Roman Catholic) was complete with bridesmaids, flowers, veil, and everything. After the ceremony the bride and groom withdrew to the sacristy with the Monsignor, who motioned for the Ambassador and me to follow. He shook hands with us at the foot of the chancel before we all moved into the sacristy where there was much to-do over signing the Witness Book. The photographers made their pictures in there. This is one custom I like. Afterward we had a reception for about seventy-five people here at the Residence with champagne and a delectable cake made by two of the Embassy wives. I am glad we were asked for that signing, else I should have always wondered what went on in there behind the scene.

Monday we were entertained at lunch at a downtown hotel by Mr. and Mrs. Hutchinson. His business is directing the operation of Kennicott Copper. They come directly from Spokane, Washington. As a matter of fact, both are Canadians, but both simply adored the United States and say that if they ever go back for any length of time, they expect to take out United States citizenship. He has a doctorate from the University of Wisconsin. She became extremely interested in American politics and worked hard in Senator Spike Jackson's campaign. Being a Canadian, she sees Australia with a different eye from that of anybody else I have met. She is not in the least impressed with all the "Britishness" of life in Australia, though she understands it perfectly. As a matter of fact, her father was a Liberal member of the Cabinet in Ottawa for more than fifty years. The aura of glamour about English customs does not exist for her. She told me a good deal about the French-Canadian situation and why the new flag of Canada, which is three stripes, the white one bearing a maple leaf between two red ones, has no blue and no part of the Union Jack, retained by most dominions and former British colonies. The French-Canadians felt strongly that it should not look in the least English or have any relation to that country. She said these same French-Canadians have no relations with nor feel any loyalty to France.

On Sunday, the second Sunday in Advent, it seemed strange to see the church decorated with pink roses and white Easter lilies obviously grown in the gardens of Canberra.

Congressman Hale Boggs of New Orleans was welcomed as our houseguest on December 7. He is just about the nicest person imaginable and we thoroughly enjoyed him. Traveling with him was his assistant, Argyll Campbell. That night we had a few people for cocktails. The Prime Minister and Dame Pattie honored us by coming and staying for an hour before going on to their dinner engagement. Then Ed had twelve gentlemen for a stag dinner with the Congressman. Next morning Mr. Boggs was up at 5:30 saying he thought his watch must have stopped. In reality, he was caught by the time change, which troubled him almost as much as it had me when I first arrived. December days are long, bright days here like we have in summer. We get almost the southern version of midnight sun.

Early Wednesday morning, we all left on the same plane for Sydney. There we had a small reception in the airport for Mr. Boggs before he departed for Hong Kong. I attempted a little shopping in Sydney, but the stores were teeming with Christmas customers and I found that due to my unfamiliarity and my uncertainty about what I wanted, shopping was more than I could handle, so I gave it up, or "gave it away," as the Aussies would phrase it. That night we were entertained by Sir Howard and Lady Beale. As you know, Sir Howard was the former Ambassador to the United States and had not been long returned to Australia. He is a lively, attractive person and it is easy enough to see why he was such a success in the United States. He visited Texas many times and was a special friend of Bill and Marty Lynch's of Dallas. When we arrived at the Beales' house, sitting on the front stairs in the entrance hall to welcome us were a pair of Texas boots and a big hat. They were gifts from Bill and Marty. Lady Beale is one of those typically petite Australian women, charming and lovely. Before dinner, they had perhaps fifty in for cocktails. The house is admirable with what they call a "very good position." That means it looks out over the harbor. There is a swimming pool and a terrace and balcony from which to watch the view of all the activity in the most beautiful harbor in the world.

Six couples stayed for dinner and I felt at ease because the service was after the American fashion. A seafood cocktail was followed by a casserole of cannelloni served by Sir Howard at the table, hot bread, and green salad; then a beautiful dessert of mangoes, jellied in a ring mold with the usual whipped cream. Australians love cream. Among the dinner guests were Sir Garfield and Lady Barwick. He is Chief Justice of Australia and a former Minister for External Affairs. Also, our friend Walter Phillips, who is American managing director for Esso in Australia, and his wife, Betsy.

The following day I had accepted an invitation from Mrs. Charles Walton, known nationwide as Nancy Bird Walton. She is a great friend of Lady Casey's. A well-known Australian aviatrix, she is also just an interesting, articulate individual aside from her connection with aviation. She picked Dottie Cronk and me up at the hotel at 11:00 A.M. With her was a young English actress, Marigold Williams. Marigold is the wife of the assistant producer of a new film that is being made in

Australia, called *The Weird Mob*. I considered her a great addition to
our day because she was both pretty and modest and also full of information, which she projected well when her opinion was asked on
any reasonable subject. I thought our day remarkably successful. Mrs.
Walton was at least vocal and uninhibited about the subjects on which
she talked. We drove all around Sydney and looked at the various
beaches, winding up our drive at Palm Beach, one of the more fashionable spots, where we lunched at her club. On the way out she stopped
and bought the lunch. When we arrived she explained to us that it was
a "do-it-yourself" club, which it was. It was attractive and absolutely
immaculate. She fixed us all a drink, signed a chit for it, and took a
bottle of wine out of the ice box, directing us to sit and enjoy our
drinks. Within fifteen minutes she produced a delicious lunch of
broiled lobster, supplemented by bread and homemade cookies from
her picnic food basket. We sat and enjoyed our lunch while watching
the bathers and surfers on the beach. Afterward we went into the
kitchen, tidied up, then got in our car and drove off to join the men of
my party, Ed Cronk and Ed Clark.

At Taronga Park Zoo we were conducted around by Sir Edward
Hallstrom, a delightful gentleman in his seventies, dressed all in black
and looking like a character out of Dickens, or perhaps off a Toby jug.
He told us he had a blind eye. He had lost the sight when he was
kicked by a giraffe, but he said the giraffe had not meant to kick him,
he was only awkward! I thought the zoo, known throughout the world,
was one of the most interesting things seen in my lifetime. There were
fifteen giraffes; all save one was born in the zoo. They also breed rhi-
noceroses. There was a pit, reminiscent of monkey island in Bracken-
ridge Park, San Antonio, where about fifty kangaroos of various types
(with prospects of producing progeny) bounced about. Of course, the
creature at the zoo that visitors are most interested in is the unique
platypus. How shy the platypus is and how hard he is to glimpse, even
in captivity! Sir Edward went straight into the platypus' little house,
brought it out in his arms, and had us examine it very carefully. While

telling us about the venom carried in its spurs and that there was a man in the hospital right then who would need at least a week to recover from that venom, he insisted that we pat the little fellow. Ed gave one small pat and walked away toward the car, but I had courage and talked to him as well. I thought of Theo and jail coffee. When he served on the grand jury, coffee was brought up from the jail. Fastidious, but impeccably polite, Theo always found a fascinating view out the window during the refreshment break. I think this should get me on Gary Moore's program, "I've Got a Secret," and my secret would be, "I have personally patted the platypus." Of course, the koala bears are the dearest things you have ever seen, sleepy, furry, fat, and cuddly, and they are willing to let everyone fondle them. Ilka Chase says, "Dear as they are, I wouldn't call them stimulating company." It is said that the eucalyptus on which they feed is soporific and that they are doped all the time.

I also saw the famous Tasmanian devil, now almost extinct. Its appearance is something like a pig with a snout and something like a large dog. The name derives from its eerie howl, which the aborigines associated with the cry of ghosts.

Sydney was in gorgeous bloom with mounds of hydrangeas everywhere. Jacaranda trees give harbor-side gardens the appearance of huge lavender bouquets. Also, the Christmas bush is beginning to flower. This is a native shrub popping up all over the hillsides that is as beloved as the daphne; the natives will pin an orange-red sprig of it on your lapel at the drop of a hat.

Nancy commented on Sydney's colony of Dutch migrants, who work hard, build homes, and get ahead fast. The Australians say they have no sense of fun. Then she went on to say, "You Americans work so hard. Why, your generals nearly upset the whole plan of things by wanting to run the war on Saturdays."

That night we went to a lovely dinner in the American National Club and I was presented with a set of silver coffee spoons with opals in the handles. Next morning I was a little bit lazy. Then to "Craigend" for a large tea put on by the Australian-American Association Women's Group. It was attended by at least two hundred women curious to see the new Ambassador's wife. Of course, it is always pleasing to know how interested the Australians are in the American Ambassador. The women started arriving at least forty-five minutes before the appointed time for the tea. It is the Australian custom to have chairs provided for all guests after they have passed through the receiving line, and most times there are small tables from which to eat.

Our time was cut so thin that we were forced to don our evening clothes at "Craigend." Dottie Cronk and I got ourselves into full-length evening dresses and long white gloves and were joined by our husbands in white tie and tails for dinner at the home of Mr. and Mrs. Warwick Fairfax. When we arrived there, the first thing we saw was a large wreath of yellow roses on the door. The Fairfax home contains a fine collection of modern Australian paintings but time was too short to really examine them. As one of the features, a cowboy singer named "Smoky" rode a fine palamino horse on to the lawn while singing "The Yellow Rose of Texas." Dinner was served on the terrace. In place of table cloths, there was green artificial grass with center pieces of yellow roses. All this was but the background for heirloom china and Venetian glass goblets. Everything was too hurried to savor fully because the main purpose of our trip to Sydney was to attend the Metropolitan auditions. Young singers contested for prizes of scholarships on which to study in New York and have an opportunity to sing at the Metropolitan. After the auditions, which ended about 10:30, a reception was held on the terrace outside the theater. An enoromus buffet of roast beef and other cold food was laid out. There was an orchestra and outdoor dance floor. However, I was forced to fold early. The day had been too long.

Saturday morning we stole a few minutes to go to the home of Lady Lloyd-Jones, which is one of the show places of Australia. She has fine Dobell portraits of all members of her family and some modern French paintings, too, including a Bernard Buffet. She has collections of everything from Staffordshire china to orchids. Her home, called "Rosemont," is a most interesting house. I hope to go back and stay longer sometime. Lady Lloyd-Jones is to me a very attractive woman, probably seventy-five years old. She is a great hostess, a friend of Mrs. Mesta, in Washington, and Marjorie Merriweather Post. From there we went to luncheon at the Rush Clarks. He represents Pan American Airways in this country and lives in a house that once belonged to Prime Minister Billy Hughes, "The Little Digger."

From there we returned to the hotel for Ed to get into his striped pants and gray top hat. We attended a fashionable wedding. Billy McMahon, a bachelor Cabinet Minister of fifty-eight years, was married to a beautiful blonde of thirty-three. Sydney society was out in full force, as were the uninvited onlookers on the sidewalk and the photographers. One of the differences between our wedding services is that here they provide a printed leaflet with the words of three hymns for congregational singing, which they perform with gusto. Other music was by a children's choir, which did not process. The bridesmaids walked behind the bride. Again, all sat twenty minutes in our pews while the wedding party repaired to the sacristy to sign the Witness Book. The reception was at the Royal Sydney Golf Club, dark and conservative. Walter Phillips is Royal Sydney's only American member. We didn't stay for the toasting or cake-cutting, as we rushed on to our next appointment, a dinner engagement with Betsy and Walter. Betsy is rich and charming, a gray-haired grandmother, but much more lively than Walter. She has the greatest figure I've ever seen on a woman of any age. She likes to get up at seven and go swimming with her golden retriever, while Walter, she says, just likes to sit and think about Esso. He's a polished Virginia gentleman, an Annapolis graduate. The Cronks had brought Ed's dark suit for a quick change, because we went on to the theater to see *Who's Afraid of Virginia Woolf?* Betsy Phillips' house (which she owned before she married Walter two years ago) is a thing of beauty—old, lovingly restored, lots of white wicker furniture and red roses on the tiles imported from Italy by the original builder. Its name is "Villa Porta Rosa." Naturally it has a rose-pink gate. Everybody's house in Australia has a name. This house has a beautiful "position" looking on the harbor. After the theater, Walter and Betsy dropped us at our hotel. We left early next morning for Canberra. The theater we attended is called The Old Tote, because it was built on an old race course on the spot where a totalizer or tote board once stood, pari-mutuel board to us.

We are laughing at ourselves as we begin to adopt the Australian vernacular. A local phrase is always to speak of your ride as "transport." For example, they will not say "Do you have a ride?" or "Do you have a way?" but "Do you have transport?" Another Australian phrase calls one's turn to treat in the bar "my shout." Betsy was "shouting" her daughter's trip abroad. For another commonplace one, which Mamma Clark would express as "he lit a shuck," they say "he shot through like the Bondi Tram." A phrase used when offered another drink or other attention is the answer, "I'm right," meaning, "No thanks." Some say the local favorite brush-off, "She'll be right," may be Australia's downfall because like the Mexican *mañana* it is used as an excuse for not finishing the job properly.

This was our gayest trip because we were relieved of official calls. We did call officially on the Danish Minister who resides in Sydney, and we did have the American Club dinner and my ladies' tea, but, other than that, we had a little more freedom of movement than we have had in the past. I thoroughly enjoyed it, though it's strenuous still. We plan to leave Canberra the afternoon of Christmas Day and spend the day after Christmas, December 26, in Sydney. That day is known as "Boxing Day." It has nothing to do with prize fighting. It refers to an old English custom of delivering boxes on that day to friends or, possibly, to the poor. Boxing Day in Sydney will be given over to the start of the Sydney-Hobart Yacht Races, and we have been invited by Mr. Lex Anderson to spend the day on his boat to watch the yacht races. I don't know whether we will see any of the tennis tournament or not. The final round of the Davis Cup matches also begins that day. I saw the Davis Cup itself displayed in the window of David Jones' store. It is a handsome, double heavy, beautifully embossed silver punch bowl.

We have been invited to spend part of Christmas Day with the Prime Minister, Dame Pattie, and their grandchildren. Then we will have lunch with my dear friends, Natasha and Sir Charles, before we take off that afternoon. I will have to confess I am looking forward to coming home, seeing you, my friends, getting an American perma-nent wave and some new clothes, and hopefully resting up from this strenuous life that I am leading here.

So, goodbye for now, and I will be seeing you probably by the time you get this missive, which is too long for most of you to read.

Anne Clark

Canberra, Australia
February 4, 1966

Dear Friends at home, dear Absent Family:

This is my first letter since we left Canberra on the afternoon of Christmas Day after having spent part of the morning at the Lodge with Sir Robert Menzies, Dame Pattie, and a large gathering of their children, grandchildren, nieces, and nephews. The table was laid and decorated in the entrance hall, which is one of the more spacious rooms in the Lodge. The tree was in the library. It was a happy, home oc-casion, a Christmas "just like the ones we used to know." They are a wonderful, charming family. I am glad I was privileged to know them and to be a part of the Menzies era. By the time we returned to Can-berra, Sir Robert had exercised his usual grace and good sense, by yielding the power to other, younger hands, thereby doing what his heart told him was best for Australia. He was the last of the great Commonwealth statesmen, and for Ed and me, two of his newest "captives of love," there will always be a happy memory for us of that last Christmas the Menzies spent at the Lodge.

The new Prime Minister, Mr. Harold Holt, will be wonderful, too, only different. "The old order changeth, yielding place to new." I have been to the Holts' home in Melbourne, when they entertained a group for drinks after the Melbourne Cup. Mrs. Holt is charming and sophisticated. She owns fine modern paintings and two fashionable dress shops, known as "Mags." Mr. Holt is a true son of Australia, in that he is a dedicated sportsman—presently, his interest is skin diving.* Sir Robert is a great gourmet, and we made a point of having special wines, brandy, and cigars when he dined with us. Mr. Holt is a discriminating and moderate drinker. He is much less of a Queen's man than Sir Robert.

We arrived in Sydney the evening of Christmas Day and were taken by our friend Walter Phillips to a family gathering of the Graces, the kin of his Australian wife. They are an old, established Australian family with business interests in merchandising, packing, moving, and other fields. There were at least fifty people, half under ten years old, and a half-dozen more upstairs in their baskets, so Betsy Phillips said. Little girls were all rigged up in tarleton costumes left over from their "concerts" (I judge we in the United States would call these piano or ballet recitals). They entertained us with impromptu pageants and concerts. Two little crippled boys were in wheel chairs. There were great aunts galore, and Mick Grace, reigning head of the family, and smart young matrons in muumuus. Everybody had a present for everybody else and thanked each other with kisses. That included us, their new American friends. Ed and I left laden with especially chosen gifts like books and records. Mr. Grace said, "You can tell we are in retail." Drinks were mixed by the drinkers themselves. A lovely cold buffet was served before the tree ceremony. They have Christmas pudding for luck with hard sauce called "brandy butter." Mrs. Grace, the

---

* This letter was written during the first week of February, 1966. Mr. Holt's tragic death while skin diving occurred in December, 1967.

matriarch, lives in her castle across the way like a duchess and refuses to come to such gatherings. She says she can't stand the din, so she receives her progeny a few at a time, for not more than five minutes.

Next morning we went out on Lex Anderson's yacht to see the opening of the Sydney-Hobart Yacht Races. Fifty yachts in full sail are a gorgeous unforgettable sight. The Andersons' year-round residence is on the harbor, occupying a "good position" with its own pier and boat docks. December 26, Boxing Day, we dined at Kiribillie House with Sir Robert and the Johnstons. The Commonweath maintains a residence for the P.M. in Sydney, a charming, restored Victorian mansion, with beautiful gardens overlooking the harbor. Next day we lunched with the Phillips and went briefly to the Davis Cup matches. We left the hotel at 8:30 A.M. for an inspection tour of the U. S. submarine *Archer Fish.* We were piped aboard. If you ever board a sub, you need either slacks or bloomers, because a crewman must stand at the foot of the ladder to help you up and down. This sub has had its fangs pulled, that is, torpedoes removed and only does oceanographic exploration. It is 326 feet long and only 27 feet wide, including the tanks on the sides. It carries a complement of sixty men.

The tennis matches are held at White City, not a particularly attractive stadium, with an old-fashioned wooden baseball grandstand. The Grace family holds ancestral seats, like owning a box at the opera or a parking space at Rice Stadium. We left about midway, with the Australians already leading their Spanish opponents. I changed into a comfortable dark cotton dress at the airport. We stored several suitcases of summer clothes in Sydney and enplaned at 5:30 P.M. for Pago-Pago (pronounced "Pango-Pango"), American Samoa. The only thing to note about Pago-Pago is a lot of Polynesians at the airport and a tax-free grog shop; twenty minutes there, then on to Hawaii. We slept fairly well because each of us occupied two seats; by removing the arm rest between, we could stretch out. Dear Rush Clark, Pan Am's Australian manager, arranged for us to have both front seats. Time zones change so fast on a jet flight. We were about an hour in Honolulu and

arrived in Los Angeles at 4:30 P.M., December 26, by clock and calendar, an hour ahead of the time we left Sydney. I shot off to the hairdresser at a nearby hotel in order to face the photographers in Dallas.
We arrived in Austin just after midnight. We had been on the way
about twenty hours.

Our time in the United States was a series of one-night stands:
Dallas, Houston, Greenville in Mississippi, San Augustine, back to
Austin, back to Dallas, and thence Washington. We spent our first
evening in Texas at the LBJ Ranch, riding there in the helicopter. The
President looked great to me. He is said to be happiest at the Ranch.

We spent another evening in Washington with him and Mrs. Johnson at a small dinner party. Warren and Mary Ellen Woodward, Bill
White, the columnist, and Jake and Beryl Pickle were also there. The
protocol in Washington is lots less exacting than in Australia, even
when the President is present. Coming home restores one's perspective.
Out there you get to thinking that the title means you *are* "excellent,"
when sure enough, you are just Ed and Anne, home again. Mrs. Perle
Mesta gave a cocktail party for us, Scooter and Dale Miller held a big
reception at the Carlton, and Justice Clark had us for lunch with the
Supreme Court in their private dining room. I saw lots of Elizabeth
and Hutch, Beryl and Jake. Senator Ralph Yarborough had a lovely
luncheon in the Senate private dining room with all our friends
present, including Senator and Mrs. Tower. Jean and Frank Ikard had
a dinner party at the City Tavern Club in Georgetown. It's as pretty as
anything in Williamsburg. I saw Ambassador and Mrs. Waller several
times and feel we are now real friends. She seemed as glad to see my
snapshots and talk about our mutual friends in Canberra as I would if
one of you walked into the American Embassy.

We left Washington in a snow storm on American Air Lines.
Changed to Pan Am in Los Angeles and were met by the whole American Consular staff in Sydney. Luck ran out there, for we had a long
wait before finally getting off to Canberra. I feel vastly different from
that day in August when I first arrived in Australia. At least, I know

where the light switches are. We started right in on the usual hectic pace—a reception at Parliament House given by the Haslucks (Minister for External Affairs). We had a luncheon for Sir Reginald and Lady Sholl on Thursday. He's about to depart for New York to be Consul General for Australia there. Hope all my English-Speaking Union friends will get them invited to Texas soon.

The Residence was on tour for a charity sponsored by the Rotary Club Sunday afternoon. They took in fourteen hundred pounds. Since the fee was ten shillings (one-half pound) each, that means 2,800 people tramped through in two hours. I decided to decline the help of the Embassy girls and do the flowers myself. Last time some of them got their feelings hurt at each other over the job. Then came a long Australian holiday. Monday was Australia Day, a national holiday. Everything at the Embassy closes for all the holidays of both our own and our host country.

Wednesday we journey to Portland in the state of Victoria. It's a town of six and a half thousands (as Aussies put it). We flew down on an R.A.F. plane, a Convair, one of the most plushly appointed planes I have ever seen, not to mention a wonderful steward serving something every minute—whisky, beer, coffee, candy, breakfast, and lunch. Our host was Mr. Malcolm Frasier, new Minister for the Army in Mr. Holt's cabinet. He is only thirty-five years old, six feet five, Oxford educated, a grazier, reputed to be the richest man in Australia. He's ruggedly good looking, unassuming in manner, and very attractive. This was his first visit to his constituency since his elevation to the Ministry, and are they proud of him! I predict he'll be P.M. someday, for he certainly has time on his side.

Portland was founded before Melbourne but, like the old story of many small towns, the railroads bypassed it. Today, Portland has seized time by the forelock and is as much on the move as Freeport or the other industrial towns on the Texas Coast. There are several new "wool stores" which are like auction barns. These are immaculately

clean and lighted in a very proper fashion, a matter of the greatest importance. The wool is bagged in jute, much better than cotton bales.
It's as carefully sewed as a sugar sack. Fine merino feels like silk in
your hand. Crossbred wool is rougher to the touch, and the difference
is like that between tweed and cashmere. One reason for not raising all
merinos is that those highbred beasts never make fat lambs, and the
two sources of profit in sheep raising, meat and wool, can be combined
with crossbreeds. The buyers inspect and make a chart of the lots, then
the actual auction is conducted in other quarters. There is no silent
bidding. Buyers must cry out their bids. The unit is *pence*. Remember,
there are twelve pence to a shilling and twenty shillings to a pound.
Merino sells for around one hundred pence and the coarser varieties
for half as much. (That's about one dollar for Merino and fifty cents
for the crossbreed fleece.) They compress the bales like cotton, except
it is called "dumping." This takes place after the sale when the wool is
ready to be loaded aboard ship.

Besides the wool market, Portland has built the most modern, fully
automatic grain elevators and new harbor facilities. Another industry
is a carnation plantation, which, alas, I didn't see. Penguins and seals
are to be seen in the harbor. These visits are so carefully arranged by
such courteous hosts that one can't help but be flattered. The Town
Clerk (pronounced "Clark") was the key man who had rehearsals to
be sure all went right. A call came to know what the Ambassador liked
for breakfast and if he had a wine choice. The Ambassador's main
speech was in the Parish Hall of the Methodist Church—Wesley, they
call it—and, believe it or not, they served whisky and beer as well as
coffee and tea. The pride of the town is a hundred-year-old cork tree,
a giant similar to our oldest live oaks. Visitors ask for acorns because
Spain and Portugal no longer permit this export.

We reached home—there, I'm calling the Residence home—about
mid-afternoon. The Canberra Planning Commission composed of about
fifteen persons came for cocktails. Served them salted pecans and hot

chili con queso, always a good conversation piece. It is hard to believe pecans are not much used down here. They do grow in Queensland but have never caught on in popularity.

I have been forced to hire a social secretary. There is just not enough of me to go round. She will keep the invitations and guest lists straight, do errands, answer the phone, fix the flowers, and help market. She will also do accounts, which are complicated. Maybe I won't feel so harassed from now on. The name is Mrs. Marjorie Turbayne. She has been secretary to a Lady Mayoress in London and to an American Ambassador's wife in Prague, so she certainly knows more than I do about this job.

Monday I will have a car delivered to me and I shall feel like a bird out of a cage. I am getting a Ford Galaxie. I just couldn't bring myself to try a car without power steering and have to master that as well as the left side of the road. I hope that, when Australia adjusts itself to the change-over to decimal currency, right-side-of-the-road driving will be the next step into the twentieth century.

The date book is full for the next two weeks, but I don't plan to write any more letters this long and wordy. I would like to add this one little item on word usage. The shortened name for chrysanthemums here is not "mums" but "chrysies," and I did forget to tell you about our arrival in Canberra two hours late after our trip home. All members of the Embassy staff, one hundred strong, were out to meet us with a brass band playing "The Yellow Rose of Texas" as we stepped off the plane into one-hundred-degree heat and a swarm of flies, on January 25.

Fondly,
Anne

Nedalla Beach, N.S.W.
Australia
March 1, 1966

Dear Mrs. O'D. and Beachcombers:

I am at the beach. Nedalla is the name and I am not exactly sure where that is, save it's a four-hour drive from Canberra through the mountains in the state of New South Wales to a picturesque rocky shore. When the Ambassador left for the Philippines Friday morning, and Congressman George Miller of California, Chairman of the Science and Space Committee, departed, I left with Dottie and Ed Cronk, our deputy, for the beach. Every year there is a conference of United States Ambassadors to Asia held in Baguio, a mountain resort near Manila. I did not go for one good reason—paying my own $800 fare.

This is my first trip out of Canberra, unofficially, and I can't tell you what a respite it is to lie around the house and on the beach in a muu-muu, with pins in my hair and dining on pork and beans and peanut butter. Ed Cronk grilled a steak tonight. It was tough and stringy compared to those at the Night Hawk, but the charcoal taste was at least reminiscent of home. We have a nice cottage unit, in the usual motif— kitchen, dining, and living rooms all together, for three pounds a day ($6.75). This is the off-season—summer is nearly gone and school vacation is over. When it is too windy to lie on the beach, we look out the big picture window at the pounding waves, the rocks, and the lighthouse. There are few shells on this beach but lots of strange seaweed. We found two sponges and a big cuttlefish. A solemn, fat kookaburra came to sit on our balcony. When fed raw meat, he came within three feet of us. Kookaburras have no natural enemies and so are almost tame. He was buff colored with some blue and white wing feathers and about the size of a big crow. The kookaburra is Australia's national bird, a member of the kingfisher family. My memory keeps returning to Anne Lindbergh's little book, *Gift from the Sea,* in which she recounted the renewed spirit she had brought back from a long stay at the beach. I feel that I, too, have had a healing of my weary muscles, brain, and spirit here.

I want all my stateside friends to read Ilka Chase's book, *Second Spring and Two Potatoes,* which is about her trip through the South Pacific. I found the part about Australia properly authentic. We enjoyed two interesting dinner parties recently. One was at the Embassy of Israel. Mr. Tesher has served as Consul General in Chicago. He knows and admires Jim Novy. Their Embassy has a flower bed in front planted to form a seven-branch candelabra. The food was ordinary catered Australian. The dinner at the Chinese Embassy was more colorful. Madam Chen, Lilyan, is as American as popcorn. She was born in Brooklyn, New York, and carefully guards her American citizenship. She's willowy, beautiful, and dresses in Chinese fashion. Dinner was served from a lazy Susan; four dishes at a time were placed on the turn-table, soup came mid-way in the meal. The dessert was a fruit cup of pink watermelon balls and an unfamiliar white grape-like fruit called LoAnne.

The week just past was "the week that was." Before our Vice-Presidential visit was set, we already had three large dinner parties on the calendar. Executives of *Newsweek* and *Time* came on consecutive days, and Esso officials the day before. Immediately after, five house guests arrived, the Vice President and Mrs. Humphrey, Governor Averill Harriman, a doctor, and a sergeant who was listed as a valet (but he didn't press or pack, fetch or tote). Poor Governor Harriman had to have all his clothes pressed, shirts ironed, and a store opened for the purchase of a hat to replace the one he had lost. A maid discovered his hearing aid barely in time to save him departing without it. The house swarmed inside and out with security officers; Frederick, the chauffeur, had to sleep in the Residence. I could never use the official car because it was all bugged up for the Veep. We had a small family dinner for the party Friday night. Later Sir Robert called on the Vice President. The boys all gathered around to hear and see Sir Robert give one of his great virtuoso performances, which lasted till 2:00 A.M.

Saturday morning. Mrs. Humphrey had her press conference at the Residence, and we took her on an official tour to the mint and to Koomari House, a school for retarded children. The Humphreys have a five-year-old retarded granddaughter, so Muriel Humphrey is vitally interested in all such work. Then we stopped by the souvenir shop where she bought a kangaroo rug. After luncheon for sixteen women at the Residence, we had a hairdresser come and get us all laundered and brushed for the reception. Two hundred people called in one hour. A quick change into black tie, long dress, and gloves followed for the Government House dinner. That's always a magnificent show with gold-braided footmen and so much table silver one's eyes won't focus for the gleam. Then there are those curtsies. Even the Humphreys, who must have attended state dinners all over the world, were slightly awed by it all.

We planned a ceremonial farewell for the Vice President. At 9:30 A.M., he was to stand on the terrace beneath the white-columned portico with all the Embassy family gathered on the sloping lawn in front to say goodbye. Especially invited were the American children because their parents feel keenly their separation from the American way of life (they don't even study American History in the schools). Though it is January (equivalent season of July in the Northern Hemisphere), the weather proved perverse. An unceasing icy cold rain intervened, so, instead, I had a hundred pair of muddy feet and a live kangaroo hopping about the house. It made wonderful pictures though. A minor semitragic result was that the borrowed kangaroo was immediately expropriated by the government. The Australians are very particular about their animals, and kangaroos are not allowed in captivity in the A.C.T. (Australian Capital Territory). Cathy Martin, ten-year-old daughter of the Political Counselor, made the newspapers round the world with the V.P. and the 'roo. We loved the Humphreys. They were so constantly agreeable and undemanding.

The new Prime Minister and his winsome though worldly wife, Zara, honored us by accepting our whole battery of invitations last week. Mr. Holt (and we are now on first-name basis—I can't decide between Harold or Harry) said we might as well show him his bedroom, he'd been at the American Embassy so much. Being a *couturière,* Mrs. Holt is beautifully turned out. All wealthy Australian women still have their clothes made by a modiste just as our mothers used to have theirs made in Louisville or New Orleans. They refer to my most costly Neiman-Marcus dresses as "your off-the-peg frocks." That was black slander about the P.M. being a teetotaler. He drinks one Martini before dinner and always has two wines with dinner. The Holts will bring a new look to the Lodge, and I am sure they will do much to bring Australia up to date. Though Zara has three married sons, she sponsors the young look. She says, as far as fashion goes, if you are over thirty, you are dead. She herself wears conservative clothes and leaves the mini skirts to her glamorous daughters-in-law. Being what I must call dumpy, she says she can't wear new-look clothes because she doesn't have the shape for them.

We had two more functions on Monday and Tuesday. Luncheon honoring George Moore of the First National City Bank of New York and Stuart Peeler of Southern Union, and a farewell dinner for Sir Robert and Dame Pattie. Then Congressman George Miller of California arrived to be our guest, requiring no entertainment, just breakfast, laundry, and valet service. The Congressman's devoted staff aide, who spoke of him as "my chairman," looked after him completely.

My dear little dog, Patsy, was run over in our drive. She never went outside and few cars came in. We don't know how it happened.

The newspapers and TV have discovered Ed's and my morning walks. They seem to think they have news value, and we have had three sessions with the media. My walking costume is for comfort, not style.

Monday morning I am having the Embassy wives' meeting at the Residence. The program is to consist of the chronicle of my trip to the States. Tuesday I speak to the women of the Australian-American Association; Wednesday we have luncheon for the new vice president of Esso, Mike Wright, who will be going to Houston soon to live. Friday there will be houseguests and my first dinner dance for sixty people. The cook remains inadequate and must be replaced. I certainly hope the Wynn girls will enjoy pointing with pride to the portrait of their Grandfather, the Ambassador, because I think their legacy of pride will be my greatest reward for a lot of hard work here.

On the drive to the beach, I saw several hundred miles of Australian countryside that I hadn't seen before. Part of the drive was on mountain roads bordered with cycads. These are a form of prehistoric plant life, some like ferns and older ones more palm-like. They are the plants that fossilized into coal. Everything else was grazing country. I never saw a row crop or a field of oats. Summer is about over. Last Sunday the church celebrated the harvest festival (in March).

I am starting a new cook Tuesday, an English woman. I hope she works, because I am about at my row's end on that score.*

Love and kisses to you all,
Anne

* She didn't, and we almost had a tong war in the kitchen.

Canberra, Australia
March 20, 1966

Dear Friends:

When I went to church this morning, I found this to be "Mothering Sunday," so-called from the rural English custom of visiting parents and taking gifts on a Sunday in mid-Lent. It's the forerunner of the American Mother's Day.

Another fundamental difference to which I must accustom myself is having autumn in March. The Michaelmas daisies are in bloom and the dogwood that flowered in November now bears small red fruit.

Sunday is usually a day of quiet, the one used to catch up on letters, reading, and repairing clothes. I believe I dispatched my last letter on February 28. Since that time, we have had all the big-business men in America, it seems. There was Mike Wright, who is moving from New York to Houston to be vice president of Esso in charge of Humble. Mrs. Wright says her cook in Scarsdale used to work for Clint Whitfield, Doug Wynn's aunt. Also General Wood of Sears and Roebuck, and Mr. and Mrs. Arjay Miller of Detroit—he is president of Ford Motors. We gave a dinner dance for the Millers and the Wallace Booths of Melbourne. This was our first such affair. Sixty guests were invited and it appeared a success. I even made yellow tissue paper roses to decorate the ballroom. I say "ballroom," but it is really the old sunroom, which recently was floored with vinyl tile, making it more usable. In fact, I hope the next tenant of this Residence is duly appreciative of all the additions made during our tenure. Besides fenders, andirons, shower curtains, a portable bar, ice bucket, some jiggers, a half-dozen bedroom clocks, and more decorative flower vases, I am this week getting a new cook stove and grill for the kitchen, and a small refrigerator for upstairs use. In the kitchen crisis, I was forced to try my own hand at cooking and I found an antique range, circa 1920. It took thirty minutes to heat one cup of water, and for these hordes of visitors coffee was made in two eight-cup percolators. To give an example of comparative prices: an Australian-made coffee urn for this 220-volt current costs $80. The cost would be about $20 in the states.

The guest book count shows 1,146 signatures, many Mr. and Mrs., and this did not include anyone who came during the Vice President's visit or the large benefit tours of the Red Cross and Rotary. Our most recent party was a reception for 150 men, representatives of the United States War College.

We made two recent trips to Sydney, once to dine aboard the *Hornet,* our enormous Pacific fleet aircraft carrier. Admiral Pete Aurand is a cousin of Jean Daniel's, also a great-grandson of Sam Houston. The other trip of five days was for the purpose of greeting the astronauts,

Wally Schirra and Frank Borman. They with their bright, pretty wives made us proud to be Americans.

Then we had a day in Melbourne where I lunched with Lady Spry. Her husband, Sir Charles, is the counterpart of J. Edgar Hoover. Several United States agents work with him directly, including Bill Caldwell of Bonham, Texas. CIA-FBI people are referred to in the trade as "spooks." I dined with the General Motors brass—Bonner, Wilson, and Knudsen.

Aussie charity goes all out for fetes. I participated in two yesterday. Much like our church bazaars, there are several every weekend. An effort is always made to get some well-known figure to "open" the show. I judged little girls' bonnets and parasols at the YWCA fete on the grounds of Government House. The Australians have a unique way of supporting their charities. R.S.L. clubs (returned soldiers) are supported by poker machines, others run lotteries, and many things, such as retarded children and old folks' homes receive a pound-for-pound grant from the Commonwealth government, that is, the government matches all the money privately raised. I went to a coffee where everyone contributed a bottle of grog to be sold for the Boys' Grammar School when its fete comes off.

"D" Day, the change-over to decimal currency, has gone perfectly. Each pound note is worth two dollars, and each ten-shilling note (one-half pound) is worth one dollar. However, the Australian dollar is worth $1.12 American. The six pence and the three pence are not as easy, but I believe the change-over will be complete long before the two years' time that has been allotted. Cash registers and coin vending machines will take more time.

We called on the ship *Seven Seas,* a floating college with four hundred American students. The daughter of Lawrence Hagy's secretary and Frank Ikard's niece were aboard, both Amarillo girls.

I haven't finished the diplomatic calls, but made the great effort to make my call on Madame Loginov, the Russian Ambassador's wife, this week. She speaks no English, so the wife of a Russian Embassy attaché interpreted. Madame is both plain and shy. She has acne scars on her face and pale blue eyes. She was cordial and promised to invite me back to see a film of the Bolshoi ballet. She gave me some Russian cigarettes and sweets to take home. In my opinion, we got along nicely because I just won't be intimidated, and chattered away about trivia, nonstop.

We lunched at the Greek Embassy, where we were served the best food I have eaten in Australia. There was a white caviar, so smooth I thought it was cream cheese. Mrs. Tsmassis speaks *no* English and *no Greek.* She is an Argentinian and her language is Spanish. Mr. Tsmassis presented his credentials a few days ahead of Ed, so we always stand just after them in official lines.

I am limping along with an inferior cook. One thing is sure, if I had my Ching back, I'd try to make him happier. The American Embassy Residence is like a hotel, and just a home-style cook won't produce good food for such numbers. For instance, Sunday is diplomatic tennis tournament, alfresco, 120 for supper. The following day we leave for New Guinea for two weeks. Tomorrow we go to Adelaide to the Festival of Arts presided over by the Queen Mother. A full wardrobe has to go—white tie and tails, black tie, cutaway, and gray topper.*

Love from traveling

Anne

* Note: For Ed, and, for little me, a formal garden party outfit and long dress for the ballet, my best jewelry, and my long red velvet coat.

Canberra, Australia

March 25, 1966

To those who are still with us:

We arrived at Canberra at 2:00 A.M. Friday morning and will leave again Monday for two weeks in New Guinea, so I am hastening

to get off a letter about Adelaide and the Festival of Arts before I leave.
I write this at the hairdresser's. New Guinea is supposed to be hot and
humid, so it's dig out the wash-and-wear clothes, raincoats, walking
shoes, everything for two weeks of travel with no time for cleaning,
laundry, or hair sets.

The Festival of Arts, held every two years in Adelaide, population
600,000, capital of the state of South Australia, is unique. Adelaide
is called the Boston of Australia. Even our own Consul, Mr. and Mrs.
Jack Linahan, were unkindly referred to by one objectionable American as "Boston snobs." Jan *did* go to Radcliffe and they *do* travel an
ancestral grandfather clock around the world, but other than that
mark of identity, I can't say that I found them anything but charming, efficient, and hospitable. The Linahans gave an after-theater party
one night for the performers, especially the Americans. These included
the Negro musicians from the Jazz Quartette; Odetta, the folk singer,
whose politics I abhor; Dame Judith Anderson, born in Adelaide, but
now resident in California; her niece who travels with her; and a
Maori male singer from New Zealand who sang "Porgy." The Maoris
are Polynesian; he's terribly attractive, very British, lives in London,
possesses a marvelous voice. I found the Maoris too light skinned to
be convincing in *Porgy and Bess,* but the performance was wonderful, otherwise. It seems I remember that the authors specified that all
performances must have a colored cast. Maoris aren't much like South
Carolina negroes, but they were closer and more convenient. I didn't
see Dame Judith perform, but she's a beautiful woman and gracious.
I am sorry to miss her in Canberra because I want her to give me a
picture for the Residence.* I think a photo of this Australian-American actress would enhance our house. There were art exhibits stuck
in every possible place, from auto showrooms to the South Australian
Museum.

The features were a collection of Australian art assembled for a rich

* I never got it.

American, Harold Mertz, which will travel to the United States later,†
and Turner water colors and etchings lent by the British Museum. In
four days we could only sample the fare. At noon in a church hall
among several fifty-minute performances you could choose "Intimate
Opera" or "Intimate Ballet." I saw an opera based on a Don Quixote
vignette with live singers and puppets both in the same show. We saw
Royal Hunt of the Sun, Porgy and Bess, and the Australian Ballet. The
ballet was attended by the Queen Mother, looking both regal and
sweet at once, in white satin, rubies, and diamonds. His Excellency, the
Ambassador of the United States, was in white tie and tails, and Mrs.
Clark attended in her best ivory brocade, long white gloves, and long
red velvet cloak. During the interval, Sir Edric Bastyan, the Governor,
plucked us out of the row of Ambassadors to accompany him to a private room where we were presented to Her Majesty. I was so surprised
I didn't have time to practice my curtsy or prepare my speech (you
know it's my custom to give great thought to the small talk I will use
when introduced to a celebrity).

We talked about the discomforts of a long air flight and the physical confusions caused by crossing so many time zones, and compared
the differences in time between the United States and Australia and
England and Australia. Three ballets were on the program. One was a
new score by Robert Helpman (the Australian choreographer named
man of the year in 1966); the sets were done by the famous Australian
artist, Arthur Boyd. It was *Electra,* all black and white, with Furies.
I am mentioning these names because they are the ones you will hear
again with reference to the Australian arts.

Of course, everyone was decked out in his finest plumage. But what
really wowed me was the Clergy in full dress. The Bishop had a purple
embroidered coat, knee breeches, silver buckles on his shoes, and a
clerical collar. The Dean of the Anglican Cathedral from Brisbane

---

† This exhibit showed in Austin at The University of Texas Humanities
Center and brought five hundred guests for a reception-showing in October,
1967.

wore the same in black with a scarlet vest. I am also distraught at missing what the impertinent newspapers refer to as the "Queen Mum" in Canberra, because the Archdeacon had asked us to sit with the Prime Minister when the Queen attends St. John's. We are the most regular attendants at his church from the diplomatic circle or even from the Australian government.

Lord and Lady Casey follow the practice of attending different churches each Sunday, and they also spend long weekends at their own home near Melbourne.

Adelaide also has National Flower Day. The school children bring flowers, which the women of Adelaide use for elaborate displays. The most magnificent is a floral carpet with a bridge across so that it can be properly viewed. There are four downtown squares, all filled with spectacular floral displays. The indoor show had arrangements named for people—needless to say, the United States Ambassador's was of yellow roses. An enormous flask with yellow-tinted water was the container. The arranger said she had wanted to use oil but it looked ugly when she tried it.

We had two other looks at the Queen Mother. For her arrival ceremony our seats were in a grandstand directly opposite her; the Lord Mayor presiding, horses, Rolls Royces, the royal standard "broken out" at just a precise moment, Her Majesty appearing in brilliant aqua blue. My feeling was that if I were a Queen, I would never carry a handbag. She was completely overbalanced by a large white one. She wore decidedly unfashionable white shoes, heels and toes out. Her Majesty is really very small and it's just all that fluff that makes her appear so pudgy.

Thursday morning we visited Chrysler's big plant, 4,300 employees with only four Americans. They were thrilled with the Embassy Imperial that Frederick had driven down. An Imperial seems to be a rare sight here.

For the garden party the visiting Ambassadors, only five of us, German, Belgian, New Zealand, and Malaysian, all had a member of the City Council assigned as host. Ours was the lady member, Mrs. Cook, the counterpart of our Emma Long. She said we could treat Mr. Cook like Prince Philip. The middle-aged Australian gentleman employed by our Consulate who came to pick up our luggage took one look at me in my "high Sunday" garden party outfit and said, "Ma'am, if you'll pardon me saying it, I do like your rig-out." It consisted of an ivory coatdress, Carolyn Curtis' gift hat and a parasol to match, those bronze shoes with a rose on the toe that I've had for years, and my sable scarf. My hastily assembled millinery wardrobe is a success. Nini Van Cawenberg, the Belgian Ambassador's wife, says she has dubs on Nancy Scott's green hat covered with the red poppies because she comes from Flanders "where the poppies grow." Local ladies all have turbans (homemade) and they think my gift hats "bought in America" are something.

We went straight to the airport, and, two hours later, put down in Mount Gambier, a town of 6,500 souls, but larger appearing business-wise—three hundred miles from either Adelaide or Melbourne. It is famous for its Blue Lake, a volcanic crater that for nine months each year is the same slate color as several other nearby lakes. Then one morning in November the town's inhabitants wake to find it a brilliant azure, an unexplained phenomenon. It continues this blue for three months, gradually fading back to gray. The town has a crayfish (lobster) industry, the largest softwood sawmill in the Southern Hemisphere, nearby sheep and cattle stations, a lady Mayor, and an export cheese factory. The Ambassador spoke to the combined Rotary, Lions, and Apex clubs on trade. Do you understand the terms "GATT" and "Kennedy Round"? I don't. The occasion was International Understanding Week. They sent greetings to the Austin Rotary and had looked up its history.

Two Australian premiers (state governors) will be traveling in the United States soon, Sir Henry Bolte of Victoria and Frank Walsh of South Australia. I hope any of our friends who hear tell of them will really make a special effort to be nice to them. I have been passing out packets of bluebonnet seed sent by John Connally, Governor of Texas. I have to carry an artificial one and a picture cut off the state highway map to explain the Texas state flower. Everyone is a gardener at heart down here and the idea of growing our wildflowers is intriguing.

Tomorrow and Sunday the diplomatic tennis tournament will be held on the Residence courts, ending with a barbecue and TV photographers. First prizes are silver bowls and trays from good old Jean's shop in New York and runners-up must settle for a bottle of bourbon and some tennis balls.

Monday we leave for New Guinea, with a stopover in Nouméa, New Caledonia (French territory). They say I might find a Dior dress there but French perfume for sure. As you see, life goes on merrily, or hectically, depending on your viewpoint.

Lovingly,
Anne

En Route to New Guinea
March 29, 1966

Dear home-based Friends:

I am starting this in Brisbane where we spent last night. Thirteen of us are flying in a DC-3. Our party consists of an Australian Captain and his wife; our American Navy Attaché, Captain Jim Mooney, and wife, Blanche; Doyle Martin, our Political Counselor; Ray Carlson, the Air Attaché, and wife, Ruth; Dottie Cronk (Ed Cronk can't join us until we get back on Australian-controlled ground, which will be New Guinea—New Caledonia, our first landfall, is French), ourselves, and assorted pilots and other crew. No grog is allowed on Navy planes, so we eat apples, drink coffee, play cards, and read or write.

Sunday, just preceding our departure on Monday, we hosted the

diplomatic tennis tournament. By no means all the players were diplomats. Ted Schroeder, former international tennis champion, who lives
in Canberra while representing General Dynamics, was our star. He
really now prefers golf to tennis because he hates to win always but is
embarrassed to lose; he's such fun and always adds color. He's an
amusing talker, using the phraseology of Damon Runyon. The climax
was a cookout supper—that is, the men broiled steaks and chops on a
rented grill fueled with bottled gas. Potato salad, cole slaw, and cokes
came out of the Embassy kitchen. We tapped a keg of beer and used all
120 rented plates. Since the Residence has nothing but gold-banded
white china, our tableware didn't seem appropriate for outdoor eating.
Everybody called it a nifty party. We even had a Russian player. The
Russians called and said, "Why weren't we invited?" So they sent a
man from Pravda who played a better game than any of their staff
members, and two bottles, Vodka and brandy, which courtesy required
that we accept. Do you think this indicates a thaw? It was a bright, cold
night, with everyone except me in slacks and sweaters, and a big fire in
the barbecue pit. (It was the first fire ever in that pit.) The staff says we
may wear out the Residence by using it too much. There are three
functions scheduled in my absence.

March 30. Arrived yesterday afternoon in New Caledonia where the
airport is thirty miles from the town of Nouméa. We were met by a
French two-star Admiral. French confusion prevailed. Nouméa is a
town of forty thousand, half French, half multiracial and other Europeans, notably Melanesian (fuzzy-haired), Polynesian (straight hair,
light-brown skin), Australians, and English. In this part of the world,
European is the euphemism for white men. A huge nickel smelter
supports everybody. The Admiral explained that the smallest picka-
ninny gets $200 a month for just *being,* like the Osages and the "head
rights" for oil in Oklahoma state. All street signs and hotel menus are
bilingual, English as well as French. Tipping is strictly forbidden and
the waitress definitely doesn't hang around expectantly. We had champagne at the Admiral's house last night. He is a widower living with

his twenty-year-old daughter, Nicole, and eleven-year-old son, Guy.
He doesn't want to go back to France when his tour here ends in the
near future. The governor of the island is called the "High Commissioner," which does not mean the same as it does to the British. We will
dine with His Excellency tonight and picnic at Admiralty House for
lunch. Nicole is taking me shopping for French perfume this morning.

7:00 P.M. The shopping was a huge success. The perfume was
cheap! Also bought two pieces of Tahitian cotton for shifts and beautiful postage stamps. Ed, as usual, let me case the joint and then went
back to do his shopping in the afternoon. Had a wonderful real French
lunch on the veranda instead of the expected picnic, with decanters of
both red and white wine and ice water on the table, French lettuce,
and delicious bread. Bread is never served in Australia, I suspect because it isn't very good. We visited the aquarium in the afternoon;
like everything else, the fish are unique, some beautiful, some hideous.
Sea anemones have one fish that is their own pet, all others are de-
voured. Some fish look like huge barnacle-covered rocks, only their
breathing motion indicates life. It is a venomous species if you step on
one while ocean bathing or skin diving. This aquarium is one of the
most fantastic in the world. Living coral is shown once a day under
flourescent light in a darkened room. Some of its denizens are literally
"living fossils." Mrs. Nicholson, wife of the Australian Consul, says
she is being forced to become a shell collector; all the women on the
island do it seriously, and it's the universal topic when the ladies gather
after dinner. All day I've been trying to recollect Nellie Forbush's line
in *South Pacific* about herself and DeBeck because that's the way I felt
about the Admiral and Anne (me).*

---

* I finally found a libretto that filled me in: "He's a cultured Frenchman
                                    And I'm just a little hick."
Later the dialogue went like this: "She: My mother is awfully prejudiced.
                                    He: Against Frenchmen?
                                    She: Against anyone not from Little Rock."
(Richard Rodgers, Oscar Hammerstein II, and Joshua Logan, *South Pacific*)
All who knew my mother can guess why such lines stuck in my subconscious.

In spite of much conversation about the heat and humidity, the climate here seems about like summer on the Texas coast where I've been hotter and sweated more. The town is quite picturesque but terribly untidy. All roofs are corrugated iron, often painted red. The vegetation has the same tropical lushness of Mexico and South Texas—palms, immense hibiscus (tree size), flame tree (royal poinciana), oleander, Queen's wreath, cup of gold, bougainvillaea, banana, copper plant, croton, and philodendron. You are familiar with all except perhaps the banyan tree. This enormous tree looks as if the roots hang down from the branches.

April 1. Honiara, Guadalcanal—six hundred miles south of the Equator. What a day, what a place! This is really the land of Sadie Thompson. The palms don't whisper, they wail, and branches fall in the night with a sound like the report of a gun. The High Commissioner, Sir Robert Foster, has a territory of 500,000 square miles, including the Solomon Islands, Gilberts, Hebrides, Christmas Island, and about 990,000 square miles of the South Pacific. The water in front of Government House is known as Iron Bottom Sound because there lie the hulls of many sunken ships. In fact, our traveling companion, Captain Bruce Loxton of the Royal Australian Navy, was aboard the cruiser *Canberra* when it was sunk under him there in 1942. This is his first time to return. There's plenty of evidence of battle still visible—rusting old ships on the beach, wrecks of airplanes, and abandoned tanks. Honiara has about four and a half thousands, as they say; only about five hundred are English or Europeans (that is, white men).

Government House here is a converted barracks with a veranda to which some native straw mats have been attached for the picturesque effect, ceiling fans, and no permanent outside walls other than shutters on the seaward side that may be closed in case of a driving rain. The plumbing is what you would expect in an old Army barracks. Nevertheless, the gentlemen put on their dinner jackets, the officers their

whites, and down we sat to a five-course dinner served by "Fuzzy-
Wuzzy chaps" in white *skirts,* scarlet boleros, and no shoes. The skirts
are "Lap-Laps." Lady Foster says she's a "colonial" born in South
Africa, most of her life spent in Rhodesia where her brothers and
brothers-in-law still farm. She is outspokenly bitter about their situation, the Labour Government, and her distaste for the Pacific. Forth-
right as she is, I found her charming, nevertheless. She says there is a
date engraved on her heart when she goes on leave to England and
when she can make a weekly visit to the hairdresser. Our morning was
relaxed, featuring a ride around the island to see a palm plantation.
I think coconut palms are taller and more beautiful than the date
palms of South Texas. Then followed a walk around the gardens to
see the orchids, a dip in the pool, and a look at the native village. The
natives are Melanesians, as fuzzy-headed as golliwoggs. "That nap is
often bleached a light red color, accomplished with the lime applied
to keep down the livestock," said Lady Foster. A boy shinnied up a
tree to throw down coconuts to us so we might drink the milk. The
constabulary are as smart as paint. They have had haircuts and wear
blue skirts, immaculate white jackets, epaulettes, scarlet sashes, and
well-polished black leather sandals. After an early lunch we bade our
delightful hosts goodbye at the Residency. Loaded with gifts of baskets,
we made a 2:00 P.M. takeoff for Sohano. The 1942 words of Gabriel
Heater, radio commentator, still ring in my ears—"There's bad news
on Guadalcanal tonight." I heard them at 1520 Northwood Road over
my "no-stoop-no-squint" Philco radio.

April 2. Island of *Buka*—part of the Papua-New Guinea-Australian
protectorate, a United Nations mandate. We were conveyed thither
by a launch from the airport at Sohano. There we were met by a dele-
gation of American nuns and Marist Fathers. Two of the nuns had once
been stationed in Lubbock, Texas, and they were thrilled over a touch
of home. They brought a parcel of little coal-black children (some
stark naked) thirty miles to see the plane. The Melanesians are the

blackest people I have ever seen. The priests don't wear clerical garb. They said they wore their clericals only as far as Sydney and left them. The only identification with their vocation are silver crosses pinned to the collar of the uniform white sport shirts. There are no public inns, so all our party are someone's guests. Ed and I are staying at the Residency, guests of the District Commissioner. Last night we were honored with a buffet. Guests were the Australian officials, plantation managers, and a few natives and their wives, some barefoot and some with shoes. One black semipygmy was the wife of the Postmaster, a trained nurse who spoke traces of English. She was about twenty years old, shy, but proud. There was plenty to drink, including South Pacific Island beer, good food, curry, and a sweet and sour fish dish.

This island has 159 inches of rainfall each year. All of the water for human consumption is caught in tanks and reservoirs. The garden is lush with fragrant frangipani, colorful crotons, hibiscus, ginger lilies, philodendron. Strangely enough, the soil on these coral islands is not particularly fertile. One plantation wife told me only coconuts grow on their land because of low fertility. Cocoa can sometimes be profitably cultivated under the palms. It helps to keep down brush, but the soil is inadequate. The kerosene refrigerator and its companion deepfreeze have made life over for these people. They don't have lights or running water, but they can get imported frozen meat and even bread. This young wife is thirty-four years old. She and her husband are both Tasmanians. He comes of a family of sheep farmers whose holdings are too small to be divided among all the sons, so out he comes to New Guinea, adventuring, hoping to make stake enough to put down a payment on a sheep property of his own. The plantation that he manages is owned by a large diversified company from Adelaide.

Next, a short flight to *Buin* (on Bougainville)—visited a school where we had morning tea (six kinds of cakes, scones, banana bread) and bought Buin baskets, world famous and beautifully made. Another plane ride, another jeep ride, and lunch with the sisters at Kieta, a mission school. I felt we were served the saved-up delicacies these women should have eaten themselves.

We arrived an hour late at *Rabaul* (on New Britain), hot, disheveled, bone weary, to be met by the District Commissioner's wife in white gloves and a smart guard of honor.

April 3. Prewar Rabaul was the most beautiful town in the Pacific. Heavy bombardment leveled everything, including trees. Everything now is new-built, the quickest and cheapest way. There is no trace of the exquisite old botanical gardens or the avenues of rain trees, and only the ornamental gateposts and steps remain to mark the site of the elegant pre-1917 German Residency. The plantations have been largely brought back to productivity. We spent most of our day at the agricultural station. We saw coconut palms, the oil-producing royal palms, cocoa, coffee, tea, cinnamon, nutmeg, pepper (which is a vine), and vanilla (which is an orchid). Every pest from toads to tapioca is credited to the Japanese. A jet-black native doctor is the son of a much decorated "coast watcher" of wartime fame. The natives are as dark as midnight and an unsmiling lot. Household servants are "cook boys" or "wash boys," and said to be a vanishing lot here, as well as Stateside. Now they work on plantations or for the government. The flowers are ones we know, growing to monster proportions. Split-leaf philodendron climb the jungle trees, referred to as "monstera." Every waving palm frond reminded me that the day was Palm Sunday and that St. David's in Austin would be cool and dark with palm leaf branches imported from the Rio Grande Valley. I was offered a chance to attend services at 7:00 A.M., *only.* I simply could not make it after those two long jeep rides. On my way to inspect the new hospital, we saw little black chaps returning from church, their Bibles on their heads, carrying a palm branch decorated with hibiscus flowers stuck on the spikes. Mrs. Kelly (of the white gloves) had cocktails and a salad supper at the Residency for fifty-odd people: plantationers, the doctors (Estonian, German, and Australian), the dentist (American), some rich Chinese merchants, and two young American citizens (black) from the Caroline Islands visiting in Rabaul for a Methodist leadership conference. My personal conclusion is: Like New York, the South Seas are a nice place to visit, but I wouldn't want to live there.

Wednesday, April 6. Wewak (Territory of New Guinea), where we passed the night with the District Commissioner, was one of the hottest spots. I have to admit to a certain astonishment when the champagne and hors d'oeuvres were served by the indigenous staff with black feet and torso bare, their only garment being a "Lap-Lap." Next morning we moved on to Mount Hagen in the Western Highlands where the climate is like the mountains of New Mexico; the natives wear only paint and pig-grease, with shells through their noses, bird-of-paradise plumes on their heads, breech cloths of woven string, and tails of palm fronds on their fannies—nothing else though it's quite cold. The effect is the same as "Les Girls" in the Follies. A crash program is on to civilize them, and build schools, roads, and a cattle station that teaches the care of cattle and rudimentary animal husbandry.

We visited four missions, two Catholic, a Nazarene, and a Lutheran. Never belittle a missionary again as long as you live. These Highlanders saw their first wheel on an airplane, and for the first time in history they make "walk about" on the roads unafraid that some headhunter from another tribe will rise from a bush to bash in their heads. Mr. Gus Wortham's little tie girt with the Santa Gertrudis emblem is now hanging around the neck of a painted Fuzzy-Wuzzy, presented by the Ambassador in trade for two bird-of-paradise plumes. The Reverend Tex Mansour, out eighteen years, is from Mrs. Hilda Weinert's school at Seguin. Among the *introduced* flora are thousands of poinsettias in full burst of bloom for Easter. Remember, Easter lilies bloom at Christmas? The rainfall is 150 inches annually but the land is still poor.

I put the question, "If the Australian administration should withdraw, how long before tribal war?" Reply, "Within forty-eight hours." Travel is educational but it requires a stout heart and a strong back. I am longing for a soaking bath, two towels, a hairdresser, and a freshly pressed frock. The humidity keeps your clothes wrinkled and dampish. Even dry towels are a luxury. The Union Jack is not flying but English civilization is still spreading by osmosis: to wit, cocker spaniels, marigolds, buttered scones, and polished boots.

April 7. I enjoyed *Lae* though it's too civilized to be an anthropologist's dream like our previous stopping place in New Guinea. Back on the coast, newly established since 1945, are infant industries, such as a foundry, an abbatoir, a technical school, a teacher training college, and a beautiful botanical garden. We visited yet another agricultural station and a cocoa fermentary. The manager of the cocoa plantation was here prior to the war. He was made into an officer and gentleman at Duntroon in Canberra before returning to the island to shoot his first Jap at ten paces. Our host, District Officer Timperly, was with General Krueger's headquarters and had learned about bourbon whiskey. Same luxuriant bloom as in Hawaii but without the tourists and neon.

Early this morning we were off to the *Kiriwini Islands.* The isle of Losuia has a Polynesian population who value their land, pigs, and women in that order. Three big air strips, miles of deteriorating roads, and acres of tarmac in the bush tell the tale of a bomber base built and abandoned after six months. Hope seemed dimmest here of all our landings. The land won't support any crops. Unless the rapidly increasing population can turn to the fishing industry, they will have to eat each other. In pidgin English, Ed is "face Man belong America—Stop along Australia." Pidgin is the universal language, based partly on English and partly on German. I have been doling out packets of bluebonnet seed like a Texas version of Johnny Appleseed. At the rate some legumes grow that are annuals with us (Crotilaria grows into a tree), five years from now the South Sea Islands may be overgrown with bluebonnet trees.†

April 9. Spent Thursday night in *Port Moresby* with Sir Donald Cleland, Administrator of the Territory. Government House there is a traditional open tropical house where we slept under mosquito bars, had delicious food, and were waited on by those quiet, barefoot black boys. Ed is wearing his LBJ hat, which spells "cowboy" to them. Everyone loves Western movies and is very anxious to meet the Texas Ambassador, whom they associate with cowboys. H.E. laid a wreath at the War Cemetery. I recall that Vice President Nixon‡ said he'd laid wreaths in eighty-seven countries. The city was closed for Good Friday and will stay so until next Wednesday. Moresby is a civilized city with eight thousand Europeans and only four Americans. Our fellow guest at Government House was Lady Braburn, a family connection of the Earl of Mountbatten. She is a friend of Mrs. Merriweather Post and calls Lord and Lady Casey as "Maie and Dick." I'd describe her as a traveling socialite. The official car is an Austin Princess that has jump seats and a running board. The fish they served was "baramundi," proclaimed by Lady Cleland the third best fish in the world. You can nominate your own first two. Prince Philip's choices are Dover sole and Scottish salmon. My personal selections are pompano and "Hot cat."

Last night a hotel in Townsville, back in *Australia.* No official functions there, I'm glad to relate. We will arrive in Canberra at 4:30 P.M. after a 1,000-mile, nonstop, seven and one-half hour flight on Saturday, April 9. We traveled 6,100 miles by air, forty-eight hours in the air, twelve nights in ten different beds; we were guested at seven cocktail parties, five dinners, several outdoor barbecues, morning and afternoon teas. Happy is the conclusion to my saga of island-hopping: no plane trouble, no weather delays, no illnesses; fourteen passengers

† In October 1968, I met a young American who told me he'd seen my Texas bluebonnets blooming at Lae.
‡ President Nixon was one of our first houseguests at the Residence.

who never complained of a headache, cold, dysentery, blisters or worn-
out feet, or got mad at their husbands and/or wives. Incredible journey, wasn't it??

Love and kisses to all my friends,
Anne

P.S. In case you have a world globe handy, look at the South Pacific
Islands, those small dots in the vast Pacific. That's where we've
been.   A.

Sydney, N.S.W., Australia
April 30, 1966

Dear Everybody:

The Book of Common Prayer assures the stranger of the
familiar Easter Services but the music and flowers are not quite like
home. The church was decked with asters, not lilies, because it is
autumn here. That evening we flew to Sydney to dine with Sir Howard
Beale and Mr. Edward W. Kuhn of Memphis, Tennessee, president of
the American Bar. By Tuesday, the Inter-Parliamentary Union guests
were arriving, fourteen congressmen and senators and their wives, including Senator and Mrs. Ralph Yarborough and Congressman Bob
Poage of Texas. We entertained with one large reception for about
two hundred guests from many nations. Next day I took all the ladies
attending with their husbands to a nearby property, "Lanyon," one of
the show places with a dear old house and appendages (convict-built),
including a "gaol" (as they spell jail). Then back we came to the
Residence for lunch. That was a party of fifty.

I loved seeing Opal Yarborough, really the first old friend who has
been here. Our families have been friends since 1930 when we all
arrived in Austin from the country for Ed and Ralph to join Attorney

General Jimmie Allred's staff as eager young assistants. Ralph is a great nature lover, so he wanted to see 'roos and emus in their natural habitat. It has come back to us that he tells a hilarious story concerning his trip to Strathnairn Station with Frederick in the Chrysler. They opened a cattlegate to drive right into the pasture with cattle, 'roos, and emus. He was startled, to say the least, when he picked up a rock only to find it to be an emu egg. The shaggy, brown, six-foot-tall emu owner of said egg took out after him. Ralph jumped in the car, with the blue-eyed emu trying to follow, saying "Drive on Frederick." Ralph said it was an unforgettable sight, the big black car flying its official flags speeding over the paddock.

We have also had as guests Mr. and Mrs. Harlan Fentress of Waco and Mr. and Mrs. Ralph Brown of Corsicana. The Browns are parents of Dick Brown, publisher of the *Austin American-Statesman.* The President sent us a film of himself made in 1942 in Australia. We show it after dinner frequently, to everyone's great interest.

We had three days in the Snowy Mountains visiting the hydro-electric dam project. If you are not an engineer, three days is a little long to spend looking at power plants, tunnels, and dams. There the rivers, which would run normally off the mountains into the sea, reverse themselves and flow back inland where the water can be used for irrigation. Power is created for cities at the same time. The Snowies are the only real mountains on the continent, therefore, the only depend-able source of fresh water, making this hydroelectric plant one of the few possible in Australia. The weather was cool, and, though the roads were rough, at least we didn't socialize at night. Our weary bones could be at ease. If you come on a tour of Australia, firmly resist more than one day of the Snowies. Our companions on this trip were John and Lupe Murchison of Dallas, Phil Bee, Oscar Griffin, reporter, and Richard Pipes, photographer, of the *Houston Chronicle.*

We reached Canberra Sunday at dusk, had sixteen people for supper, and started the day early Monday, the twenty-fifth of April, which was

Anzac Day, the fifty-first anniversary of the landing of the Australian and New Zealand troops at Gallipoli. The Ambassador attended a solemn requiem mass. All of us went to the service at the War Memorial where male and female veterans of all the wars marched so proudly and smartly—even a few from the Boer War. Many were original Anzacs and, of course, with them marched veterans of World War II, Korea, and Vietnam. The representative of each country having a Mission in Canberra laid a wreath. The Governor General, the High Commissioner of New Zealand, Sir Charles for the United Kingdom, and my H.E. (in striped pants) for the United States had especially prominent parts to play. Anita Hazlett, wife of the New Zealand High Commissioner, was stunning in her black costume. She'll be such a beautiful widow she'll never walk home from the graveyard alone.

After that the day grew progressively gayer. A luncheon party at the Turbaynes and dinner at the New Zealand High Commission completed the festivities for us. The only thing comparable in the United States would have been Confederate Memorial Day in about 1910. All the merriment died for me when the news came that Mme Van Hieu of Vietnam had died in childbirth about nine that morning. She it was who, with her constant chatter using a twenty-five word English vocabulary, had furnished the diplomatic corps with all its genteel amusement. Ed and I decided not to wait to unravel the protocol, but went immediately to their Residence, doing what came naturally to us in such circumstances. Ambassador Van Hieu wept on Ed's shoulder, making me know we'd been the first to dare to offer condolence. The Vietnamese are so small and really friendless, and going home to Saigon is going to they really know-not-what. I pray that Buddha can comfort His Excellency and Madame's little old mother.

We set out Wednesday for the picnic races at Gunnedah, north of Sydney. Everything came off except the races. During lunch a hard shower made the track too slick for the nags to run. The riders are all gentlemen jockeys, usually sons of the owners. The horses may be any age; all are grass fed; the purses are minimal but the betting is lively, with bookmakers under their traditional umbrellas. They at least are "pros." In spite of the complete cancellation of the races, the spirits were not dampened for the ball at all—a white-tie affair lasting until 4:00 A.M. Picnic races are the greatest snob thing in Australia, just for the country people, though they have recently lowered the barriers enough the let in bank managers and doctors, but *not* solicitors. Country towns and country hotels in Australia are an experience. You carry your own bags. They give us American VIP's such an effusive welcome it is embarrassing.

We had a nice Sunday on Sydney harbor where we rescued the crew of a capsized sailboat. That was exciting. Went to the evening service in the Cathedral where Admiral Paul Ramsey, United States Navy, read the lesson and we sang "Eternal Father, Strong to Save," the sailor's hymn. This service opened Coral Sea Week.

Monday night Ed spoke to the Apex Club in Gosford, fifty miles north of Sydney. They gave him the works—motorcycle escort, band in red coats, even the Christmas lights were turned on (according to Frederick, "ten thousand lamps for you, Meester Ambassador"), presents, flowers, and a printed copy of "The Yellow Rose of Texas" so that everybody could sing.

This trip I have done a few things to amuse myself. I had my fur hat made over; went to a Lunchtime Theater, fifty minutes of action while you eat tea and sandwiches off your lap; and went to Paddy's Market—birds, orchids, old clothes, sea shells, "bits and pieces," a once-a-week event every Friday. Only bought three shells.

Sydney is as big as Rome, twice as big as Washington, the fourth largest city in the British Commonwealth. It's Australia's swinging town. But each time we return to Sydney, it is newly exciting. Already I have told you of the myriad beaches, the surfers' and swimmers' paradise. These symmetrical horshoe-shaped white sand beaches were made by the pounding South Pacific, and are famed for elegant homes as well as modest cottages on the promontories. D. H. Lawrence wrote about this aspect in his novel *Kangaroo*. But it is the harbor all my water-bewitched friends must see to believe. At night it is like a huge jeweled tiara, its shores scalloped with sparkling diamonds and sapphires. Cab drivers have their favorite hilltops where they drive tourists to view the bridge, the high-rise apartments and housing units spreading up and down the hills and around the innumerable bays. Ships and ferries are dwarfed to toy-size in the very vastness of the harbor. On any warm day, thousands of motorboats, yachts, and brilliant-sailed baby sailboats flit around like butterflies. Dominating the harbor scene is the multiple-arched opera house on the city side. It, too, is a sailing ship—its concrete arches years in the building, its completion projected years in the future—a thing of puzzling grandeur.

We went to a dinner given by a Sydney merchant for the new Lord Mayor, John Armstrong. He's Labour Party. The group was different but interesting. Our last night was spent at the Coral Sea Ball at the Trocadero. Admiral Paul Ramsey attended with full panoply, to represent the United States. We will have a repeat of the Coral Sea Ball in Canberra on Friday. Next guests are Laura Lee and Jack Blanton, our young cousins from Houston. They are traveling with a group called Young Presidents (business, that is). They will be followed by Maurice Acers and his wife, Ebby, from Austin and Dallas.

Love and kisses,
Anne

P.S. I had Opal carry home to Luci Baines Johnson our wedding gift—
a rug made of fine Merino sheepskins, a local favorite, handsome
and serviceable. A.

NOTE: This is the first of Mrs. Clark's round robins since they returned to
Australia.—Mrs. O'D.

Canberra, Australia
July 14, 1966

Dear Hearts and Gentle People:

We have been back in Australia ten days. Hard to believe that
for a year now (lacking one month) Ed will have been His Excellency.
I am still only the "pig tail," but it seems to wag every minute. Six
weeks in the United States passed on wings. Though I was deprived of
butler, chef, chambermaid, steward, chauffeur, and secretary, life was
easier with just Bertha and Richard, my kind, untaught East Texas
staff whose stock answer to all directions or requests is, "well-M'am."

We left Australia on May 19, my birthday. I admit I am fifty-seven.
And on this Friday, July 15, Ed will be sixty. We came straight to
Houston, gained a whole day crossing time zones. Australians do not
name the time zones with titles like Central Standard or Mountain
Time. By the way, I've never heard a time zone named outside the
United States. I wonder if the next zone passed flying west after Pacific Standard has a name. The Scurlocks and Fishers had a lovely
party for us in Houston. Ed saw many of his old friends and I spent
the day at Carl's Beauty Salon. Sunday we drove to Straddlefork. On
Monday, rainbows shone in all our skies because our daughter and her
adorable "pee-wees" joined us there. Then we went to Austin, com-
muting daily to Georgetown for the ceremonies and festivities surrounding Ed's "investiture." Frank and Charmaine Denius shared the
hosting of a most elaborate garden party with Grogan and Dorothy
Lord at the Lord's beautiful white-columned house. There I felt I was
truly home, in the Southern part of Heaven with "the sweet magnolias
climbin' round the do'."

It was a proud day for me to see my husband hooded and conferred
for his very own achievement, mid the applause of five hundred old

United States Embassy, Residence, Canberra (courtesy Chas. P. McGaha).

United States Embassy, Chancery, Canberra (photograph by Adrian Lautenbach, Beam Photographics Pty. Limited, Canberra).

Ambassador Clark signs the oath after having been sworn in as Ambassador, August 9, 1965. *Standing,* Mrs. Clark, Secretary of State Dean Rusk, Australian Ambassador Sir Keith Waller, Senator Ralph Yarborough, Senator John Tower (courtesy U. S. Department of State).

The Clarks arrive in Canberra, August 15, 1965. Jeff Pretyman, Keith Douglas-Scott, the Ambassador, Jack Lydman, Mrs. Clark, Mrs. Lydman (copyright Manuka Photographic Centre).

At the Sydney home of Sir Warwick Fairfax (before he was knighted), December 10, 1965. Mrs. Clark in white, Lady Fairfax, the Ambassador, Sir. Warwick standing alone to the right (photograph by Brian Bird, courtesy *Vogue Australia*, copyright Condé Nast Publications Ltd.).

Government House, "Yarralumla," Canberra
(Courtesy Australian News and Information Bureau)

The Prime Minister's Lodge, Canberra
(Courtesy Australian News and Information Bureau)

At the wedding of Minister William McMahon, Sydney, December 11, 1965.

At the King Ranch, Milton Park, Australia, August, 1966
(Courtesy Chas. P. McGaha)

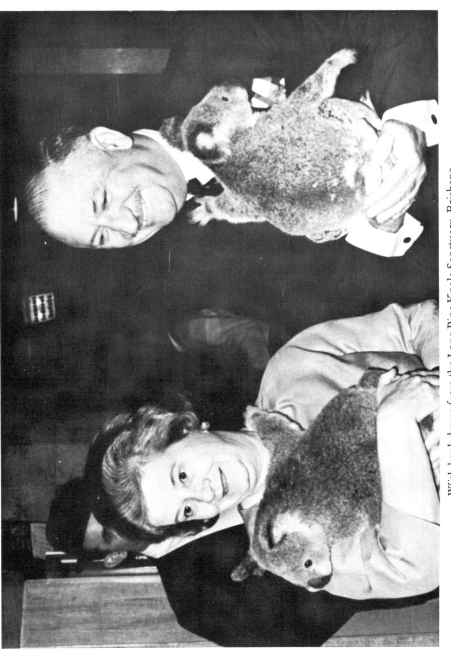

With koala bears from the Lone Pine Koala Sanctuary, Brisbane.

Government House, Sydney

Parliament House, Canberra
(Courtesy Australian News and Information Bureau)

Dame Pattie and Sir Robert Menzies, the Ambassador, Senator J. William Fulbright (Copyright Manuka Photographic Centre)

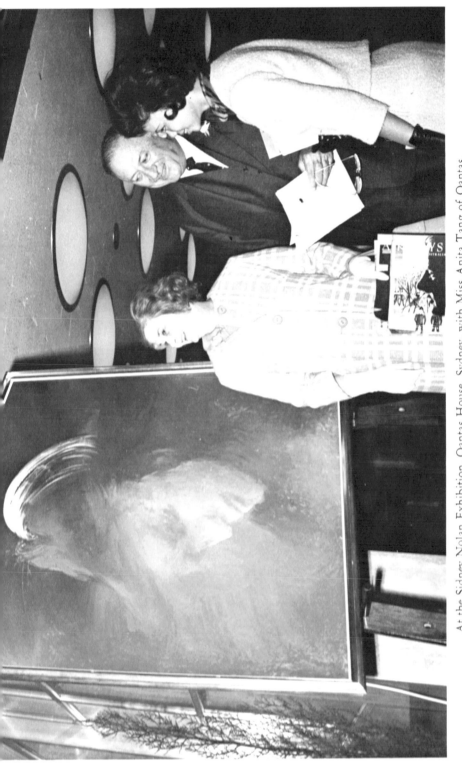

At the Sidney Nolan Exhibition, Qantas House, Sydney, with Miss Anita Tang of Qantas, Honolulu, April 29, 1966 (Qantas Airways photograph).

Sydney Harbor

Commissioning the *Investigator*, February 4, 1967. Mrs. Clark and Mr. Harding, manager of State Ship Yard, Newcastle.

At the Coral Sea Ball, May, 1967. Mrs. Clark, Admiral David McDonald, Mrs. Stewart Jameson, Senator John Grey Gorton (now Prime Minister).

t the Residence, on December 6, 1967. Mr. Freddie Roe, Dame Zara Holt, the Ambas-dor, Mrs. Roe (the daughter of Sir Norman and Dame Mabel Brookes), Prime Minister arold Holt, Mrs. Clark, and Mrs. Busst of Queensland, a friend of Mrs. Holt.

The Ambassador enjoys a toast by Prime Minister Harold Holt at the Residence, December 6, 1967.

Government House, Melbourne (courtesy, *The Herald,* Melbourne).

Government House, Brisbane (courtesy State Public Relations Bureau, Premier's Department, Brisbane, Queensland).

At Lex Anderson's farewell party, Sydney, December 17, 1967 (courtesy Chas. P. McGaha).

and dear friends. I believe it was J. K. Galbraith who said that though
the businessman and the academician are natural antagonists, no businessman ever felt himself a complete success until the warm June day
when he walked down an aisle to be awarded the ultimate honor of an
honorary degree. One of the newspaper men asked Leila if she knew all
these people, and she replied, "If they aren't kin, I have at least known
them since I was born." We spent two weeks in Washington, broken
in two pieces, two days in New York, several-odd days in Austin (not
enough). We welcomed the Prime Minister of Australia on his first
official visit to America. If you have any way to get yourself invited to
an "arrival ceremony" for a head of state on the White House lawn,
hurry it up, for it beats a state dinner all to pieces (nineteen guns for
the Prime Minister, arm loads of red roses for Mrs. Johnson and Mrs.
Holt).

Leila and Martha Wynn saw us off to New York at Andrews Field
where we boarded a Qantas plane—the same plane all the way to Sydney with stops in San Francisco, Honolulu, and Nadi (pronounced
Nandi). I don't believe they feed you as much on Qantas or ply you
with as many drinks; their main ploy was hot or cold towels scented
with cologne, which must have been passed twenty-five times.

We plunged right into activity here at home in Canberra. Charlton
Heston was our houseguest. He requested a tennis game, which was
arranged, and afterward we served informal supper for twenty-four
persons. Next morning he read poetry—Robert Frost, Thomas Wolfe
—and the Preamble to the Declaration of Independence. Afterward,
we assembled in the reception room of the theater and toasted the
President and the Queen. Thus we celebrated July the Fourth. Our
guest list was a wide one, all the Americans and as many diplomats and
Australian officers as the theater would hold.

Last week we attended a dinner at the Embassy of N.A.R. (Egypt)
and flew to Sydney for dinner at the home of Mrs. Diana Van Kahorn.
She is a young, beautiful Australian, once married to a German baron

and resided in the States. She says, though she is now living on the Australian money of her Australian father, she'd like to live in the United States again. Line up, any of you single fellows.

July 17. It is really cold now in the Southern Hemisphere. I feel it because of the change. We wear our warmest clothes and have a fire in the sitting room all day. The thousand rose bushes stand bare, so H.E.'s yellow roses are sometimes missing. On Ed's sixtieth birthday, July 15, something happened that he never expected to see—it snowed! Canberra is quite quiet. Parliament is not in session, so no ministers are in town. The diplomatic colony is a "fruit basket turn over." Three very nice heads of missions are leaving soon: the Chinese Ambassador with his American wife, the Dutch Ambassador with his French wife, and the Ceylonese High Commissioner with his half-Scottish wife. The United Kingdom High Commissioner, Sir Charles, and his Russian wife, Ed's Nasturtium, are on leave; we miss them most of all. The Belgian and the German Ambassadors are both in Europe. At least four members of our staff have been replaced, Naval Attaché, Administrative Officer, Agricultural Attaché, and the assistant to the Political Counselor. Two years is about the standard term, and it really boils down to about eighteen months and then a home leave. Our United States Information officer, the Chinese Ambassador, and one of the Counselors at the German Embassy, each with five and one-half years' service, are the oldest resident members of the Diplomatic Corps. Mexico is establishing a mission here now just in time to present the Ballet Folklorico next Sunday. The chargé has served in the United States, is pro-American, speaks fluent English, and has an American wife, Elizabeth.

Ed has been taking some of his new staff members to lunch at the Commonwealth Club, an old organization in bright new quarters with picture windows and Danish modern furniture. They like to run it, though, as if it had leather chairs and old mahogany. Diplomats can acquire membership promptly, but locals have to wait interminably.

There are two separate coat racks, one for life members and one for associates. Ed insists on flouting rules about the number of guests he may bring to lunch but they haven't ordered him out yet.

I am happily looking forward to a visit from my friend Fredeen Herring. She and the travel agent have worked out a schedule for her to stop off in Hawaii and Papeete; she will arrive, she thinks, at 2:50 on Sunday, July 24, but, on account of time and date lines, she can't be sure. It could be Saturday or Monday, and it could be 3:50 or 1:50. It's always thus.

I hope my next report is more fun-packed, and full of good tidings, news like a new cook, a trip north, and nice guests.

Love and kisses,
Anne

Canberra, Australia
August 11, 1966

Dear U.S. Friends:

I've forgotten how long since I paused in my correspondence with you. I am guessing it was about mid-July. For most of the intervening time we have hovered about the fire in the Residence. There has been a series of farewell parties for three heads of missions —Schurmans (Netherlands), Chens (China), and Muttukamarras (Ceylon). We had a Sunday luncheon for thirty-six to farewell the Chens. My friend Fredeen Herring of Houston arrived in Sydney on Wednesday, July 27. We met her there and attended the thirtieth anniversary of the founding of the Australian-American Association dinner. It was white tie, everyone wearing his full set of medals and honors. The Governor, Sir Roden Cutler, and Lady Cutler, were in attendance. It was he who was formerly Consul-General in New York. He wears both his Victoria Cross and his artificial leg with style. Quite an impressive fellow, he's at least six feet six. We had only shortly before made our first official call at Government House in Sydney. When the Ambassador had called officially last year, there was an Acting Administrator, whose wife was *persona non grata* to the United States (by this I mean she was pinkish and vocal; she was omitted, so I did not call).

Government House in Sydney is the oldest and most regal of the official residences. It was built about 1830 with cupolas and turrets, parquetry floors, enormous sliding doors, and tiny iron grates in the fireplaces. We were received in a diminutive parlor with ceiling taller than the length or breadth of the room, but made cosy by a glowing fire of briquettes. There were splendid portraits, four handsome sons and a Great Dane. Sir Roden is barely fifty, very young for a governorship, which usually caps a career because, like an ex-President, it is considered unsuitable for him to engage in much activity afterward. He just must not be in commerce. The new Governor of Queensland is also Australian, as is the new Archbishop of Sydney. The English are fast being pushed from the seats of power here, though they hold on to some ceremonial positions.

The Texans in Sydney gave a dinner for us. The William Bohlmans of Schulenburg (she was formerly Bailey Carroll's secretary), the Chuck Schwartzes of the Union Oil Company, and Nadine and Bill Bell of Brown and Root.

The Hazletts of the New Zealand High Commission had a lovely after-theater party for Joyce Grenfell, famous English comedienne-monologuist, a Cornelia Otis Skinner type. Some of her most successful sketches satirized or sentimentalized Americans. Her mother was a Virginian, the youngest of the Langhorne sisters (Lady Astor was the eldest). Fredeen and I loved her, though we suspected that perhaps it was us she was taking off. One number was built of American folk songs and she used the lullaby "Pretty Little Horses." Grandfather

Downs sang this to Ed as a child, and Mamma Clark sang it to Leila. Very sentimental.

We had ninety American teachers one Sunday for coffee and invited the two Austinites, Inez Jeffrey and Madge Rudd, to stay on for lunch. Get them to describe the Residence for you. Ed and I joke about the number of "Click-Clickers" there are in any touring group. If you have any venture capital, I suggest Kodak stock. Tourists lug thousands of dollars worth of equipment. The Instamatic Camera is the merchandise marvel of the era.

Benno Schmidt of Abilene and New York was our houseguest last week. We gave a black-tie dinner. Sir Howard and Lady Beale from Sydney, Dame Mabel Brookes from Melbourne, Mary Fairfax, the Egyptian Ambassador, and the Vietnamese Ambassador were guests. A few days later we heard that Benno's sixteen-year-old son, Tom, was killed in a motorcycle accident at Esperance in Western Australia.

Next morning we set off on a real safari, first stop Bathurst, a small city in New South Wales. I had accepted months ago an invitation to open the fete at All Saints Cathedral there. When it was learned that H.E. was coming, too, I was pushed off stage and the town went all out with the Bishops and Canons and Headmistresses guiding us through their various domains. It makes you feel very humble and proud to be an American. If visiting Ambassadors are received in the United States with the royal treatment we receive in Australia, I wonder why they aren't traveling the country all the time. I can remember only three coming to Austin in thirty years, a German Ambassador when Allred was Governor, an English one in Price Daniel's governorship, and the Minister from Luxemburg for a Headliners' party. My only problem was the cold, cold weather. The girls' school that I visited was an iceberg. It is one of Australia's oldest, 120 little girls from nine to seventeen in blue uniforms who are mainly country girls from the properties in New South Wales and Queensland. My memory drifted back to pigtailed Jane and Anne Metcalfe and Virginia Eatherly and

Sister Mary Paula, at our convent school in Greenville. I wondered if the little Aussies were as homesick as we had been.

Next morning at 5:00 A.M., take-off, then breakfast at the Australian Officers' Mess, Fairbairn, Canberra, where we changed planes and added more members to our party. There we had the happy surprise of greeting Sir Robert and Dame Pattie on their return from England, where he had been for his installation as Warden of the Cinque Ports, succeeding Sir Winston Churchill. All-day flight landed us in Alice Springs, the great red heart, the center, of Australia. We were guests of the District Officer, Mr. Conway, who administers that end of the Northern Territory. The first and biggest rain in years changed all the plans for our visit. We visited the Flying Doctor* and the Aboriginal Museum but could not go to the Murray River Property, as planned. The streams grow dangerously swift for a few hours, just as our Pedernales or Guadalupe, so we were kept in town. The one thousand miles of asphalt road through nowhere is called "The Track."

Sunday noon we departed for Darwin, capital of the Northern Territory, the last capital for us to visit. It is two thousand miles from Alice. Because so many of our troops were stationed there during the war, Americans tend to think of Darwin as a city of more size and importance than it actually is. Population is about twenty thousand persons. We stayed at Government House, guests of the Administrator and Mrs. Dean. It's an old stone house with encircling verandas and wicker furniture, built about 1870 with beautiful views of the harbor. The house is smothered in Mexican fuchsia-colored bougainvillaea. Slow turning ceiling fans and blessed warmth were noted, as I had suffered in Alice from the chill. India under the British must have been like this. The Ambassador laid another wreath at another war cemetery. This one I will remember because here we saw the famous bowerbird's "display" beneath a shrub. (Read your nature books about that; it's too

---

*Flying Doctors constitute the unique medical service that cares for the isolated populations of Australia. Settlers on the vast stations talk by radio to the doctors, who come or send an ambulance as a last resort.

intricate to describe here.) Suffice it to say, Norman Terrell, our staff
member who is a "birder," said he had slogged all over Australia hoping to find one. Then, by surprise, he saw this creation by one of
Australia's unique and famous birds, or rather his identifying signs,
in a very civilized, much visited spot. We also visited Rum Jungle, a
large uranium mine. It is a rich lode where the ore assays out two to
eleven pounds per ton. Uranium is a yellow powder resembling sulphur
and is stored in steel drums, awaiting a peaceful use—we hope.

Two nights of blissful warmth and we set out south again to chilly
Brunette Downs, King Ranch, Australia. The Convair dropped us at
Tennant Creek, where we boarded a twin-engine Cessna, one and one-
half hours to the five-million-acre station with fifty thousand head of
cattle. The King Ranch of Texas is a partner in this operation along
with Australians Peter Ballieu and Sir Rupert Clarke, both of whom
are in the States at the moment visiting their Texas associates. Brunette
is ninety-four miles from the nearest telephone. The lifeline out is the
plane by daylight, supplemented by an undependable telegraph system
relayed through Alice Springs. The manager and his wife, Mr. and Mrs.
Weiss, have been there only three years. She is an excellent hostess who
wears a long dress for dinner at night, and a creative cook who serves
three desserts. The homestead is a sweet white cottage, furnished in the
exact opposite of "Ranch Style," with white walls, flowered chintz,
and cut flowers flown in from Brisbane, fifteen hundred miles away.
Mr. Weiss was lured out of retirement to make the property produce
money after $1,500,000 had been poured into improvements, such as
"bores" (wells), fences, and equipment, the most costly of which are
road trains (three-piece trailer trucks carrying 150 head of cattle each).

I learned a lot about Santa Gertrudis breeding and aborigines and
saw native companions (a rare dancing crane), kangaroos, and white
cockatoos. Set off early the second morning for Mount Isa, where we
rejoined the rest of the party and visited another mine, 53 per cent
American-owned, which produces lead, zinc, and copper. Had morning
tea at 11:30 at VIP guesthouse with company officials. The menu in-

cluded caviar canapes, three kinds of sandwiches, and chocolate cake, plus coffee, tea, whisky, and gin. Didn't leave us long to inspect the mine and its fine new shaft. I was glad, as the mine looked black and sinister to me. We hope to arrive in Surfers' Paradise (Coolangatta) by 5:00 P.M. Truly we are Thursday's children who have far to go—over fifteen hundred miles today. As I gazed down at the earth from the plane, I thought the surface of the moon must look like this, barren and pock-marked, the back of a far-beyond land.

A Week Later

We arrived at Surfers' only slightly late, met by a full-scale party, headed by the Mayor. I heard again those dread words, "Hurry and change. We are having a small reception for you immediately." So I clutched my basket of yellow roses, climbed into the first car behind the police escort, and roared off along their Gold Coast (equivalent of any Ocean Drive, Any Coast, U.S.A.). Frederick had brought the car up to meet us. Most of our engagements were in Brisbane, fifty miles away, and we needed the car. Surfers' Paradise is a lovely Florida-type resort of souvenir shops, restaurants, and privately owned beach houses. It was "Show Week" in Brisbane. This is something like the Dallas Fair, save most of the emphasis is on the cattle and agricultural displays. All the landed gentry come in from the country and spend the whole week. They give big dinners. We went to one given by the Santa Gertrudis Breeders. The dancing had started when we left and bade fair to last all night. Queenslanders are like Texans. When the grass is tall and beef is a dollar a pound, they are a merry lot. Our host, Mr. Barney Joyce, owns the enormous station called Eisenvald, where Prince Charles did his country visit. His nephew-manager, named Coates, has recently visited Albany, Texas, and knows Mozelle Howsley. Lennon's the hotel where the American soldiers spent all their leave and MacArthur had his headquarters, has returned to its prewar status as the St. Anthony, the Peabody, or the Ritz of Queensland. The graziers are glad to have it back for their own.

The Ambassador and even I were invited to award trophies and to tie ribbons on those prize bulls. The Hereford judge was the most elegantly tailored English gentleman I've ever seen, actually from Hereford, England, itself. The sleeve buttons on his coat really unbutton so he could turn his sleeves up when handling cattle. Next day we drove in again for the races. At the races there were separate enclosures for men and women. We even lunched separately and the gentlemen joined the ladies only at tea. Such a beautiful course with swans (those elegant black ones are native to Australia; any black ones you meet elsewhere were exported from here). Lunch was served in the members' dining room with champagne and tea between the races. Girls come around and take the bets while men with little satchels come to pay off. Many of the horses were owned by the members personally, but, even so, I did not get any reliable tips. I did not cash a check, or, as the Aussies say, "collect a dividend." I never saw a more elegantly turned out group of people, especially the men. An Australian woman speaks of "my best race-meeting frock," not of "my high-Sunday-go-to-meeting dress," as Mary Carpenter puts it. Sunday morning we rose in time for nine o'clock service at the Anglican Church. It was the family service and the Vicar pointed out to all the little tots in the church that they were seeing the American Ambassador. I frequently ask myself if this is my same old Ed they make such a fuss over. I am torn between being humbled and amused. We spent the day with Marjorie Turbayne's brother-in-law, David Turbayne, and wife at their lovely beach house. There were a number of Australian friends and kinfolk there, too. They are all marvelous talkers and can expound on any subject and be interesting in many fields from auto racing to Shakespeare. Several sets of darling children were there with their English or Irish governesses, young and pretty girls, not staid old nannies.

The afternoon entertainment for me consisted of visiting the bird sanctuary. At four each afternoon, hundreds of rainbow lorikeets (parrots) flock in to be fed. Imagine Venice populated with the gayest

parrots in place of pigeons. They sit on your head and shoulders, jab-
ber, gurgle, and murmur, and eat out of your hand. In fact, I'm fond of
the birds out here because they are so obvious—loud, large, and highly
colorful and so many flocks. There are no wild felines in Australia, so
no natural enemies for our bird friends. There were baby kangaroos
who would also eat out of your hand. The 'roos all appear gentle and
all the babies are called "joey." I may be able to send you snapshots of
me and the 'roos. Next morning we rested before departing at 2:00
P.M. for Canberra. I've spent most of the week reviving, unpacking,
writing thank-you notes, and preparing to start again at 9:00 A.M.
tomorrow when Elaine and Bob Burck arrive. I'll be glad to see some
Texans.

Fondly,

Anne Clark

September 27, 1966

Dear Friends:

        That is if I have any still interested in our life "down under"
and "inside" the Embassy. We returned from the Northern Territory
and Queensland on August 15. Most of the next month centered
around our American visitors. Fredeen stayed five weeks in all. Having
a friend to talk things over with was wonderful. She left from Sydney
September 7, to return to Houston across Asia and Europe, traveling all
sorts of odd lines like Cathay Pacific and Air Ethiopia. Two flights
were cancelled before she left Sydney, an Air India and a BOAC.
My advice is stick to Qantas or Pan American. We had three other
groups of American visitors in the month. Bob and Elaine Burck of
Dallas (Braniff), who conveyed a silky terrier back to Leila. The
Wynns call him Digger and say he's in danger of being loved to death.
Then we met the Houston Hartes in Sydney. They were on a Matson

cruise. They gave a lovely party aboard the *Monterey* themselves and had us invited by their Australian friends to many nice parties in Sydney. We stayed at the Australia Hotel, the "home away from home" of the New South Wales country gentry. As Delta planters go to the Peabody in Memphis and South Texas ranchers to the St. Anthony or Gunter in San Antonio, so every city has its hotel for "country" people —who are the world's greatest snobs.

The Australia Hotel is like a breath of England. We gave a luncheon there for the Hartes in the Opal Room. One of Mr. Harte's great friends is a Mrs. R. R. McDonald Parr (Gracie), born in El Paso and a successful entrepreneur in radio, producing canned programs of what I took to be soap operas. She says it's a dying enterprise, but still profitable.

Ed went to Norfolk Island from Sydney, taking a planeload of staff. Part of the *Bounty* mutineers emigrated hence from Pitcairn. They say it is exactly like story Number 2 in *Tales of the South Pacific*. Nearly everyone is named Christian, descendants of Fletcher. The Norfolk Island pine is the leading export, considered then and now as making the finest sailing ship masts. Their only other VIP visitors had been the French Admiral Picard-Destelan from Nouméa, and the Archbishop of Sydney, so the novelty of an official visitor made them especially hospitable. There is a duty-free port whence all the party brought home perfume, watches, and cameras. Since whisky and cigarettes are tax free to diplomats, they are not tempting.

Lyndal and Gus Wortham of Houston arrived in Canberra before Ed's return. My Saturday entertainment featured a trip to Cootamundra country races, ninety miles away. Never have I seen the countryside so green and beautiful (the drought has broken). Even in those boondocks, they roll out the red carpet or at least fly an American flag, assign us to the president of the Club as his special guests, have delicious picnic lunches under a tent, and allow me to present the trophies. Bookmakers are there in plenty. You can also place bets on Sydney and Melbourne races; local races are conveniently timed for this. The grandstand (where no one sits, they hang on the rail or stay in the bookies' circle) is wedding-cake jigsaw with all new paint as white as the frosting on a real cake. Those sports-worshiping Australian members of the Bowl Jockey Club do all this maintenance work themselves, volunteer.

Sunday morning our guests were the Hawaiian Dillinghams (old missionary family). We served milk punch. I doubt that the Australians really like it. They prefer their gin and tonic, or whisky and soda. Afterward, I persuaded Huang to feed us some of his family fare (Chinese). Mr. Gus said it was the best food he ever ate. That night we had the usual black-tie dinner for our guests. I asked the Indonesian Ambassador and wife for color. They didn't disappoint me; even he came in his little black velvet cap. Madam wears national dress. Monday Peter Ballieu (Australian King Ranch partner) sent a small plane for us. Had lunch at their Milton Park stud farm. Beautiful wife, Edwinia, and beautiful old house and garden. Mr. Gus went on to visit ranches in Queensland, but Lyndal came back to Canberra with me. Lyndal stayed until Wednesday and I tried to show her as much and have her meet as many people as possible. Even managed a kangaroo and at least a look at Lord Casey laying a cornerstone. I cannot produce the Governor General or the P.M. at will. It takes luck to arrange those meetings. I have been reading Lord Casey's books; one is called *Personal Reminiscences—'39 to '45.* I learned more about the behind-the-scenes events leading to Pearl Harbor, El Alemein, and the dissolution of the Empire than I ever knew. It's anything but tedious reading. I am also reading again *South Pacific.* Now that I have visited the places, the story comes alive.

A colorful occasion, of which I can only give a recounting: gentlemen's dinner—"Dress Mess"—at Duntroon Military College. Ed mouthed mightily at the idea of white tie and tails for a stag dinner, but came home starry-eyed. Lots of visiting American brass. What did they do? They danced on the table! When his regimental music played, each officer hopped on the table and danced, sometimes a dance as intricate as the Highland fling, never disturbing a piece of cutlery or a glass. Colonel Divers, our Military Attaché, did the honors for the United States. He danced three times—"Star Spangled Banner," "Infantry Song," and "The Yellow Rose of Texas."

Another spectacular was Morning Prayer at St. Paul's Cathedral in Sydney. It happened to be the anniversary of the Battle of Britain. Service representatives laid a wreath and did the slow march, a trumpet played last post, and the Archbishop of Perth spoke, not preached, on how England reacted then and how he hopes she will rise to the present economic crisis. He was fighting in Burma in 1940 on this date. The choir boys sang like angels, and I felt small and humble leaving the Dean's personal pew while the rest of the congregation waited on our going.

We went to dinners in Sydney, Melbourne, and Albury on Sunday, Monday, and Tuesday, returning late at night via Embassy plane. Dinner at Albury was with Mr. and Mrs. McRoberts, ten miles out. Everyone made sure that we were aware this was the property where Princess Alexandra visited when last in Australia. Thursday we dined with Air Marshal Sir Alister Murdock and Lady Murdock. Bobby Murdock is beautiful with brown eyes and light hair—though the dainty feminine type and twice a grandmother, she's an enthusiastic surfer. I can't imagine her with a ruffled hair.

They are special favorites of mine. Friday I had a night off, but Ed went to Sydney to the English-Speaking Union. Saturday we had lunch for twenty, honoring the Vietnamese Ambassador, who leaves soon for Rome. He is the brother of President Thieu. Representatives of the *National Geographic* came to take photos. They like people in their pictures. We asked all our Embassy people to wear bright colors, and the officers to "rig out" in their most colorful uniforms.

Through all this, I have been preparing for "Operation Westward Ho." We left for Perth by train from Sydney Saturday night—four days and nights on the train, fourteen days away from Canberra.

We were a party of six people—stopovers everywhere, black tie, striped pants, ranch clothes, whisky, cigars, gifts, place cards and a thoroughly exhausted———

Anne

Canberra
September 27, 1966

Dear Mrs. O'D. *et al.*:

After three nights on three different trains, I will start my description of our transcontinental journey. We entrained at 9:00 P.M. Saturday night in Sydney, detraining at Melbourne at 8:00 A.M. next morning. Photographers and reporters at both ends. This is a new gimmick for an Ambassador: H.E. was invited to read the lesson at St. Andrew's Cathedral where Dean Francis Sayre (grandson of Woodrow Wilson) of the National Cathedral in Washington would preach. We were met at the step by the Dean and seated behind the Governor of Victoria, Sir Rohan Delacombe. All lunched at Government House with Delacombes *en famille*.

After lunch I visited a charity antique show. Ed napped at the hotel and we entrained again at 8:30 P.M. This time we enjoyed the use of the Vice-Regal car built in 1937 for the Duke of Kent. He had been designated Governor-General. He never came to use it because soon after he was named, war came and he was killed in a plane crash. Next morning we detrained at Adelaide after having tea, toast, and fruit served on the train. Consul Jack Linahan had breakfast arranged with a railroad official. We had morning coffee with the English-Speaking Union and lunch aboard the train. The train we rode to the border of

South Australia was changed at Port Pirie. Three different gauge railroads come into this town. Each state has a different gauge. This is a holdover from the days before federation when each state was a separate Crown Colony. They are trying to switch over now to standard gauge. Here we boarded the transcontinental train operated by the Commonwealth. All trains are either state or federally owned. Our car this time was a period piece built in 1922 for H.R.H. Prince of Wales (now Duke of Windsor), when he came for an official visit. We also have a sleeping car and club car at our disposal. This has been a twenty-eight hour haul. We crossed the Nullarbor (Latin for "no tree")— miles of literally nothing, no mountains, just red earth and salt bush, the longest straight stretch of track in the world, 306 miles.

Our last change was at Kalgoorlie, a gold-rush town, still a going country town, not a ghost, though it was finished in 1902. Here it was that President Hoover lived and worked as a mining engineer. Here Consul and Mrs. Mayfield of Perth joined our party and next morning at 11:00 A.M. we finally disembarked at Perth. I met an English woman, professor in the university, who told me that when she first came out here, she used to sit and gaze at the Indian Ocean, thinking this was the very edge of the whole world, and in her loneliness and homesickness she sometimes wondered if she might be slipping off that edge. My feeling about Perth is much the same.

We were at Government House. Sir Douglas Kendrew was our host. Lady Kendrew is away in England. It is a lovely old house, set in a thirty-two–acre garden, recently refurbished with great taste by Lady Kendrew. The ballroom holds eleven hundred, and a supper room, with its own kitchen just below the ballroom, holds eleven hundred, so more than two thousand people can be entertained at one time. I am looked after by Elsie, Lady Kendrew's maid—unpacking, pressing, bath drawing, and zipping. Ed is looked after by Harry, the valet—clothes laid out, studs put in. They have a staff of eleven plus Captain Patrick Spence, the aide, who opens the door and meets all trains and planes. Captain Spence is also charged with looking after the dogs, two long-haired dachshunds called Freddie and Lulu.

After lunch with H.E. the Governor, we went to the Royal Agricultural Show for the grand entry. A field as big as Memorial Stadium was literally filled with animals, their attendants, and everything from goats to smart gigs. For the first time, Santa Gertrudis cattle and quarter horses were shown. That night, H.E. entertained at dinner for twenty-four. Now I am speaking of the Governor, not the Ambassador. In Lady Kendrew's absence, Sir Douglas plans the meals. He doesn't care for sweets, so no dessert, instead a hot shrimp savory was the finale. Bonbons are always on the table, anyway.

Next morning I had my wild-flower walk in King's Park with a lady botanist. They have made a South African garden and a California garden. Will someone send me some material on Texas wild flowers so maybe I can get a Texas garden going.

Lunched at Parliament House, had afternoon tea with Lady Paltridge, and supper with Bill McGovern, one of our Consuls. Ed went to the Law Society dinner. All Saturday we raced—in the afternoon at the "gallops," and at night at the "trots." I won two quinellas in the afternoon, which financed my day. Ed had a bad day. He was like the poker player who shouts, "Deal." Each session had a race named for the Ambassador, and the American Flag flew over both stands. Sunday we took two swings at church, morning and night. The morning was Navy Day; at Evensong, Ed read the lesson from Ephesians: "I am your Ambassador in chains." Monday, I had another "fern foray," or wildflower walk with Lady MacFarlane-Reed. Luncheon was with Australian-American Association, with H.E. addressing them. That night we entertained about 150 at a buffet supper in a club. Tuesday the men all flew off for a twenty-four–hour stay at Exmouth on the Northwest Cape, where there will soon be a big United States Navy installation. I was hostess at noon for twenty-four women at the Consul's residence, and in the afternoon we went to the Art Gallery to see an exhibit of Rodin and some Australian painting. They would like to see a major American exhibit here. This director suggested Jackson Pollock. He has never seen one of his paintings.

Hardly any Australians have really seen any American art. I mean the real, not the reproduction. I think it a great mistake on the part of our State Department to let all their cultural programs die before they reach this lovely, friendly corner of the world. Time and distance are the excuses, but it is not too far to find our warmest allies or to be the site of much American investment. All we seem to get is burnt-out entertainers like Mickey Rooney.

Western Australia reminds me much of West Texas in the attitude of its people. They are a bit on the defensive, old fashioned in manner and ideas, but changing fast. You should see our hotel, white iron grillwork on red brick, dark leather inside, maroon red carpet with pink roses, presided over by Elsie Plowman. She is the owner-manager— plump, blonde, neat, and an avid racing fan. She taught me how to hedge bets. Always bet twice as much to place as you bet to win. We also find the door locked at night and must ring the bell for the night porter to open up. Tea is served at 7:00 A.M. by a squeaky-voiced middle-aged Mary Poppins type maid. The teapot always has a crisp, freshly laundered white cozy over it. Breakfast is later.

When all our men returned from Exmouth, the buzz over the Presidential visit began. Looks like it's on. However, we continued our planned visit to Esperance, a new area being opened for farms. It is four hundred miles from Perth. Here, Benno Schmidt has his Orleans Farm in partnership with David Rockefeller. Original exploration here was French, hence the place names. Only a few years ago, it was discovered that trace elements of copper and zinc plus yearly superphosphate applications could make this heretofore barren land lushly productive. Rainfall is sufficient. We stayed at Orleans Farm with Tony and Phyllis Moore as our hosts. Tony is highly intelligent and highly articulate. He knows to the threepence what it costs to produce a pound

Presented by
Mrs W. O. Fairfax
This recipe of a Soufflé created by her chef
in honour of
Their Excellencies Mr & Mrs Edward Clark
U. S. Ambassador in Australia

Soufflé Edward Clark

5 egg yolks	3 oz. finest cocoa
6 egg whites	5 oz. castor sugar
¼ pint of milk	2 oz. Kirsch
2½ oz. plain flour	2 oz. Benedictine
2½ oz. unsalted butter	1 oz. French ground ginger
1½ oz. instant coffee	¼ oz. nutmeg

4 oz. mixed glacé fruits

Marinate chopped glacé fruits in Kirsch. Dissolve and mix in milk, 4 oz. of sugar, the cocoa, the nutmeg, ground ginger, instant coffee. In a saucepan melt the butter, add flour and cook till it does not stick to the bottom of pan. Add milk mixture and cook till the resulting paste is again free from the saucepan. Away from the stove add the egg yolks one by one. Beat the egg whites until stiff and add the remaining ounce of sugar to them. Then fold the whites into the chocolate mixture. Pour into a soufflé dish. Allow the fruits, drained of the liquor in which they have been marinated, to sink into the mixture and bake in oven for 25 minutes at 400°. Have a little Benedictine and Kirsch mixture ready, warmed, and when the soufflé comes out of oven, light it and pour on top. Serve promptly together with a sauce boat of chantilly cream flavoured with Benedictine.

Presented at a midnight dinner after the performance of *Il Trovatore*, Canberra, October 12, 1966.

of wool or a fourth-cross Santa Gertrudis heifer. Tidbits for the Book of U.I. (Useless Information): The rare black sheep that appear at a rate of about twenty a year among their three-thousand-head flock are kept to graze the paddocks and act as a barometer of the trace elements. When their fleece loses color, it's time to add more zinc and copper. Stud bulls are priced in guineas, as are all the luxury goods, professional fees, jewelry, paintings, and medical fees. "Old Jack," their valuable pride and joy, is as gentle as a house pet.

A fine barbecue was given for us at the woolshed, with a caterer brought out from Perth and the ladies in long skirts and high heels. Art Linkletter and his party were guests, too. Next day we visited his shearing shed; my first time to see the shearers. They are contractors who bring their own team, even their cook. The owner must supply them with proper quarters, strictly prescribed by the Union. After shearing, the woolshed is tidied up and becomes a meeting hall, movie theater, or ballroom. Linkletter's New Years' Ball is a highlight of each year. Art Linkletter spends about a week every year here, but is amazingly well informed about the operation. Rhonda Fleming and Robert Cummings also own properties here, freehold, which they aren't developing. The state would like for them to pass to a new ownership, who would be ready and willing to put the land into operation. The homestead at Orleans Farm is new, neat, and unpretentious—formica-topped tables—but glowing with Benno's fine collection of Australian original paintings by Dobell, Streeton, Sidney Nolan, Friend, literally dozens of them. I puzzled over why he has invested so much in paintings that he sees only briefly twice a year.

Our second night in Esperance, we were entertained by Blake Senior, general manager for Esperance Land and Development Company, another American company. All the managers are young people, good looking, honorable, and brave. Some children travel one hundred miles a day to school. I still say it is a hard life for women and horses.

A 9:45 take-off Saturday morning with refueling stops in Forrest and Adelaide should put us in Canberra at 7:30 P.M. On Sunday morning an advance guard of sixty Presidential "preparers" arrive, and we have a full calendar of dinners, luncheons, and receptions already set up, plus official houseguests, the Administrator and Mrs. Roger Dean of Darwin.

I may have to run away to Straddlefork. This life really belongs to the professionals.

Fondly, but frantically,

Anne

October 18, 1966

My Darlings, Leila and Doug:

Your joy is unbounded, I know, now that a son is born to you. Your father and I share your happiness, but mostly our thoughts are with *our own baby,* and our relief is great that one more hazard in your life has been passed over safely. How many times through these last weeks the words of the Prayer Book have echoed through my head, "Defend, O Lord, this Thy child." All the hustle and bustle, the hullabaloo over the Presidential visit seems so trivial compared to the miracle of new life. Carolyn Kellam Curtis had a little girl, and Jesse's mother died at an advanced age. Thus is the drama of old life passing the new life coming in.

I have gone about my way and usual activities because all the plans for the visit are being handled by the Australian government or the teams of staffers out from Washington. There are too many of them here. The Australians are very good operators and will handle everything beautifully. They know protocol better than any of the Americans. They can and will follow it to the letter. The diplomats are quite upset because there are no plans to include them in any functions, and

I am fighting for our Embassy personnel to have an opportunity at HIM. Anyway, I will tell you all about it later.

I love you, Anne Wynn, Margaret, Martha, and wee William,

Mother

October 28, 1966

Salutations:

"When Earth's last picture is painted, and the tubes are twisted and dried,"* one of my most unforgettable experiences will have been the opportunity of traveling with a visiting head of state—my own President—being enthusiastically received by hordes of smiling, cheering people. In fact, the reception was so uniformly good that it ceased to be newsy after three days, so the papers picked up a small incident that might have happened anywhere at home. "Man bites dog" is always news.

Apparently, I was too far behind in the processions to make American TV screens, though everybody here said I was very visible and had my hair combed every time. I did have the rather terrifying experience of being caught in a crowd and nearly crushed. A perfectly good-humored crowd, but I was nevertheless hysterical when a friendly pharmacist opened his door and pulled me inside his closed shop. I came in on two feet, but a couple of other women were carried

---

* When Earth's last picture is painted,
 and the tubes are twisted and dried,
When the oldest colours have faded,
 and the youngest critic has died,
We shall rest, and, faith, we shall need it—
 lie down for an aeon or two,
Till the Master of All Good Workmen
 shall put us to work anew.

Rudyard Kipling, "When Earth's Last Picture Is Painted," Stanza 1.

The President of the United States of America and Mrs. Johnson will be present

The Government of Australia

requests the pleasure of the company of

His Excellency Mr. Edward Clark and Mrs. Clark

at a Parliamentary Luncheon

at Parliament House, Canberra, on Friday, 21st October, 1966

at 12 noon for 12.15 p.m.

R.S.V.P
Hospitality Section
Prime Ministers Department
Canberra. Phone 71411 Ext. 268   *Dress: Lounge Suit*

---

in. This happened in front of Lennon's Hotel in Brisbane. That is the place where Americans are always most happily received, so I was not surprised at the near-mob scene.

One of the jolliest sights was a knot of people clustered beneath a big sign, "The Beagle Club." They were accompanied by about forty beagles, which they held in raised arms for the President to view, being aware of his love for that breed. In the end, the President never visited our Residence, though Mrs. Johnson allowed me to infringe on her rest period to visit there and plant a tree on the grounds. We followed the English custom and had all the staff lined up in the foyer to greet her: Huang, Ming, Chan, LeeLee, Hsu, and Foo. Huang's children, Ching Mai and Ching San, were unfortunately in school. You see, I have a small Chinatown on the premises.

The President left us a shower of gifts: a lady's silver cigarette box and a gentlemen's size, too, both suitably inscribed. Ed received a Tiffany watch and there was a tiny Acutron clock for me. The Holts received silver julep cups (very American).

Just before the departure, we had a thrilling church service at the Cathedral in Townsville. After being met on the steps by Bishop and Dean, we processed behind the clergy with cross and crosier, clad in their richest green vestments, all singing "The Church's One Foundation." It lasted only twenty minutes. The theme was all Peace—collects, lessons, and brief sermon. As usual, I sobbed when I saw the big United States Air Force One lift off. I always do whenever I see a plane go home. Everyone kept saying how tired we must have been, but not so, because the whole responsibility of the tour was carried by the Australian government. All I had to do was *be there*—I didn't even have to wave!

I caught on quickly that I should be ready one hour ahead of schedule, because each morning the President had someone phone from Canberra Rex Hotel: "Tell Ed to get down here right away." This is a highly characteristic action of the President's.

Our only responsibility was the barbecue, run by Colonel Divers, the Army Attaché, and Mr. T. A. Fields, the owner of "Lanyon." It was carried off with military precision. There were seven hundred people and no Walter Jetton, our Fort Worth catering genius. All home cooking, "we furnished," as my San Augustine washwoman always put it.

Arrived home Sunday night and were met by our stay-home staff, who came to the Residence for a rehash and supper. Tuesday I had luncheon for twenty-four girls from the office, and Wednesday I went to Sydney to make a speech, yet! On the program for the United Nations, I was third speaker and nearly panicked when the first two made almost all my speech. Luckily, I had some lines up my sleeve about Senator Tom Connally's part in founding the United Nations. Bless him!

This week I have been to two black-tie dinners, two cocktail parties, and the opening of a railroad station, had several people to tea, and gave a lunch for twelve at the Residence the day I was in Sydney. A Dr. and Mrs. Alford of Buffalo, New York, called. She was a Miss Kittinger of the well-known furniture family. They wanted to see the Wil-

In honor of
The Prime Minister of Australia and Mrs. Holt
and
The President of the United States of America
and Mrs. Johnson

The American Ambassador and Mrs. Clark
request the pleasure of the company of

at a Barbecue
to be given at Lanyon Station, Tharwa,
on Saturday, October 22, 1966, at 3 45 p.m.

LOUNGE SUIT
Please present this card on entering

R.S.V.P.
October 20
7-1351, ext. 225

liamsburg Craft House furniture, made by her father and brother.
We have more than she does.

We have arranged a lunch for thirty and a dinner for twenty-four
as a starter when we return next Wednesday. We are meeting Mary
Scott and Jim Nash of Austin in Melbourne for the Cup.

Monday, October 31

We are now halfway through Cup Week. Mary Scott says she likes
"Sirs and Ladies." We've been to the Derby, to Mrs. Stevenson's lovely
cocktail party, to the opera with Lady Bolte, to High Mass with the
Nashes, which included being met on the step by the Dean of the
Cathedral and seated in arm chairs with velvet cushions, to Sir Rupert
Clarke's "lunch party" (the Australian term) at "Bolinda Vale,"
Clarkefield, his country seat. He is the only hereditary baronet in
Australia. In the corner of their drawing room is a small blue velvet
chair with "ER-II" on it. That was his chair at the coronation, and

(so I heard) all the peers could bring their chairs home for a keepsake.
Sir Rupert is the Australian partner for King Ranch. He is also chairman of the board for Schweppes Table Water.

Lunch was served under a big tent, but with tables. I sat between Sir
Rohan Delacombe, the Governor, and Sir Henry Bolte, the Premier.
Last night Dame Mabel's big dinner took place. Also in a tent, all
swathed in gold satin, with so many waitresses and waiters that we were
reminded of penguins in flock. Mary Fairfax and Lady Lloyd-Jones are
each here with their chauffeured Rolls Royces, alone. So I just divide
my crowd and let some ride with each of them and the rest of us go
along, like peasants, in the Embassy Chrysler Imperial. I recount all
these things just to show how well they treat any representative of the
United States.

Cup Day itself is one of those spectacles that should be seen at least
once in a lifetime, like Carnival in New Orleans or Inauguration Day.
Eighty thousand people turn out. It is a full-scale holiday in shops and
offices. I enjoyed it more this year than last because I, at least, knew
where I was, how to make those great big old fifty-cent bets, when it
was tea time, *et cetera*. Also, I knew lots of faces. It was a little difficult, though, because they came from all over Australia and I was often
unsure of where we'd met—Perth, Sydney, Brisbane, or Adelaide.
Some of the costumes are a bit bizarre, like the Fifth Avenue Easter
parade. Diplomats sit in the stands reserved for Committee members,
lunch in their dining room, drink in their bar.

I went up to the members' stands to visit my friend, Marjorie
Shelton, twenty years a resident of Washington, returning to visit her
mother and to present her young daughter to Melbourne relatives and
friends after a ten-year absence. She says the hats are less spectacular
than prewar. She observed the rite of picnic lunch under the trees,
champagne and chicken from the "boot" (trunk) of a Rolls. You will
all laugh when I tell you it was thought terribly democratic for the
American Ambassador's wife to join their group and sit on the steps,
even beside beautiful Lady Curtis, wife of a former Lord Mayor. His

Excellency finally had a winner on the Cup after two days of steady losses. After that, he was really telling funny jokes. Big Jim said if they'd only paid for fourth places, he'd have been rich. We finally did the two Nashes in. Both had to take to their beds and poop out on the Livingston Ball, where they dance the Highland fling and the champagne flows like a river.

Ballieus, Osbornes, and Fairbairns live up to the line about "the privileged class enjoying its privileges."† The saying is that Ballieus and rabbits multiply in Australia. Two governors, the Prime Minister, too many dames, knights, and ladies to mention, Commander Brash, and Colonel Tim Rodriguez (pronounced Rod-re-gay), who is supposed to be the most rigidly correct of the Government House aides, were all dancing the twist.

Off this morning early (at 8:30 A.M.) when the Embassy aircraft "closed the doors" (their term for take-off time). We are about to land in Canberra where I will have thirty for lunch, receive visiting United States Air Force officers, and attend a black-tie dinner tonight with Air Marshal Sir Alister Murdock. Tomorrow I drive to Yass to open a church fete, and that night we entertain with a dinner for Mary and Jim. They will find Canberra quiet after rich, gay Melbourne.

Happy Thanksgiving to all. Did you know that we have a dear little grandson, William Thomas Wynn of Greenville, Mississippi, weight eight pounds, birthday October 16?

The proud grandmother,
Anne Clark

† Philip Barry, *The Philadelphia Story.*

January 3, 1967

Dear Friends and friends of friends,

Since last I wrote, Ed has returned from his trip to "The Ice," excited and pleased with his adventure. I occupied the eight days of his absence completely with a seamstress and Christmas preparations, plus a number of engagements, staff parties, Sunday lunch at the Philippine Embassy, and ladies' lunch with Anita Hazlett, who put me to shame by revealing that she adds the raising of chickens ("chooks" Aussies call them) to her other activities, which include a very busy social life, lots of New Zealand visitors, tennis, golf, and bridge. Had dinner at Canberra House, where I dined with two interesting Britishers, Lord Jellicoe, grandson of the World War I Admiral, and Mr. Bonham-Carter, grandson of Lord Asquith and son of Lady Violet Bonham-Carter. By all rights, Bonham-Carter's brains and heritage entitle him to a place in the British Cabinet, but his loyalty to the Liberal Party prevents his even having a seat in the Parliament. There hasn't been a Liberal government in Britain since Lloyd George wrecked the party in the twenties. These two charming gentlemen were in Australia looking over the possibilities for investment in pipelines. They delivered to me a gift of Steuben glass from George Patterson of the Buckeye Pipeline. Mr. Patterson is a friend of Frank Ikard, who visited us last year; he is also a friend and admirer of Ted Schroeder; we got them together to talk tennis here.

After the Ambassador's return, we plunged into the usual official duties. We had luncheons for Congressman Charles H. Wilson of California and Roger Blough of United States Steel. We gave a farewell reception for John Erskine, who is returning to the United States. I had a Christmas luncheon for the Embassy officers' wives and asked each to bring an Australian friend. Sheila Vincent read a Christmas story and Virginia Zwald played and sang carols. The weekend of December 17 and 18 was taken up by our diplomatic tennis tourney, ending with a Sunday-evening barbecue for the ninety players and their spouses. We dined at the Japanese Embassy and had a lovely, formal, six-course dinner with nothing Japanese save the silver salt and peppers on the table and two ladies, Mrs. Chiba and the Counselor's wife, decked out in kimonos. Mrs. Chiba says she doesn't wear hers often because just putting it on, with obi, takes an hour, and, for cleaning, they must be sent to Japan where they are ripped apart and then repainted after the cleaning process. We went to the Argentinian barbecue, which was picturesque, and to a black-tie dinner with the Indonesians where each napkin was folded (like Japanese paper folds) in a different pattern, bird or boat or flower. Christmas week we had cocktails or eggnog for the press and the whole Embassy staff, including gardeners, drivers, *et cetera*, and an afternoon for the children with magician and Santa Claus. I used Mary Koock's Coffee Ice Cream Punch,* and we gave out promptly—150 men, women, and teenagers drank 500 cups in half an hour. They thought it a real novelty. We went to the children's Christmas service at St. John's at 7:00 P.M. on Christmas Eve. The church was decked in pink and blue summer flowers with Easter Lilies among them, no wreaths, no evergreens. After the prayers, sermon, and hymns we processed out to the lawn where a live tableau of shepherds was arranged. Then back through the graveyard to a crypt beneath the church where there was a live crèche with real lambs. Only about a dozen people could enter at once, and the illusion of the stable in the hillside was complete.

Sunday we lunched at Canberra House with Sir Charles and Natasha, his White Russian wife, who reiterates that December 25 is not *her* Christmas. She's Russian Orthodox, and her mother is a nun who took her vows at the age of forty-seven. Lady Johnston's mother is abbess of a convent in Jerusalem. They always have those paper crackers on the table, and were apologetic for the cold plum pudding.

Early Monday we flew to Melbourne and were guests at Government House for three days. Government House in Melbourne is sup-.

---

* Recipe for Mary Koock's Coffee Ice Cream Punch:

1 qt. bourbon whiskey	1 qt. strong coffee
1 qt. whole milk	½ gal. vanilla ice cream
1 pt. light cream	1 qt. light rum

Start with everything cold, including the punch bowl. Add ice cream in chunk form. [Recipe used by permission of Mary Koock.]

posedly a copy of Osborne House, Queen Victoria's small palace on the Isle of Wight. It has 160 rooms with a ballroom for 1500. My room had a name on the door, "The Magnolia Room." Covers and curtains are deep cream and the window looks out on a magnificent magnolia tree. The grounds have ninety acres, two grass tennis courts, a swimming pool, and a croquet court. I am always impressed with how hard the Governor and his wife work to present the best image of their sovereign, whom they represent. Their thoughtful hospitality and courtesy are unfailing. They are at the door to receive you and up to see you depart, no matter what the hour. Maids unpack (almost too thoroughly), press gowns, polish shoes, lay out clothes, turn down beds, and overwhelm you with attention. The inevitable dog here is a black Labrador. Lady Delacombe does massive flower arrangements and needlepoint while H.E. plays tennis. Lady D. is prevented from participating in sports by a severe case of arthritis.

We were present at the Davis Cup finals, Australia versus India. Besides ourselves, the Johnstons and the Indian High Commissioner and his wife were guests. The matches are played in an uncovered bowl seating fourteen thousand. Champagne lunch was served under a beautiful marquee. I wonder if American TV ever caught us. We sat directly behind the Governor General and the Prime Minister. Tennis really brings out all the VIP's here. We spent one day at the races where they had representative international jockeys; the United States had no one—they wanted Willie Shoemaker, but he declined.

Thursday we paused in Canberra to pick up more passengers, went on to Sydney, and returned to our own beds that night. Friday we drove to Batemans Bay on the beach for an overnight with General Sir John Wilton and Lady Wilton (Helen). It was relaxed. We went barefoot, tied our hair up, washed our own dishes, and launched our own boat— No pomp! I saw the first evidence of any real religious activity ever in Australia. Something called C.S.S.M. (Children's Special Services Mission) was holding a "beach mission" where several hundred children attend, something comparable to our vacation Bible schools. The leaders were all volunteer college students, handsome, pretty, and earnest—very spontaneous—usual things from hymns to "Farmer in the Dell." Returned to Canberra in time for New Year's Eve party, but still made it to bed before midnight. The Aussie holidays are quite prolonged. Any holiday that falls on Sunday, or even Saturday, is made up by taking one more day on the end. Thus December 25 and 26 came on Sunday and Monday, which would not have been working days, so they took Tuesday to make up for Christmas that fell on Sunday. New Year's worked the same. January is the month of the long school holiday. Every person who can possibly do so (and most can) goes away to the beach; no pearls can be restrung, no film processed, no clothes altered, let alone carpets cleaned, because every kind of workshop is shut fast the whole month.

Our APO mail has been very slow and I have not yet received all the cards and packages that I know will come sooner or later. I still say Christmas is a state of mind and that weather isn't the key. I have a new silky terrier. I call him "Happy" for Happy New Year, the day he came to me.

Meantime, to all friends of the Clarks, we wish a wonderful year and blessings on you all. We hope to be in Texas when the dogwoods bloom, eating catfish and sipping a cold Texas beer.

Anne Clark

Canberra, Australia
May 19, 1967

Dear Ones, soon to be seen:

On the eve of my eighth crossing of the Pacific, and my birthday (I won't tell which one), I want to catch everyone up on what's been happening. I seem to have written last just after Christmas. Ed went home for two weeks in January, and I didn't go. When he returned, he brought Anne Wynn, my eleven-year-old granddaughter. She stayed until we all three returned to the United States in March. While Anne was here, the Residence rang with merry shouts. The American children and all my Australian friends' little moppets had free run of the house. Huang's little Ching Mai became a best friend. Once I took them all to church and they looked like a picture out of the Sunday School book. Anne made her first curtsy when she was presented to Princess Alexandra outside the church. Travel may be educational, but, for her, it was just an opportunity to make lots of new friends. We took her with us to Newcastle, where I had been invited to "commission" a ship—not a christening because it was already afloat, so I just unveiled a plaque and named the vessel *Investigator*. It's really a large off-shore drilling rig. I was recommended for this delightful duty by David Searls, of Houston. There were a number of Americans and Texans in Australia just for the occasion.

We had some very pleasant visitors. Ambassador and Mrs. William McCormick Blair of Manila. He belongs to the International Harvester McCormicks in Chicago, and she is an international beauty and fashion plate. Tall, brunette, slim, elegant, no jewelry, Paris clothes, needle pointer, collects paintings, not over thirty years old. Deda Blair is a winsome, thoughtful person and I was captivated by her. En route home, we stopped in Manila and Baguio for the conference of American Ambassadors to Asian countries. Among those there were such newsworthy people as General Westmoreland, Admiral U. S. G. Sharp, Ambassador Cabot Lodge from Vietnam, and Ambassador Goldberg. The Philippines seem tragic to me. Manila, which should be the jewel of the Pacific, is full of decay. Mexico looks much more prosperous and tidy.

Among the interesting visitors we've had lately have been Hedley Donovan, editor of *Time*, General Freeman, John J. McCloy, and Roy Emerson, the tennis player.

We spent three lovely, restful days on Lex Anderson's boat on the river—gathered oysters and mussels off the rocks. We've had several

tours through the Residence for charity. However, since I am now re-
peating many of the events of last year, things don't seem so exotic or
exciting.

We spent six weeks in the United States. This was the home leave to
which we are entitled every two years, the one on which the government pays my way. The first ten days we spent in Washington where
the exciting Mertz Collection of Australian Art was opened with fanfare for a three-week stay at the Corcoran Gallery. We had a large
group of friends from Texas, Mississippi, and New York with us. Mr.
Mertz gave a lovely supper party at the Carlton for the whole group,
several hundred people. The President and Mrs. Johnson received all
our friends at The White House. The person who enjoyed that party
most was my granddaughter, Margaret. Since she is a godchild to the
President, he paid her special attention with presents and photographs.
I spent a week with my family in Mississippi; my mother is ninety and
I had never seen my six-month-old grandson. Then we spent three
busy, happy weeks in Texas; the bluebonnets and dogwood were in
bloom. Lastly we were in New York for a week. I saw three Broadway
shows, including my favorite, Mary Martin in *I Do, I Do*, and dined at
"21," the River Club, George Moore's apartment, and Harold Gray's
Park Avenue apartment. The River Club has the best food in New
York; don't miss it if you ever have a chance to go. Our coldest weather
was experienced that last week in April in New York. I had a tour of
the Met with Mrs. Lewis Douglas.

We made the long flight straight through from New York to Sydney
with brief stops in Los Angeles, Honolulu, and Pago Pago. No matter
what the hour, the airport at Pago Pago is always full of Samoans, barefoot and enormously fat. They come to see the planes go just as the
people used to go to the depot in San Augustine to see the train. We
arrived in Australia on May first.

This is the time when we are celebrating the anniversary of the
Battle of the Coral Sea. Twenty-five years ago this crucial engagement
saved Australia from invasion, and the Australians join hands with

their American friends to celebrate the event annually. Admiral and Mrs. David McDonald, Chief of Naval Operations, spent two weeks in Australia as guests of honor. We attended balls and luncheons in Sydney, Melbourne, and Canberra. They were our houseguests two days and couldn't have been nicer. We were immensely proud of the people who turned out to celebrate with us. The lord mayors, the governors, the premiers, the very nicest people everywhere. Which, of course, includes our wonderful Australian-American leaders. Dame Pattie and Sir Robert were with us in Melbourne, as impressive as ever; she as dainty and fragile as old lace and he as massive and eloquent as his friend, Churchill, except that Sir Robert is the handsomer of the two.

Saturday we returned to Canberra and received one of those happy jolts that those of us in the Johnson official family have learned to expect at unexpected intervals. Mr. President, himself, booming out on the telephone, across the miles, plain as day—"Ed, come home—bring Anne—let's talk."

So, tomorrow we are off and expect to be home for three weeks—some of the time as guests in The White House. Mr. Harold Holt, the Prime Minister will be in Washington June 1, and the Ambassador will be chief shepherd of his visit. Before I see you all, I hope you have this message from

Your correspondent down under,
Anne Clark

November 26, 1967

Beloved Friends and Compatriots:

It's been a long time since I wrote a round robin back to you and this may be my last. I guess everybody who really cares knows that I had a two-month holiday in Texas and Mississippi with my friends and kinfolks. I hadn't really been with any of them in all the two years since Ed took up this post, in spite of several visits home, and I was beginning to crack under the strain of unfulfilled longing for home. I returned with Ed October 30, after having had the pleasure of seeing him honored as a "Distinguished Texas-Ex," and knowing that the President had agreed to his release in January.

We made an all-daylight flight this time, leaving Austin at 8:00 A.M. on Monday and arriving in Canberra at midnight on Tuesday night—but only twenty-four hours had elapsed. This is the crossing on which you lose a day. However, I was much more able to readjust my sleeping hours, and by Saturday morning I was able to charge off to Melbourne to the Cup with a fair amount of enthusiasm. Remember this is the Kentucky Derby of Australia, but even more of a social event, men in gray toppers, ladies in ostrich feather hats. Jinx Faulkenberg was our guest part of the time. She was in Australia on a United States Department of Commerce American fashion promotion. She was certainly a happy choice for the "compere" (that's the Australian word for commentator). We all dined together at Sir Robert and Dame Pattie Menzies' home in Melbourne. Jinx came because her friend Mary Martin wanted her to deliver to Sir Robert her fond greetings. Sir Robert is said to love Mary Martin third best to Dame Pattie and his daughter, Heather. Dame Pattie has managed to make her modest Melbourne home look just like the Prime Minister's Lodge. Of course things like the painting by Sir Winston Churchill help. Dame Pattie cooked and served the dinner herself. I wonder if Mrs. Eisenhower is doing the same. I know that when I return to the United States, I am going to miss all my gentle Chinese staff: Huang at the door with H.E.'s hat and rosebud each morning; little Foo trotting out with endless cups of coffee for our callers; LeeLee pressing and mending and turning down beds; Hsu's meringues with spun sugar icing—but somehow, I think I can muddle through with an occasional assist from Daisy Yett and Bertha Maxey, and Sarah Lee and the Night Hawk. Last Sunday one of the

Embassy wives sat by me in church and thoughtfully turned the pages of my Prayer Book. However, I often quote Satchel Paige, who said, "The social ramble ain't restful," and it has just about taken the entire crew to keep me functioning. Of course I'll never have another Marjorie. A personal secretary is better than a personal plumber. She could make the plumber come!

I won $360 on the sweeps on the Melbourne Cup. At the annual lunch at Sir Rupert Clarke's country seat, "Bolinda Vale," we all put in a couple of dollars—and I drew the favorite, Red Handed. It's better to be lucky than smart, I say. Sure enough he romped home for me. You horse players watch Tobin Bronze, a great Australian horse who has been bought by Americans, and came in third in the International Stakes at Laurel in his first United States try. He'll be racing at Santa Anita soon. Will miss the available and perfectly legal bookies, because we often went down to the T.A.B. and had a little "flutter" on Saturdays.

The Ambassador and a large part of his staff (all male) spent a week in Western Australia visiting the mines and stations. The wives here looked after me admirably, having me to dinner and lunch and driving me to church and parties. One affair was a big charity lunch in the country on the Bedford Osborne property. Bedford Osborne's mother was an American actress, Maude Jeffreys from Memphis, and he has relatives living in Bolivar County, Mississippi. Their garden is beautiful with those typically English borders of foxglove, delphinium, roses, and geraniums all growing together. Members of the Y.W.C.A. prepared the food, a "salad" lunch, which means anything cold, including sliced chicken and ham, preceded by an alcoholic punch and wine with the lunch. A fresh setting of the buffet table followed with the "puddings," that is, desserts, as they are always called. The benefit lunch at a country property or an Embassy, which is sometimes called "bird and bottle" when it consists of chicken and wine, or the outdoor fete similar to our bazaars, or a tour of Embassies seem the standard way of raising funds here in Australia. They appear to me badly in need of a new idea.

Ben Carpenter of Dallas, Leon Locke of Hungerford, and Harry Gayden of Houston, traveling about studying Brahma cattle, were our houseguests last week. However, Mr. Carpenter spent the entire visit in the Canberra hospital. A vicious attack of renal colic laid him out. Three weeks of bumping around Queensland and the Northern Territory in a Land Rover will jolt a man's insides apart. Our dinner party had to go on without him, and we even had to leave him to go to Melbourne where Ed received a citation as a Tennessee Colonel from Governor Buford Ellington, delivered by Mr. Lindsay Clarke, the Australian managing director of Alcoa. The dinner was at the Melbourne Club—founded in 1830 and hardly changed since. The Boston Club or the New York Union Club have nothing on the M.C. for staidness. The last of six courses for dinner was preserved ginger—specialty of the house. The quaint old building is carpeted all over with a red Wilton carpet with medallions, giving it a very Victorian air. While in Melbourne, I made a speech—twenty minutes of drivel, and they can barely understand me even on that level. The U.S.I.S. doesn't allow me to say anything beyond eighth-grade level. We also went to Sir Rupert Clarke's cocktail bash, which he gives yearly in his capacity as Honorary Consul for Monaco on their National Day. Her Serene Highness, Princess Grace, was not there. A number of countries have honorary consuls in Melbourne, which gives the consul certain "perks"—like a diplomatic license plate and tax-free whisky (or at least enough for that special party).

Saturday we went to Cooma to a country race meeting. The nice grazier, who is president of the Racing Club and our host, was running his favorite filly—who came in for us so H.E. could bestow the trophy and the bourbon and make a quick exit in order to get on to Melbourne for the St. Andrew's Day Scots' Dinner. It is stag, but formal, with at least half the diners in kilts.

Before Ed arrived home at 3:00 A.M., the phone had rung three times—"The United States of America, The White House." These calls always unnerve me. This time it was only Walt Rostow inquiring about the Australian Senate elections, and the time in Washington was ordinary business hours.

Tonight, we are awaiting the arrival of George Champion—chairman of the Chase Manhattan and his entourage—four of whom will be houseguests. He's asked for a golf game tomorrow but the weather has turned beastly cold and is blowing a gale. The season should correspond to early June, but it is still changeable. Sometimes it is hot with lots of flies, sometimes very cold. The flies here have to be seen to be believed.

From now on we have a full program—farewell parties, farewell calls, farewell presents—Canberra to Sydney to Melbourne. Up and down like a Yo-yo. Plus the fact that we are stealing three days to visit the Barrier Reef—eighteen hundred miles to the north. It is one of Australia's great natural wonders and the only spot still untouched by Clarks, so off we go. I hope the professional packers are as good as they are said to be because I see no chance to wrap so much as an ash tray.

It's been a great experience, and I shall certainly never be the same, though I do hope that when I cease to make dining out part of my employment, I may trim off the pounds I've added the last two years. They say every family has a book in it—*Life with Father, Papa Was a Preacher, I Remember Mama*—I think I shall call mine *Excellency from East Texas*. I hope the Aussies miss us a little, for we shall certainly leave a bit of our hearts down under.

As ever,
Anne Clark

NOTE: Following round-robin letter from Mrs. Anne Clark.—Mrs. O'D.

December 19, 1967

Friday, November 17, Ed and his party returned from the West. What's happened in this past month must have been witnessed to be believed. The last three days have been our saddest. Prime Minister Holt has been our intimate and dearly loved friend. By reasons of protocol this gay and friendly man was my dinner partner more than fifty times. I often wished he could some time have had a young and beautiful lady sit next to him, but he always made it seem fun and the conversation was stimulating. The last time was December 7 when we had luncheon for the Scurlocks and McGahas. The afternoon before, the Holts, with their houseguests, Mr. and Mrs. Freddie Roe (Dame Mabel's daughter, Elaine), dropped in for cocktails. The San Francisco Chamber of Commerce nearly died of surprise; then the Holt party all agreed to come for lunch the next day. Dear Zara asked us to tea, even took Ruth and Elizabeth to see her bedrooms; all this I tell to show how deeply personal is our loss. We received the tragic news in Brisbane when the plane stopped to refuel at 3:30 Sunday afternoon. We were en route to Canberra, after three days at Brampton Island on the Barrier Reef. We stole those three days for the trip from our busy schedule because the Reef is one of the wonders of the world.

As I suspected, when you've seen one reef, you've seen 'em all. I now have a high regard for the San Marcos Aquarena. Unless you are a scientist who cares deeply about the difference between a golden cowrie and a tiger cowrie, or a snorkeler and a spearfisher, don't bother. It was sixteen-hundred miles by plane to Mackay, fifteen minutes by small plane to Brampton Island, four hours by boat (50 miles) out to the Reef. We spent about fifteen minutes looking through the glass windows of the small boat, shifted ten persons in mid-Pacific from a dory to a dinghy, in order to spend three-quarters of an hour on the reef poking with a stick for shells. Then we all returned by dinghy to the big yacht. That's a lot of traveling for a piece of coral and a box of sea shells. That's one gorilla I've seen.

Tomorrow at 4:00 A.M., the President of the United States arrives, but he will stay in a hotel. The entourage is just too numerous for our Residence. I am glad I still remember the days when we all slept on the same sleeping porches up at the Lower Colorado River Authority cottage on Buchanan Lake, and so am not as flustered as I might be.

I made a speech at the A.A.A. Women's group on Tuesday. Wednesday night back to Canberra. We attended the annual A.A.A. Thanksgiving Dinner, and Thursday at 5:00 P.M. we had a service on the terrace at the Residence with three clergymen and "Come Ye Thankful People"—weather bad for outdoors as usual—both wind and flies.

Loved dinner with the Ceylonese. She's a blonde Scottish woman, the best and pleasantest bridge player in Canberra and he, who bears the name of Clarence Oswald Coorey, is chocolate colored with white hair and a Cambridge degree. Flew to the Cooma Races on Saturday. Returned by car, and H.E. proceeded to Melbourne to St. Andrew's Day Scots' Dinner where even dignified gentlemen got boiling drunk on the Scotch-covered haggis, and by the time Ed arrived in Canberra at 3:00 A.M., the phone had rung three times from 1600 Pennsylvania. It was only Walt Rostow inquiring about the election results in Australia. I wish they'd consider time change—9:00 A.M. there is midnight here.

Mr. and Mrs. George Champion and Jake Jacobson of the Chase Manhattan were houseguests for three days: dinners, lunches, laundry, hairdressers, *et cetera.* Tuesday to Sydney for Sir Howard's dinner and Rob Norman's reception. The New South Wales Bank owns a fine old estate (formerly home of our friend Tom Field's parents) where they conduct a continuous school for their young bankers. The house was so grand that it had a dance floor mounted on springs to give a bit of bounce to the dancers. I guess the waltz needs that more than the frug. One more dinner at Sydney University and I made a speech at the

Women's A.A.A. at "Craigend." I made another in Sydney the following week to the American Woman's club. They have an appetite for
boring trivia. We dined that night in Canberra with Mr. Dudley Bra-
han (Cal-Tex) and were presented with a painting of an Australian
landscape—paintings, I have! Dinner at the Chinese Embassy was an
experience: twelve courses, every other one a soup—with continuous
"skoaling" in hot, strong liquor, glasses constantly refilled from a tea
pot, table beautifully appointed, lazy Susan. The Argentine Ambassador broke any existing ice by converting the lazy Susan into a roulette
race track using the silver horse place-card holders as counters. Count
on the Latinos to be gay.

I had to pass up the Cootamundra Races, a three-hour drive. H.E.
was so outdone with all the Embassy officers holidaying (taking their
"in-country leave" before year's end) that he just took Huang and Foo.
They loved it. Took Professor Learned of Harvard to St. John's Church
with us on Sunday and lunched with the Stewart Jamiesons, a former
Australian Ambassador to twenty-six countries, now retired, president
of local A.A.A., so nearly blind he holds papers on his nose. Out of
storage for twenty-five years have come their heirlooms from two old
families, portraits and Royal Worcester—even an early Sidney Nolan
(he is currently Australia's most popular and expensive painter)
bought in London for $200, now worth 5,000 guineas. Wednesday we
had our lunch (Chinese) for new Consul General in Melbourne, Dick
Service, born in China of Y.M.C.A. parents. By their suggestion, we
had a famous Chinese dessert "Peking Dust," consisting of meringue,
fruit, pureed chestnuts, spun sugar. Dick speaks Mandarin, an ac-
complishment that enchanted Hsu, Huang, Foo, and Chan. At 3:10
the Scurlocks and the McGahas arrived. We bounced them around for
ten days, dinners and lunches at the embassies of Singapore, Vietnam,
Korea, Philippines, and Italy, also trips to Sydney and Melbourne.

Sunday we went to Lex Anderson's annual party at his lovely home
on the harbor. This time it was a farewell to us, on a heavenly day
with guests arriving by sea and land, food and drink galore. The

kicker was a presentation book filled with on-the-spot Polaroid colored
snaps signed by all guests, then speeches and the orchestra switching
from "The Yellow Rose" to "The Saints Go Marching In." Then
came a huge banner with four flags—United States, Australia, Texas,
and the Ambassador's personal ensign, designed by Lex. On the banner
was "Big Ed for Governor, He's a bonzer bloke." We quickly boarded
a big white launch, rode off into the sunset with scores of hands waving
and voices singing "Jolly Good Fellow"—and me weeping copiously
—our destination "Admiralty House"—Sydney residence of Their Excellencies, Lord and Lady Casey. Her Excellency had arranged for me
to call, since I had not seen the place. She showed us all over, including
upstairs, that I might see the Opera House from the balcony where she
painted *my* picture. You know, she did it for me with the United States
dime-store materials I brought her. A quick call on Betsy and Walter,
and dinner with the Norton Belknaps. Mary and Norton have lived in
Japan. While there, they collected beautiful Japanese antiques and
table appointments. Norton himself made the apricot soufflé. I'm trying to get him nominated for the Wine and Food Society. Our farewell
visit to Melbourne was as usual *formal*. Calls on the Lord Mayor and
Lady Mayoress, on the Premier and Lady Bolte, champagne at 10:00
A.M., lunch at the Lyceum Club (I was hostess), a call on Mrs. Lindsey,
who has built for her father, Sir Robert Knox, a miniature replica of
the American Embassy—red brick, white columns, black-and-white
foyer, denticulated cornices, mantel pieces, and all. She once paid a
thirty-minute visit here. Thank God for Geoffrey Smith—Sir Henry
Bolte's protocol man. He won't let you make a mistake. Any public
figure who has an aide so devoted and capable is blessed. Dined at Sir
Rupert's with the Prime Minister also a guest, Sir Henry Bolte, and Sir
James Forest. Ed said the gentlemen's after-dinner séance was the most
stimulating he'd ever enjoyed.

Next night we dined at Government House—ladies in tiaras—
marvelous meal that started with melon and black caviar and went to
chocolate profiteroles, and that fruit course where they eat and peel

bananas with knife and fork, but, as I say, the English furnish me with lots of genteel amusement. His Excellency, Sir Rohan Delacombe announced, "There's a lady under the table," and a large, black Labrador named Zara quietly nuzzled all our knees in turn—I thought of Posh and his story, "Hands on the table, Senator."

Said goodbye to Scurlocks and McGahas at 8:00 A.M., plane dropped me in Canberra, Ed went on to Sydney. I stayed with the packers; they gave me Wednesday, Thursday, and Friday, and halted till after Christmas. Dined with Sir James Plimsoll, Secretary for External Affairs, bachelor art collector—line up, you old girls, he'd be a great catch—off to the Reef early Friday with picnic hamper and party of ten, including Sir John and Lady Wilton, Chief of Staff. Helen W. is my greatest friend—and so I am back to the beginning of this letter, which I will finish after Mr. President departs.

Christmas Day

Decided not to extend this one. It has been the "week that was," but I am still alive, and Ed and I still speak. Considering the strains on us all, that's a triumph in itself.

Fondly,
Anne

December 26, 1967—Boxing Day

Report for the Week of December 19 to December 26:

This is a big day in Australia, really bigger than Christmas. A day for sports. In Brisbane they begin the Davis Cup matches, in Melbourne the International Cup Race Meeting, and here in Sydney the opening of the Sydney-Hobart Yacht Races. An American businessman is giving us the use of his yacht for the day and we will host a luncheon cruise for twenty-six to watch the take-off. The harbor will be full of all kinds of boats. Fifty big yachts in full sail compete in the race.

But to go back. Monday, December 18, thru Friday, December 22, were nightmare days. A nation in mourning, ourselves deeply grieved, and the President of the United States enroute, in residence, and departing. We cancelled all parties save the one for American children until after the funeral and got the Residence all shipped up only to find the party would stay at the Rex Hotel, after all. However, the President did us the honor of dining here and entertaining the Vietnamese President and his party. My Chinese staff did one of their grand Chinese meals. I was the only woman at the table. The dessert was Peking Dust, and though I "barracked" (Aussie word meaning to back or cheer for) for simple fruit, Huang said "President may never see Peking Dust again." Marjorie Turbayne (our social secretary) said this was hers and Huang's hour. At one point, we had fourteen security people eating in the kitchen and six in the library. I believe the President was able to do more useful work and consultation with allies than ever before; because the atmosphere was sober—no cheering mobs, no toasts and dancing—great conferences could be held. President Thieu is the brother of the former Ambassador of Vietnam here, the one whose wife died in childbirth. President Thieu told me that he is adopting the baby.

All this was on Thursday night. Meantime, that morning I received the Irish Ambassador's wife, and at eleven the Engelhards arrived. Some of you may remember them when Pat Rutherford gave that big wing-ding in 1959 or 1960. Charles Engelhard is the platinum and diamond mogul of South Africa who lives in New Jersey. Because they were great personal friends of the P.M. and Zara, who always visited them when in New York, they were invited to come on Air Force One. Jane E.'s brother-in-law, Rupert Gerrard, is an Australian, nephew of Sir Rupert Clarke. Jane wanted to see the Lodge after Zara had redecorated because she, Jane, had helped her shop for it and had made several presents to it. While they were lunching with me, we were telephoned to buy the President's gifts for Mrs. Johnson and the girls. My support was Frances Legge, the new Agricultural Attaché's wife. She's from Fort Worth, and has known the Engelhards long, too. As you know, an old Fort Worth hand wasn't intimidated by even the Engelhard diamonds—thirty carats in a ring, seventy in a brooch.

Meantime, in the confusion, the Residence had been overlooked in the way of extra staff. We had no chauffeur or telephone answerer. Remember, my dear Chinkies say only " 'Allo—not here." You should have seen Marjorie and me ploughing around, East Texas fashion, picking up children, groceries, and all that, pulling the Engelhards in and out of the car—Mr. E. weighs about 280, has a hip disorder, and uses a stick, though he's barely fifty years old. Through it all, he remained every inch the Princeton gentleman, opening car doors, and standing aside until everyone was placed. I made it through on sheer bravado, but, at first opportunity, I let the whole staff have the back of my tongue for their oversight.

Friday morning we enplaned at seven for Melbourne where the service was held. When we called with the President on Mrs. Holt, I lost control and blubbered like an idiot. The proper Australians, even in such an hour, carried on. Zara's three sons stood bareheaded on the curb to greet the President and escort him to their mother. They were Harold's stepsons but bore his name and, along with their wives and children, called him "Pa." We had ordered from Abercrombie a special skindiver's watch with an adjustment for tides as our farewell gift. Ironical, isn't it?

Inevitably, we were lost from the President at the Cathedral, since we sat with the Diplomatic Corps in our regular place, one seat away from Sir Charles and Natasha. So, when we returned to Government House, we went in the side door with other diplomats and I was deprived of being presented to Prince Charles. I managed to get a small bite of lunch at what Lady Delacombe called the "free for all" buffet laid out in the small dining room. There, I sat by Prime Minister Holyoke of New Zealand, Sir Jack Bunting, and Mr. Heath (England's

Foreign Minister), but only for five minutes. The call came, "President's leaving," and up jumped Anne, and off we went to the airport. In the car rode Mr. McEwen, "The Caretaker Prime Minister." He's a great man, seventy years old, widower, childless, statesman in the mold of Cordell Hull and Dick Russell, and Country Party leader—which is the minority portion of the Coalition Government, the Liberal and Country Parties. He will serve only until the Liberals choose their leader. The power struggle is on—"The King is dead, long live the King"—but all the contenders are great friends of the United States. The Aussies are the kind of allies that stick. In the fight, you won't have to look back to see if they are still there.

As big old Air Force One lifted off, I again brushed away my tears but not as ruefully as I had in the past because I knew I'd soon be coming home, too. Our President certainly acquitted himself well. The Australians were deeply moved by his coming. They adore him here. They are proud but sensitive about being small, the same population as Texas, the same area as the United States. The only white people for ten thousand miles. I heard it said that this gesture, on the President's part, gave us a new view of ourselves.

We lit out ourselves for Canberra, braced up, found a free evening, as we'd already cancelled a Sydney dinner party; on Saturday I shopped for Senator Yarborough's kangaroo cuff links, went to the hairdresser, missed my daughter's Christmas call, and at 5:00 P.M. received two hundred people—Embassy staff, wives, and children, gardeners to colonels. Served Mary Koock's Coffee Ice Cream Punch and it was a great success. Sunday night, Christmas Eve, Ed read the lesson and led the procession at the children's service at St. John's. We all go down into a small cave-like cellar where there is a live crèche with real lambs bleating. It looks just as I imagine the stable did in Bethlehem.

Christmas Day we had drinks with Sir Thomas Daly and his cute Heather—lunch with Sir Charles and Nasturtium, a family party with coatless gentlemen. Another guest was Lord Talbot, former United Kingdom Ambassador to Laos. Then rushed to 3:30 plane, changed on plane, were met by Walter and Betsy, called at Government House, Sydney, on Sir Roden, the tall handsome governor, and Lady Cutler. They have three handsome sons. Someday he'll be Governor General. Immediately went to the Grace family Christmas at Mick Grace's. Has to be seen to be believed. All ages, dozens of people, everybody provided with a huge sack to haul home his gifts. Santa came by water. There was a new American daughter-in-law, Smith graduate "prototype." Our presents were overwhelmingly beautiful, a pair of kangaroo rugs, a painting of the American Embassy by a well-known artist. I had found a litter bag with "Clark-Downs" on it and Mick Grace was enchanted to learn that the Ambassador was also "in retail." Boxing Day we hosted a cruise for about thirty people. Jerry Lapin, a California-American, provided his grand launch and food from the Caprice Restaurant. I couldn't sell him on box lunches, so it was buffet laid out— with waiters to serve all the grog, including champagne. The Premier, Mr. Askin, came aboard after firing the opening cannon. Again I kept thinking of the line about "the prettiest sight in a pretty world is the privileged class enjoying its privileges." Remember actor James Stewart saying it in *The Philadelphia Story?* Those hundred yachts with spinnakers (colored sails) are unforgettably beautiful. Dinner that night with Belknaps and today back to Canberra.

It all sounds glamorous and it was, but I am so tired I ache all over. I merchandised too many accounts and climbed too many boat ladders, drank too much champagne, ate too much caviar, and wonder if I can make the rest of the week, including wedding reception tomorrow. Father of the bride, Ed Cronk, just broke his ankle on the tennis court. I guess H.E. will give away one more bride before he leaves.

Happy New Year to all and may you someday see an Australian Christmas with daisies, hydrangeas, and bikinis.

My love to you all,
Anne Clark

January 1, 1968

Dear Ones,

This is the end—a new year, a new life, a wonderful experience that has opened my eyes, widened my horizons. I know that I shall miss Huang and Foo and LeeLee and Chan and Ming and Hsu, and especially Marjorie. Never again will I have a secretary to write the place cards, make the phone calls, and cope with the moral, financial, and health problems of the cook. Nor will I encounter friends with the polite consideration, the gentle manners—"Oh, Mrs. Clark, not to worry" or "never mind" is standard when things fly apart. My old and dear, my tried and true ones in the United States are going to say, "Get with it, old girl."

But the minute the car in Honolulu pulled over to the right side of the road, I said to myself, "I'm home." Don't be misled by leis and brown faces, Hawaii is as American as popcorn. Last night was New Year's Eve, but I was too tired to do more than watch the fireworks from the balcony of our suite at the Royal. The music and popping firecrackers below went on all night but I had my first really good "z-z-z-us" (Aussie Eng.) in a month. For the first time, I had no appointments, no bags to pack, no dates with the hairdresser, no planes to catch. I've promised myself that if I ever detach myself from diplomacy, I will never, never be on time anywhere. In two and a half years, I've oftener been too early than too late. Either was equally bad. The well-mannered Australians always had a committee standing on the stoop to meet us. This was equally true at Government House, a church, or a bank. If too early, and they hadn't organized, they were humiliated; if late, they might be standing in the rain. The Embassy airplanes were the worst—our schedules said "Doors close at 5:05 P.M. (after some argument they altered from 1700:05) and the crew had to file a flight plan, so, if we were late, they didn't leave us, but colonels and majors were biting their nails. There was a big black book on my desk the size of a lectern Bible. The left-hand page had H.E.'s day

planned and the right-hand page had mine. To each page were clipped
the letters from expected visitors and the invitations for the day. The
Ambassador's schedule (pronounced "shedule") for the day came up
with the coffee and morning papers. Also on the desk was a "bush telegraph"—a plain old spike with notes and reminders from Marjorie
and me to each other, bills, unanswered letters, cards from unacknowl-
edged gifts, and other miscellany. It took all of this to keep us going.
Sometimes my packing was an exercise in logistics—clothes for formal
calls (morning coats, silk toppers, furs, gloves, and hats), outdoor
clothes, such as sneakers for a boating excursion; evening clothes,
which might include both black and white-tie ensembles. There were
the gifts to be carried along, usually whiskey* and books, but sometimes photos and bits specially chosen for the individuals; the calling
cards to be left in proper sequence, two for the Ambassador, one for
me; often a hamper lunch for the plane, sometimes the grog for a party
(which we bought cheaper at Embassy prices). The weather was always a problem, as unpredictable as Texas. We had to have back-up
clothes in case H.E. split his pants or someone spilled a glass of red
wine down his evening shirt or the waiter dropped a glob of Hollan-
daise in the lap of my evening dress. Even our final departure involved
wardrobe problems—summer clothes had to be saved for the final days
in Canberra and winter clothes had to accompany us for our arrival in
Washington. If I'd been coming from any place except good disease-
free, pure Australia, I'd be in quarantine now. Nobody had checked
my health card and my vaccination had run out. Even the Ambassador
often carried three hats: homburg, topper, and sports model. We are
traveling with seventeen pieces of luggage plus a brief case, four coats,
and my inevitable paper shopping bag. We have the biggest suite here
at the Royal that I've ever seen, full of flowers and leis and pineapple
from the Governor of Hawaii, the Dillinghams, the Scurlocks and

---

* The spelling of "whisky" presents a problem. Only Scotch, which is spelled
sans *e*, is served in Australian homes, but the Ambassador always made his
presentations in bourbon, which is spelled with the *e*.

McGahas, dear Rush Clark, and the resident manager of the hotel. I wish I knew someone here to impress. Tonight we dine with Admiral and Mrs. Sharp, mogul of CINCPAC, but, being American, we are back to business suit and a summer dress.

On December 27, the day after Boxing Day, we were in Sydney until 3:00 P.M. I repacked, went to the furrier to sort out my fur coat maze. I am taking home three kangaroo coats and the furrier had them all wrong. I had to leave them to be delivered to the Consulate and held my check until I could check them just before we enplaned. We were left with parts of five days in Canberra. Our official farewell by the diplomats was held at the Philippine Embassy, where we received our engraved silver tray, then went to the Cronk wedding rehearsal supper. Had a Chinese lunch for the departing Martins on Thursday with all our Brampton Island party and Mary Ed Cronk's wedding reception for four hundred the same night. It was our fifth wedding at the Residence. It was full-scale Australian-American, the customs of both countries combined. We had up a party tent and an outdoor dance floor, hard liquor and champagne, speeches, full-scale supper; it lasted till 1:00 A.M. The young wanted to stay and dance all night, but I didn't encourage it. We shook all four hundred hands in and out again. Next morning the packers returned, the pictures came down, the silver punch bowl went, and my last trunk departed. At 6:00 P.M., forty top staff members came for drinks and to receive their farewell gifts—silver boomerangs, appropriately inscribed—and afterward we went to a restaurant for dinner tendered by the staff, gay and full of jokes, but poignant, too. Saturday we lunched with Walter and Betty Smith, who had chosen some of our best Australian friends, and that night from six to seven-thirty we had our own postponed farewell reception. We think about three hundred showed although the word had been spread by word of mouth only. We had Old Fashioneds and Pimm's Cup served from punch bowls in five places. The Old Fashioned has become known as "Mr. Ed's drink" but Pimm's is something the Australians know and trust.

Huang, being an English butler, understands Pimm's—also "pink gin"—but is absolutely devastated by mint juleps and milk punch. After two and one-half years, I'd almost won the point of plenty of ice in the drinks. When the last thirsty newspaper couple had been shoved out, we took off to dine with Billy McMahon, Treasurer of the Commonwealth, aspirant for the office of P.M., and his beautiful wife, Sonia. It ended on the happy note of his asking Ed to be godfather to the expected baby who has not yet made the newspapers. Bill would have been the natural heir to the post, but devaluation and a clash with Black Jack McEwen, leader of the Country Party, intervened.

Next morning, after my last-minute packing, we went to church where H.E. *preached*. His text was "Ambassador in Chains" from Ephesians, and a tribute to the P.M. *"Here he lies where he longed to be; / Home is the sailor, home from sea, / And the hunter home from the hill."*† There was a full church and a Rector who wiped tears away. He said, "Ask your President to send us another Christian Ambassador." That was our reward for pulling out on many blue Sundays to represent our country in God's House, as well as the Statehouse. Several previous Ambassadors had personal reasons for never attending any church. Back to the Residence for a drink and farewell with the tennis players, the Australian gentlemen who use our court on Sunday morning. Sir Allen Westerman is their leader. He's a real Aussie sportsman, an unattached widower who spends Sunday at tennis and

---

† Under the wide and starry sky,
  Dig the grave and let me lie.
  Glad did I live and gladly die,
  And I laid me down with a will.

This be the verse you grave for me:
Here he lies where he longed to be;
Home is the sailor, home from sea,
And the hunter home from the hill.

  Robert Louis Stevenson, *Underwoods*, Requiem, Stanzas 1 and 2.

Saturday afternoon at the Commonwealth Club playing "snooker" with Dr. Mark Faunce, Sir High Ennor, distinguished scientist, and an old friend who is an undistinguished Aussie businessman. Then my dear Chinese staff staged their last Chinese lunch for us. The round table seats twelve, so the Turbayne family and Cronk family filled the table, and by 2:15 we were enroute to the airport, where a large crowd of diplomats, staff, and well-wishers assembled for the traditional "hip, hip, hooray" and "jolly good fellow." We reached Sydney forty minutes later, where we had more of the same, save for H.E.'s unprecedented private audience with P.M. McEwen (he will serve temporarily) and where we did have a private room with bar and savories and more presents received and given. Dearest Walter Phillips and Rush Clark saw us in and out again, both ever-present—ever-helpful—ever-wise. Happy, in his doggie pack, went to Cargo and straight to my friend Sis Byram in Austin without stopovers.

All the Dillinghams are away, but they sent their car and driver, Benny, a Filipino (I am not sure whether he's a chauffeur or a vice-president). He's highly intelligent—took us for a long drive, had all information—all subjects, people, dates, and prices. He even took us to the home of the absent L.S.D. (Mr. Lowell S. Dillingham), where we had drinks on the veranda and admired the Bonnards, Vuillards, and tropical birds; lastly we went to the Episcopal Cathedral (built and inspired by Queen Emma in 1863), where we saw the memorial to their late father, Walter Dillingham, a stained-glass window that fills the whole west end of the church. Mother Dillingham has been memorialized with a fountain in the park, and the big pink Italian palace-mansion has been given to a school. "Sic transit gloria"—in this case, it applies only to real estate; the business and the sons (minus one brother who was a flier killed in World War II, and another sportsman who broke his neck hunting) are carrying on splendidly.

Tomorrow we enplane early for San Francisco, where we remain two nights. Ed will speak to the American-Australian Association (note the reversal) and we will dine with the Quigleys—whose Phi Beta Kappa daughter was Leila's classmate at Smith—and on the third day we set off for Washington City so that Ed can turn in his suit.

I guess it won't be long until I'll wish I was back in "that pleasant little island where it's always afternoon and nearly always tea time" and I'll be lonely for Lady Casey and her pictures, and Lady Huxley and her new words ("Parousia" is our newest), for dear Frederick and his "Compliments of Frederick to Madame," for Betty Smith, who turned the pages in my prayer book, for Dame Mabel, the hostess with the mostest—but just now I'm looking forward to seeing the dogwood and the bluebonnets bloom, to a catfish dinner at Jack's and Charlie's, to my Mother with her airs and graces and pride at ninety-one, to Mamma Clark's serenity and practical advice, to my gentle sister, to all the Wynns, Leila, Doug, the girls, and Bubber Billy, to the gaudy neon and the decorations (I'll miss the Christmas ones but Valentine is not far behind), to Sara Lee and Top Chop't at the Night Hawk, to Virg and Dolly, Jeannette and Sis. What's wrong with that? In the words of D.B.H., "Nothing."

Fondly,
Your Ex-Ambassadress, Anne Clark

EPILOGUE

Now my Australian adventure is concluded. The golden coach is a pumpkin again. Queen Anne is Cinderella. There are many shimmering memories of a foreign land to be put down in the round tower of my heart, but I thank heaven for the United States of America as well as little girls.

On Saturday, March 16, as we drove toward Straddlefork Farm, I was startled to hear the radio announcer's voice telling the world that the steamship *African Star* was burning in the port of New Orleans. My heart sank because I knew that all my household goods had left Australia aboard that vessel. I thought sadly of my mother's silver tea set, the paintings I'd taken with me and those I'd acquired during my stay, the sculptured head of my daughter, the Aubusson tapestry, the Chinese screen, my lovely Steuben figures, the many mementoes we had accumulated by gift and purchase. I had to live with my suspense over the long weekend until on Monday a series of phone calls assured me that my shipment had been unloaded two days earlier in Houston, and the *Star* was enroute back to Sydney. My relief was tempered by the tragic fate of the passengers and crew of sixty who died in the disaster.

I slip easily back into my old patterns, tho' I like to remember fondly my friends, the knights and ladies, the princesses and the captains of industry who crossed the portals of our Residence; the foreign service wives earned my admiration by the competent support they give their husbands' positions.

Sir Walter Scott expressed for me a still relevant truth when he said, "Breathes there the man, with soul so dead, / Who never to him-

self hath said, / This is my own, my native land! / Whose heart hath
ne'er within him burn'd / As home his footsteps he hath turn'd, /
From wandering on a foreign strand?" I hope in a small way that I
have made a bit of a contribution to my country's welfare as I tagged
along behind my energetic husband, though oftentimes he was drag-
ging me footsore and protesting. I learned much from Lady Casey,
Lady Wilton, Lady Johnston, and Lady Waller, from Dame Pattie and
Dame Mabel, from Betsy Phillips, Jodie Lydman, Dottie Cronk, Marg
Martin, Betty Smith, and Marjorie Turbayne. I am grateful to them all.

I hope that I may return for a second spring in Western Australia,
for another flutter on the Melbourne Cup, to hear an opera in the
Sydney Opera House, for another plate of Sydney Rock oysters, to
hear again the kindly reassurance of "Not to worry, Mrs. Clark."
Though I have learned that he who travels never goes all the way home,
I have kept at least a toe hold in Texas, which absence made me realize
is really the Southern part of Heaven.

APPENDIX

I

Remarks of Mrs. Edward Clark at the Opening of Fete
for Retarded Children, Koomari House, Canberra*
October 23, 1965

Since our arrival in Australia two months ago, my husband and I have been engaged in a very busy program of acquainting ourselves with Australia and Australians. In this short time, we have traveled to New South Wales, Victoria, Western Australia, and Tasmania; shortly we will visit South Australia and Queensland.

In the course of these visits, and here in Canberra, my husband has had the honor of addressing a large number of groups and organizations representing a great variety of the Australian community.

This, however, is the first occasion on which I have been asked to represent my country officially, and I am so happy that my "inauguration" should come here in Canberra, your beautiful capital city, where I now feel so much at home. I am delighted to be here today before a group that so deserves the admiration and support of the community.

The reputation of Koomari House as one of the most progressive and worthwhile organizations of the area came very quickly to my attention as a new arrival to Canberra; I understand that in addition to the work already being done, as soon as funds are available Koomari House will be expanded to include resident facilities for retarded children.

The importance of such a facility to this growing area is obvious. Each of us is moved to sympathetic understanding for the burden of the minds of parents who must plan for the welfare of children who require special care and training.

Therefore, it is with great warmth that I, on behalf of the Handicapped Children's Association, express heartfelt thanks to the service organizations, community groups, and individuals who have given their time throughout the year and with redoubled effort in preparation for this fete, which will, I am sure, be a great success.

Now I do declare this fete opened, and I wish you all a happy afternoon.

* This is typical of the press releases from the Chancery. Remarks are small talks; a speech or address is lengthier. Opening fetes is a regular part of any public figure's duty. A lady must wear a pretty hat—mine blew off that day in mid-speech.

Remarks of Mrs. Edward Clark before the
Canberra, Australia, Y.M.C.A.
December 14, 1965

Madam Chairman:

Christmas is the season of friendship. I shall miss my old and dear friends this Christmas season, but I hope that I have new ones to stand in their shoes. I hear a great deal about the strange weather of the Australian Christmas. It all goes to show how rigid and misinformed our minds can become— our Blessed Lord was born in the hot country of the Middle East. The Gospel stories say not one word about snow or sleet—or frosty mornings. It does not say the angels sang about the weather. I can imagine that Bethlehem two thousand years ago was just as warm as Canberra in 1965.

You know, the United States is a great big country. We have many climates and many heritages. Though we are primarily Anglo-Saxon English, at least I speak for myself and my background, we are a lot farther from England time-wise than you. None of us have English educations or have spent much time in England, so the folk customs are well diluted by now. As you know, I grew up in what we call the "Deep South" and then I married and have lived the greater part of my life in Texas—that's the Southwest. I could stand here and tell you how I'm dreaming of a White Christmas where sleigh bells jingle, and snowflakes glisten, but it would be rather phony. I never heard a genuine sleighbell in my life, and I have seen only one or two white Christmases. That ballad, relatively new, was written for a musical movie called *Holiday Inn* based on all the holiday celebrations. It was sung by Bing Crosby. You know he can sell a song and he has made that almost as familiar as "Silent Night." In the movie, the singer was a homesick sojourner from the Northeastern part of the United States, New England, stranded in Southern California, where the sun shines and the flowers are in bloom at Christmas time. A California Christmas would be more like your Australian Christmas weather-wise.

Some of the Christmas memories of my childhood no longer exist. "The old order changeth, yielding place to new." But for a moment I will drag you, though you might not want to be led, down memory lane to my childhood Christmas on a cotton plantation on the banks of the Mississippi River. Picture, if you can, a rather lonely little girl. I was the child of my parents' old age. My older brother and sister went to a boarding school before I can remember, and I, myself, went at seven. We didn't have snow but rather frosty, damp, cold rain and mud. The first sounds were fires being made in the bedrooms by the colored man, general factotum on plantations of the era, called the "Hostler." His real work was to tend the stock, chiefly mules, who worked the cotton plantation, but he also doubled in brass as house servant, tending those miserable fires. Children always jumped and shouted "Christmas gift." Theoretically, if you "caught" somebody by saying it *first,* the loser paid the forfeit of a gift. In practice, you know who always gave the present. The first order was for children to examine their stockings with their Santa Claus presents—always the best ones. The stockings contained small gifts, apples, and oranges—which we had only at Christmas in those days. Neither grow in that area. There was always a coin in the toe of the stocking; depending on the affluence of the family, it might be a gold piece, or a silver dollar, or maybe just a quarter— a two-bit piece we used to call them—comparable to your two bob. The stocking usually had a doll on the top—and beside it stood your best gift, like a bicycle or for me, a country child, it was once a new saddle. Later in the morning we had a tree ceremony in which everybody participated, including servants and older members of the family. Gifts were exchanged and packages opened. My godfather always gave me a silver spoon. By the time I married I had a complete set of silver given me on various anniversaries. In those days, the tree had real candles and in our country, like yours, fire was a definite hazard to be constantly dreaded, so there were always buckets of water and blankets about in case of a blaze.

Our Christmas dinner was usually a goose, because Mother raised them, not turkeys. It was often supplemented by a well-cured ham or hog's-head cheese, and possibly quail and venison. Dessert was fruit cup of coconut and oranges and pineapple. We call it "ambrosia."

In the afternoon we often had callers from neighboring plantations. We served them eggnog. You do know eggnog, as we make it with whipped cream and bourbon whiskey? Or, if they could possibly get away, the men went hunting. When the cotton crop is gathered in the South, every male who is able-bodied takes to the hunting grounds. It used to be bear; now it's deer, or quail, or ducks, or doves. That night we had—hold on to your chairs —fireworks—Roman candles, skyrockets, firecrackers, and sparklers for the little ones. They are not considered dangerous. I will have to admit this is all memory's picture—nostalgia for a life that no longer is—but that was my childhood Christmas.

As I moved along the years, left the South for the Southwest, the country for the city, our Christmas customs changed. We borrowed some things from our Mexican neighbors across the border. We have *piñatas* for the children. *Piñatas* are made of colored crepe paper—they may be shaped like anything from a bull to an Easter bunny. They are filled with small toys, gum, and candies, and each child in turn is blindfolded and given a broomstick and tries to break the *piñata,* which hangs from the ceiling. A scramble for the contents follows. Then there are the *luminares* we put out: paper bags filled with wet sand, the top folded into a cuff, and big fat votive candles inside. Sometimes a whole neighborhood will cooperate in putting out *luminares* along the curb. Sometimes we might just outline our own driveway or garden wall. Fruitcakes are part of Christmas. I used to bake dozens but I stopped some years ago when I started receiving many each year from business friends. My friends are very creative about making their own decorations. They make beautiful velvet stockings with sequins and beads—their own beaded ornaments, their own snipped-tin ornaments. They gild leaves, they make wax fruit, they make and decorate candles. They deck the halls with boughs of holly. I think often that our Christmas flower—the poinsettia—came to the United States as a gift from an American diplomat, the first minister to Mexico. His home was in Charleston, South Carolina, and he died in 1850. His name was Joel Poinsett, and he brought back the lovely flower and gave it his name. I'd love to think I could be immortalized by a flower from our service in the diplomatic world.

Cynical as people are these days, I must say, in America a good deal of Christmas is still a religious festival. We make a great thing of decorating the church with greens and garlands, and have special music during Advent at the noon hour. Every household has a crèche as part of the permanent collection of Christmas decorations. Each year I'd ask my daughter, "Are you ready for your special fine crèche to keep?" intending to buy one made at Oberamergau or a fine porcelain set—and she'd say, "No, the children like to handle ours, so we just get new cows and sheep and angels from the dime store each year, and they make their own manger from a cigar box." But last year we spent our vacation in the Tennessee Mountains, where they still practice country handcrafts like hand weaving and woodcarving. We bought a *genuine American set* of crèche figures. They are made from corn shucks after the manner in which the Indian children made their dolls. I know one family that has an impromptu pageant done by the children—a box of old costumes they improvise from—a wicker wine basket with a flashlight for the Blessed Babe in the manger. The older children who can read will speak the parts of the herald angels. The rector reads from St. Luke—Mrs. Carter pushes a tot forward saying "Come on, second Angel, speak louder." They did it with their own children and friends and now they are into the second generation. Last year, one of my granddaughters was Mary, and Mrs. Carter gave her a silver cross to commemorate the occasion. Our Jewish friends celebrate Hanukkah—with presents every day for a week. My granddaughter, Maggie, was beside herself when Bruce Friedman started receiving his gifts, which culminated in a gold watch—I mention this because the Jewish Community is so much a part of American life, and it's interesting to see the way in which they have amalgamated their own customs with the rest of our American way of life.

The Christmas story is part of our custom. There are the old tried and true ones: Dickens' *Christmas Carol* and the "Night Before Christmas." My Southern upbringing included Roark Bradford's *How Come Christmas*, and Irwin Russell's "Christmas Night in the Quarters," both in Negro dialect. Then there is Henry VanDyke's *Story of the Other Wise Man*, O. Henry's *Gift of the Magi*, and the more up-to-date *The Little Mixer* and *Miracle at 34th Street*—that's Macy's corner in New York City. However, my own favorite was the one my father always read. We call it *Is There a Santa Claus?* It appeared as an editorial* in the *New York Sun* many years ago, 1897, and is said to be one of the most famous editorials of all time. Would it bore you to hear it once more?

*   *   *   *

Dear Editor:
    I am eight years old. Some of my little friends say there is no Santa Claus. Papa says, "If you see it in *The Sun* it's so." Please tell me the truth, is there a Santa Claus?
Virginia O'Hanlon

    Virginia, your little friends are wrong. They have been affected by the skepticism of a skeptical age. They do not believe except they see. They think that nothing can *be* which is not comprehensible by their little minds. All minds, Virginia, whether they be men's or children's, are little. In this

* Editorial by Francis Pharcellus Church.

great universe of ours man is a mere insect, an ant, in his intellect, as compared with the boundless world about him, as measured by the intelligence
capable of grasping the whole of truth and knowledge.

Yes, Virginia, there is a Santa Claus. He exists as certainly as love and
generosity and devotion exist, and you know that they abound and give to
your life its highest beauty and joy. Alas! how dreary would be the world
if there were no Santa Claus! It would be as dreary as if there were no
Virginias. There would be no childlike faith then, no poetry, no romance
to make tolerable this existence. We should have no enjoyment, except in
sense and sight. The eternal light with which childhood fills the world
would be extinguished.

Not believe in Santa Claus! You might as well not believe in fairies. You
might get your papa to hire men to watch in all the chimneys on Christmas
Eve to catch Santa Claus, but even if you did not see Santa Claus coming
down, what would that prove? *Nobody* sees Santa Claus, but that is no
sign that there *is* no Santa Claus. The most real things in the world are those
that neither children nor men can see. Did you ever see fairies dancing on
the lawn? Of course not, but that's no proof that they are not there. Nobody
can conceive or imagine all the wonders there are unseen and unseeable in
the world.

You tear apart the baby's rattle and see what makes the noise inside, but
there is a veil covering the unseen world which not the strongest man, nor
even the united strength of *all* the strongest men that *ever* lived could tear
apart. Only faith, poetry, love, romance, can push aside that curtain to view
and picture the supernal beauty and glory beyond. Is it all real? Ah, Virginia, in all this world there is nothing else real and abiding.

No Santa Claus! Thank God, he lives, and he lives forever. A thousand
years from now, Virignia, nay, ten times ten thousand years from now, he
will continue to make glad the heart of childhood.

Arrival Statement of Ambassador Edward A. Clark
on Return to Australia from the United States
January 23, 1966

Friends and Allies:

I bring you greetings from the President and the people of the United
States. I have just returned to Australia from a three weeks' visit there. I

visited the President both at his ranch in Texas and at the White House in Washington. He remembers with great happiness his wartime service here and always says that the only person he'd trade jobs with is me. Next to being President of the United States, he'd rather be Ambassador to Australia than any other job in the world.

I visited our four banks in Austin, Center, San Augustine, and San Benito; my law office in Austin, Texas; my own lands in the piney woods of East Texas; and my grandchildren in the state of Mississippi on the banks of that great inland waterway, the Mississippi River. I visited the office of the State Department (External Affairs to you) in Washington, our national capital. I visited the big cities of Texas, Dallas and Houston. I talked to bankers, oil men, big ranchers, and little tree farmers—a cross section of America. The words of Sir Walter Scott re-echoed in my heart, "This is my own, my native land"—but oddly there was another echo in my heart, another dream intruding in my slumbers—of the broad and beautiful land that is now my second homeland. My friends, I am happy to be home again with you.

Beyond your imagination is the interest and affectionate feeling I found in the States for Australia. Such words as, "Those folks think just like us." I met a man traveling around the world from Australia. He told me that, next to Australia, he'd like to live in West Texas. A great musician asked two questions: "What time is it in Australia?" and, "How can I buy some land—I'd like to own a small piece of that continent." A former soldier proudly introducing his beautiful wife said: "Australia gave me my greatest asset. I love that country." If the distance were not so great, I'll warrant the exchange of visitors would be so great we'd have to expand our hotel facilities to take care of them in the United States and in Australia. As Sir Stanley Burbury in Hobart said after his trip around the world, "Time and distance are nothing; only money." We are going to have to find a way to reduce that cost with group flights or some other imaginative scheme so that there can be more exchange between our two friendly peoples.

Then there was the big question asked from top to bottom—from the President to the most callow school boy—"*Do the Australians support us in Vietnam?*" I was able to look them all dead in the eye and proudly proclaim, "*They do!*" Australians know where their interests lie and they carry their share of the load. Diggers voluntarily, willingly, have shouldered their Mathildas again and, just as they did at Gallipoli, at El Alamein, in New Guinea, they are marching beside American doughboys—pulling their share with equal efficiency and cheerfulness—because they know the United States and Australia are defending the same frontier—that frontier is not the Rhine, but Vietnam.

Address of Mrs. Edward Clark to Australian-American Association Women's Group, Canberra, Australia March 1, 1966

After going to several meetings of the Australian-American Association Women's Group, I found myself with the courage to say "Yes" when a committee called to ask that I say a few words to you at this meeting. You didn't look to me as though you would judge me too harshly or expect me to show myself as a great wit or polished speaker.

When I was in Washington with my husband preparing for our great adventure to a new world and a new life, being vaccinated, shot, coiffured, filled with advice, and farewell party-ed to the point of exhaustion, all the professionals in the State Department said to me nothing concrete like, "Buy five hundred visiting cards and a carton of match clips for the table." Instead, they said, "Mrs. Clark, be yourself." That's one field in which I'd had lots of practice, but since nobody provided me with any training for a substitute role, here I stand *again—being myself*. The only direction that I found specific and helpful in all the mountains of printed material was, "Every man should have a black four-in-hand tie and every lady a black dress and hat for funerals." So I did put those items in my trunks and, since my husband has had an occasion to attend one state funeral, I was glad to be ready, provided with the tie.

I do want to say how much the Australian-American Association has meant to us. It was not an organization with which I was familiar, though I believe it may have chapters in the northeast part of the United States. In Washington there is a Southern Cross Club for transplanted Australians and their friends, and the English-Speaking Union is extremely active everywhere. Your Ambassador, Sir Howard Beale, traveled all over the United States to speak to its meetings and became well known everywhere through it. All my friends in Texas know him well and many remember Lord Casey's charm and helpfulness when he was Australian Ambassador to the United States. I have come to know and cherish the Wallers and Caseys.

But it is the Australian-American Association that has extended the hand of friendship, the warm welcome to us. I mean to my husband, the Ambassador, and to me, wherever we have traveled in Australia. From that dreary, foggy morning last August when I first set foot on your continent, there have been the representatives of Australian-American with a nosegay of flowers, a bright smile, a sincere "Welcome to Australia." In every one of your six state capitals, sometimes in the cold gray morning, sometimes at an uncomfortably late hour in the evening on windy, dusty airports, a lady in a beautiful hat and a hearty gentleman with the little gold eagle and kangaroo pin have made us glad we came.

Would you like to hear a bit about life in an Embassy and how it differs from my past? I had lived for more than twenty years in one house—something like the Residence, save miniaturized—a two-story brick, attached garage, same rooms downstairs, only smaller. Upstairs I had only three bedrooms and three baths, where the Embassy has five, and instead of nine acres of gardens, I had 90 feet across the front street and 120 feet on the side street. My trees were oaks and elms, bigger than your gums. We watered with an automatic sprinkler. A part-time gardener came each Tuesday, rain or shine, and the same colored maid, named Daisy Yett, looked after us in her own fashion. Both had been with us more than twenty years.

Austin, Texas, our hometown, is a city of 250,000, the sixth largest city and capital of the state of Texas. It is fifty miles to the L.B.J. Ranch at Johnson City where the President makes his permanent home. The drive ordinarily takes an hour if you know the way and are a good, fast driver. The last time I was there, on December 28, 1965, we flew up in the President's helicopter, a matter of fifteen minutes.

Our climate is similar to Canberra's. We live in a cup, surrounded by misty, purple hills. We call it the "City of the Violet Crown." The hills are covered with live oak and cedar, so they never turn red and gold in the autumn. Our summers are longer and hotter, so we are more wedded to air conditioning than you. In the fall we follow The University of Texas football games. In the spring and summer we go boating or fishing on the beautiful Highland Lakes, all manmade, which form a chain stretching seventy-five miles from Austin.

When I arrived here, I found that my first official duty was a series of calls on the wives of the other diplomats. These follow a set pattern, by appointment and last only thirty minutes. I leave two of the Ambassador's cards and one of mine, drink one cup of tea, sign the book, and depart. Next week, Madame Ambassador of Country X returns the call. At first, I was bitterly resentful of the seventy-five half hours that I had to spend thusly. Then understanding dawned. All protocol has a reason, like manners and etiquette. After spending thirty minutes twice with a woman, just the two of us, I know her—her face, her name, and at least a little about her. I was so pleased with myself last week during the visits of our Vice-President and our Congressman Miller that I was able to recognize and call by name every head of mission.

At home I always answered my own door and telephone, and I frequently do here. It's easier and I find that I can save my staff for harder tasks—besides, I like to see the people who come to the door, even if it's just a messenger or a delivery man. They are Australians, too, and it is our purpose to be Envoy to *all* the people.

Then there are the dinners. I have enjoyed some magnificent food, some superb wines, and some sparkling company, but I am often again rebellious about the seating. For instance, last week the Prime Minister, Mr. Holt, honored us by accepting several invitations consecutively (the V.P.'s visit followed one already laid on). I felt it a shame he had to sit by me every time, and that I couldn't one time give him the prettiest or the wittiest woman in the party for a partner. Maybe I'll be glad of that rule sometime. At least no one can be offended when he has to sit by a bore if it's protocol prescribed.

When I arrived at the Residence, I thought the house really very beautiful, but I was overwhelmed by the scale. The dining room seats twenty-four, compared to one that seated ten. I soon found myself missing my own things. There was not a clock in the Residence or a wood basket. It was three months before those things arrived that had been shipped by ocean freight. Now that I have distributed my ash trays, flower vases, and photos of my grandchildren, I feel it's my home. But we also regard the house as the property and home-away-from-home of all Americans. Unless there's some good reason, we want them all to see the Residence, and we want you to see it, too. I have invited the group to meet with me in the near future. I can never make you of the Australian-American Association as welcome as you have made me. You are deep in the round tower of my heart, from where, like the Bishop of Bingham, I shall never let you depart.

Remarks of Mrs. Edward Clark at Adams
Presbyterian Church, Canberra, A. C. T.
March 19, 1966

Madam Chairman, Reverend Sir, Ladies, Gentlemen, and Young Friends:
I want you to know that I feel very much at home in this environment
because I've spent so many hours of my life in the parish halls of my church,
serving suppers, washing dishes, stuffing envelopes, hanging Christmas
greens, polishing brass, even painting furniture. While I am not a Predes-
tination Presbyterian—I am a bigoted Protestant Episcopalian. I find the
company of working church people my happiest fellowship. For another
reason, I want to be here. While my representation of the United States
is strictly unofficial—nobody appointed me anything, my husband is "His
Excellency," not I—I have determined that any time I can serve the Church
in any way, I shall be there as a representative of the United States of America. No matter what you have been told by the cynics about materialistic,
pleasure-loving Americans, we still are a God-fearing, church-going, pray-
ing, worshiping people (by the millions).
Our first colonies were founded for religious reasons and several were
complete theocracies. No gathering opens without some kind of invoca-
tion of God's blessing. I saw it at the football game I attended on New
Year's Day in Dallas—fifty thousand gay, pleasure seekers stood with bowed
heads in the frosty air to hear a prayer for sport and for our country. I rose
at 6 A.M. on a January morning in 1965 in Washington to attend church
services before the inauguration of our President. Our money has on it, "In
God We Trust." We salute the flag as one nation "under God." I intend to
demonstrate that side of America whenever and wherever I am able.

> Lord, in the daily round, the common task,
> The little niggling needs that each day brings,
> Give me a spirit that will rise, I ask,
> Above the tyranny of little things.
> Of *little* things, the petty jars and frets,
> The trivial cares that make a woman's day,
> The disappointments and the small upsets
> That prick the nerves, and tongue and temper fray.
>
> Give me, O Lord, the vision that can see
> Beauty in homely tasks, in work well done,

Give me the courage that will cheerfully
Accept my lot, nor wish an easier one.
Give me perspective, that the little things
May keep their little places, nor overbear
The faith and hope that are the spirit's wings
To rise in Thee, Dead Lord; grant this my prayer.*

May I now declare this fete officially open.

* Florence Reddaway, "Housewife's Prayer." Published by The Society for the Promotion of Christian Knowledge, London.

Remarks by Mrs. Edward Clark at All Saints Cathedral, Bathurst
August 8, 1966

Thank you for this invitation that has made possible for me a visit to historic and charming Bathurst.

It was just a year ago that I stepped off a plane in Sydney to a completely new world—where summer was winter and birds laughed and light switches were off—up. My husband and I were very private citizens and I was completely preoccupied with my own house, garden, husband, and grandchildren. In almost the twinkling of an eye I became in my own modest realm a representative of the United States of America. So I must always be careful that I present it properly and honestly.

One of the places that I can easily feel at home is here in the shadow of an Anglican Church. Many hours of my life have been spent in environs of the church doing the Martha tasks of church work, that is serving suppers, laundering altar linen, arranging flowers. My association with the Church of St. John the Baptist in Canberra has been a source of great satisfaction to me.

One of the things that I hope to represent in Australia, as part of the American way of life, is the wide participation of Americans in church affairs. I believe that we are divided into more denominations than you in Australia, but, nevertheless, I feel we are all united under God's banner to seek a better life for all peoples—east and west, north and south. I hope

that I am bringing you today a bit of America and a bit of my own Protestant
Episcopal Church when I declare this fete officially open.*

* This was delivered on a bitter cold day. Neither the parish hall nor the
church had much heat.

*Address by Mrs. Edward Clark at the United Nations
Combined Women's Organizations Luncheon, Sydney,
in Honor of the Twenty-first Birthday of the United Nations
October 26, 1966*

Your Excellency, Lady Casey, and Guests:
   This year we are celebrating for the United Nations what is an important event in any life. The United Nations is twenty-one. There is a saying
in our country that "if you see a boy twenty-one years old walking about,
you are looking at a miracle." If the maturation of a single individual is so
fraught with hazards, consider the obstacles that must have been passed
over for an organization composed of 118 nations, which are, in turn, fed-
erations of millions of persons. So, if the body seems battle-scarred and
frayed, be not dismayed. No young person ever developed in just the way
that his parents envisioned him as an infant.
   I well remember the birth of the United Nations: Senator Tom Connally of Texas was then Chairman of Foreign Relations for the United
States Senate. He was a dear personal friend, a senior statesman, and a
great Texan. All his activities seemed special and personal to us. He was
one of our original planners and signers of the Covenant. The organiza-
tional meeting was held in San Francisco. It was the United States' first
real journey into the international world.
   You, of course, recall that after World War I we had rejected the League
of Nations, the dream of our wartime President, Woodrow Wilson. Most
people felt that *had* the United States been a member of the League our
power might have been sufficient to tip the scales and have prevented World
War II. So, in the long hot summer of 1945, Americans were less jealous
of their sovereignty and more willing to take an extra step toward the preservation of the world's peace. Women had joined the armed services;

women had worked in munitions plants; women had endured the separation of their families that the five years of war had entailed.

Women have always been the civilizing influence in the world. It was they who took men off the war path and made them settle down and plant gardens and build shelters for the protection of their young. Their influence built the first estates, and from thence the first cities. I like to think that it was their influence working through their menfolk that brought the United Nations into being.

Now that bread is baked in a bakery and blankets woven in a factory, the protection of a woman's family has moved from the hearthstones to the halls of government. The common tie of Judy O'Grady and the Colonel's Lady has been stretched to encompass women of black, brown, yellow, and white races, of Buddhist, Hindu, Christian, and Mohammedan faiths.

Though the stripling youth, which I personify as the United Nations, may not have attained perfect success as the peace-keeper we had envisioned, still its successes in many other fields have been spectacular. Peace building has aspects other than the political. After the most comprehensive agreements, peace will still be built on quicksand if the majority of the human race is unhealthy, illiterate, hungry, and impoverished.

To change this, there are fourteen nonpolitical, specialized agencies of international significance. Both Australia and the United States are governed to a far greater extent than you realize because of our treaties with the United Nations. Every country, every letter we post, every radio or television broadcast is governed in some way by the regulations voluntarily accepted and laid down by the United Nations.

UNICEF is the United Nation's Children's Fund. Through it children of the world are helped to become healthy and useful citizens. So important is it thought to be that last year it received the Nobel Peace Prize. You must have received or bought its Christmas cards.

W.H.O., World Health Organization, concerns itself with stamping out disease. Tuberculosis and malaria have yielded to its onslaught. Plagues and epidemics don't get visas. Their controls must be handled on an international basis. Your children are safer for W.H.O.

The United Nations Committee on Human Rights, of which Mrs. Eleanor Roosevelt was a respected and influential member, has contributed much to lifting the status of women, their property rights, their marriage rights, their admission to colleges and universities. The International Civil Aviation Organization makes weather forecasting and information rapidly available. Maritime organizations make sea travel and shipping safer. There is a Universal Postal Union, the only Postmaster General in the world with only one Post Office, and an International Telecommunications Union. All these organizations are vitally connected with the United Nations. Though their headquarters may be in Geneva or London or Montreal their common heartbeat comes from the glass tower overlooking the East River in New York. That heart is almost exactly halfway around the world from Australia, yet you contributed one of the first presidents, Dr. Evatt.

As you can see from my brief outlines, the United Nations story is far more than the big building on the East River with Mr. Khrushchev pounding his shoe on the table. It is a story of men of good will working in thousands of ways to make the world better, healthier, and more comfortable. I am its warm supporter and am optimistic about its lasting health and long life. So, to the United Nations on its twenty-first birthday, I wish many happy returns.

Remarks of Mrs. Edward Clark at Church Fete,
St. Clement's Church of England, Yass, New South Wales
November 3, 1966

I always consider it a privilege to be invited to visit a heretofore unvisited community. In the year and three months that we have made our home in Australia, I have learned to love your sunburnt land and to love its picturesque country towns. I love their pretty names like Queanbeyan and Cootamundra and Yass. In the United States I am a communicant of the Protestant Episcopal Church which is the American branch of the Anglican Fellowship.

I received last week the bulletin from my parish church. Last year, by request, Australian dried flowers adorned the altar there for our American Thanksgiving, which is the fourth Thursday in November. It is the harvest festival that comes in our autumn and we always dress the church with grain and fruits.

My church friends at home follow the doings of my husband and myself with great interest and it makes me very happy and proud to report to them that I participate in church activities.

We Americans, even though pleasure-loving and, some say, worldly, are still deeply committed publicly and privately to the ethics and organizations of the Judeo-Christian way of life. It is a spring that runs strong and deep, and you will find us instinctively turning to it in time of joy or sorrow. Christianity is a joyous thing, and, therefore, it is meet and right that we have this happy afternoon together, which I hope will yield material profit as well as Christian fellowship. I now declare this fete officially open.

Save the Children

Remarks of Mrs. Edward Clark at the Residence of the High Commissioner for New Zealand November 5, 1966

Madam President, Hostess Mrs. Hazlett, and Friends of Children Everywhere:

It is because of the practical idealism of a lady with the picturesque name of Eglantyne Jebb that we are gathered this afternoon to support the organization she founded forty-seven years ago. In 1919, soon after World War I, after years of local efforts on behalf of children, this determined and enlightened English woman was so moved by the plight of starving children in Vienna that she formed the organization known as Save the Children. The task of raising one thousand pounds to provide tinned milk for the little Austrian sufferers seemed stupendous then—now it seems modest. This year millions have been distributed through this organization in the freedom-from-hunger campaign. Save the Children is concerned with the relief of children everywhere without regard to race, creed, or color.

Our immediate objective is relief for the orphans and war widows of Vietnam. Some of these war widows are only fifteen years old. Children need shelters, food, and hospital care. A convalescent rest center for them is our hopeful plan. Children are the innocent victims of the struggle for order and freedom in Asia.

So, with love and compassion in our hearts we will spend a few pleasant hours here together, partaking of a delicious tea, inspecting and buying the handicrafts of our friends, and thereby playing our part in the alleviations of misery.

With an admonition to spend generously and to enjoy yourselves in a good cause, I declare this fete open.*

* Mary Scott and Jim Nash were present when I delivered this one. Jim and Ed made the auction by bidding lively on the items offered.

*Remarks by Mrs. Edward Clark, Accepting the Bark Painting
by Mrs. Margot Pullman on Behalf of Mrs. Lyndon B. Johnson
at a Charity Luncheon—Australian Bark Artistry Exhibit
Southern Cross Hotel, Melbourne
November 30, 1966*

What a pleasure to be able to accept a gift* that I know will be so appreciated and enjoyed by the recipient!

The absence of gardens, houses, and villages has led many to underestimate the ability of the Australian aborigines, but their paintings on rocks, trees, weapons, and barks make us realize that they are able to express themselves in line, form, and color beyond the ability of most of us.

I know Mrs. Johnson well enough to be sure that she will appreciate this native art form with an unjaundiced eye, for the First Lady of the United States is a true nature lover.

I once heard her say that her only complaint about life in the White House was that never, never could she walk in the garden or breathe the air of outdoors, unnoticed and alone. I myself have spent many hours with her, watching the sunset over the hills from the terrace of the L.B.J. ranch house, wandering the paddocks in search of Indian arrowheads, or driving in the late afternoon looking for the wild deer at their feeding grounds and water holes.

She has a framed collection of arrowheads and uses it as a decoration in the big family sitting room, the one with the huge stone fireplace, and the coffee table made from a rough-cut slab of a Sherwood Forest tree—the

* The bark painting pioneers a new art form made solely of bark and lichen collected in the Victorian countryside. By Mrs. Mary Swensen and Mrs. Margot Pullman.

same Sherwood Forest that Robin Hood made famous. In this room the bark painting will no doubt find a place, and be at home there.

Many First Ladies of the United States are permanently enshrined in the hearts of their country people. Dolly Madison for wit and charm and for saving the White House paintings when the mansion was on fire; Eleanor Roosevelt for her great humanity; Jacqueline Kennedy for her taste and youthful charm. There was even one First Lady who will be forever known as "Lemonade Lucy" because she allowed no intoxicating beverages served in the White House.

When Lady Bird Johnson takes her place in history I am sure it will be because of her beautification program, the trees she has planted, the seeds she has sown, the ugliness she has helped to obliterate. The Lady Bird program does not emphasize beautiful botanical gardens but roadside plantings, removal of junk yards and tasteless signboards, preservation of forests, waterfalls, and pure running streams—the kind of beauty by which the life of even the humblest citizen can be enriched. Mrs. Johnson sighed wistfully that her busy schedule allowed her no time to enjoy the Australian countryside or to examine carefully the planned order of Canberra. Her baptismal name is Claudia, and she says Lady Bird is only a nickname that stuck. Long ago her intimates shortened it to "Bird" and I think it stuck because it was so appropriate to her interests and character.

May I thank you on behalf of this winsome lady for this precious piece of Australiana. I hope to see it many times when it hangs at home in Texas, and we have both retired to our private worlds with our neighbors and kinfolk.

United States Embassy Residence Kaleidoscopic Calendar
for the Year 1966

Co-authored by Anne Clark and
Levan Roberts, United States Information Officer

The Ambassador and Mrs. Clark left the Residence on the afternoon of Christmas Day, 1965, and left Sydney on December 27 for the U.S.A., where they remained until January 23, 1966.

On January 30 the first big function was an Open House for the Rotary Club, at which one thousand people viewed the house. From that time on the pace has never ceased. Another two thousand came through on October 2 for the benefit of the Red Cross.

Four important official delegations have visited the American Embassy in 1966, the first being the visit of Vice President and Mrs. Humphrey, including Roving Ambassador Averill Harriman, who had made a brief visit earlier in the year, and their entourage, which arrived February 18. On April 12 came the Inter-Parliamentary Union with fourteen United States representatives and senators and their wives. These included Senator Ralph Yarborough and Representative Bob Poage of Texas, personal friends of the Clarks. In June the SEATO Conference met in Canberra, immediately followed in the same week by ANZUS. Secretary of State Dean Rusk was quartered at the Residence, even though Ambassador and Mrs. Clark were again away in the United States. A visit planned to last only a few weeks lasted from May 19 to July 1, because Prime Minister Holt made his first official visit to Washington in late June. The Clarks returned in time for the July 4 Celebration, the Ambassador with the new title of Doctor of Laws (Southwestern University, Georgetown, Texas). Charlton Heston, Hollywood star, read poetry and patriotic selections for our National Day Function and stayed overnight at the Residence. The fourth official visit was that of the President of the United States and Mrs. Johnson. A wonderful occasion for all Americans and for the country of Australia. At least two congressmen, Miller of California and Wilson, also of California, have been houseguests.

Other American houseguests have been Mr. and Mrs. Arjay Miller of Detroit; Mr. and Mrs. Jack Blanton, Mr. and Mrs. Gus Wortham, Mrs. Lafayette Herring, all of Houston; Mr. and Mrs. Maurice Acers, W. W. Coates, Paul Bolton, Mary Scott and James Nash, all of Austin; Bob Burck and John Murchison of Dallas; Harlan Fentress of Waco; Ralph Brown of Corsicana; Benno Schmidt of New York; and Admiral and Mrs. Ramsey, Mrs. William Shelton and daughter, of Washington, D.C. Administrator and Mrs. Roger Dean of Darwin and Dame Mabel Brookes of Melbourne have also been guests.

The wedding reception for the daughter of Colonel and Mrs. Walter Divers was held at the Residence June 30, and in November an informal party preceded the wedding of two staff members, Madge Polumbo and Marine Sergeant Burlen Baker.

The heads of nearly every important business firm in America have visited the American Embassy during 1966. These included the chairmen of Time-Life, *Newsweek*, First National City Bank, Sears and Roebuck, Ford Motor Company, Alcoa, Standard Oil Company, Continental Oil, Union Oil, Phillips Oil, Humble Oil Company, United States Steel, General Foods, all the United States airlines, and Jim Farley of Coca Cola. A number of American labor leaders also have been visitors to the Residence. One of them, Harry Goldberg, vice president of the AFL-CIO, thrilled dinner guests with an impromptu concert of classical numbers on the Residence concert grand.

Mr. and Mrs. Clark have farewelled far too many of the staff members, leaving only two senior staff members who came before them. Ten Ambassadors have departed Canberra this year. Several warm friends from the Australian government, notably Sir Robert Menzies and Sir Frederick Scherger, have been farewelled from the Residence. Marjorie Turbayne joined the Residence staff as Social Secretary, February 1, and three Chinese have joined the staff at the Residence to make life more pleasant—LeeLee and Chan came from Hong Kong in August, and Hsu, a marvelous chef, from Taipei in September.

Ambassador and Mrs. Clark have had two parties for our staff's American teenagers and two for our wee people. The Christmas season will close with a children's party and a reception for all the Embassy people and their families. Two diplomatic tennis tournaments have been held during the year under Ambassador and Mrs. Clark's sponsorship. A number of delegations of Defense Department people have dined and lunched at the Residence; innumerable press conferences have been held in the sunroom; the Australian-American Association, senior and junior branches, and the Federal Congress of the Australian-American Association have been entertained. The ladies group of the Australian-American Association used the Residence for a large benefit bridge luncheon. Dozens of groups of traveling Americans and Australians have inspected the Residence and been refreshed with the American standbys—cokes and coffee: young Methodists, young Mormons, school children from Wagga Wagga, basketball players, golf players, the Melbourne Horticultural Society, the Air Ambulance ladies, United States teachers, and comparative education groups varying in membership from two or three to eighty-eight. The Embassy wives meet at the Residence once a month to discuss a topic of local or international interest. An official luncheon for the Prime Minister of Malta was held on November 11. Two large dinner dances were given, and lunches, receptions, and black-tie dinners were too numerous to mention.

It is the wish of the Ambassador and Mrs. Clark that all members of the Embassy staff regard the Residence as their "home away from home" and bring their friends to call and see the house. This applies whether the Clarks are in town or away and has resulted in the Residence being the most vis- ited chief-of-mission home in Canberra: 3,515 people signed the guest book up to December 15 and another 3,000 came on tours.

A number of additions have been made to the physical properties of the house. The Checker official car gave way to a Chrysler Imperial; the drive- way was made easier to negotiate by the removal of the grass island; a large car park back of the garage was constructed for the Presidential visit; Mrs. Johnson left her Kilroy mark by planting a tree to add to those already planted by Mrs. Roosevelt and Hale Boggs, the Democratic Whip of Con- gress, who put down a Texas pecan; a grandfather clock chimes in the foyer. Three brass fenders gleam at the fireplaces, and an ormolu clock and candlesticks grace the drawing-room mantlepiece; a Victorian epergne cen- ters the dining table; a black-and-white vinyl floor brings new usefulness to the sunroom; a bar in the corridor between library and sunroom makes thirst more quickly quenched; seating capacity has been increased by sev- enty-two gold ballroom chairs. Upstairs blue-and-white toile covers, crisp white curtains, and white counterpanes make the master bedroom more cheerful, and the bathrooms now have gay shower curtains and rugs. The flower room has been converted into a dull but useful serving pantry with bar, shelves, and stationary bottle openers. The tapestry, paintings, and Steuben glass, which are the personal possessions of the Clarks, make con- versation pieces along with their many personal souvenirs that have enter- tainment value rather than material worth.

The front door stands easily ajar, the phone jangles often, activity buzzes, there's a perfume of yellow roses, ice water is on the table, and a general air of Texas breeziness and Old South hospitality and warmth permeates the atmosphere.

Ambassador and Mrs. Clark took seriously the advice of the President, who said, "Be yourselves."

Commissioning by Mrs. Edward Clark at Newcastle
February 4, 1967

Mr. Chairman, Mr. Minister, My Lord Mayor, Fellow Americans, Kind Friends:

Though there are no new seas or unexplored rivers in the 1960's for the Christopher Columbuses and the Captain Cooks of today to sail upon, there *are* the unknown depths of the waters for our present-day adventurers. This craft is rightly named, for the adventurers who built her and the explorers who man her will be known in history as *our* pioneers. I now name this vessel *Investigator* and may the Lord "preserve thy going out and thy coming in from this time forth and even for evermore."

Australia and America: Two Countries We Join in Loving

Remarks by Mrs. Edward Clark before a Luncheon of the
Australian-American Association, Melbourne
November 21, 1967

Madame Chairman, Fellow Australians, and Fellow Americans:

As I look around I see so many of the faces that have made my stay in Australia happy and serene. I tell everyone at home, when I visit the United States, that Australia is the ideal post—certainly for the kind of American system that my husband represents and that I, in a small way, try to support.

Three things stand out. We have had no language barrier—even our Southern accents have been understood here. In fact, some of my Aussie friends say "Good mawnin', you all," to us now. We have had no health problems—never felt better in our lives. When American visitors are slightly inconvenienced by your strict quarantines, they must also be thankful that a ten-day visit is not spoilt by spending half of it coping with some indigenous ailment, as frequently happens in the Western half of the Southern Hemisphere, and that they don't take home with them some parasitic pest that might take years of battling. The only time I really raised a voice of complaint was about the bird of paradise plumes from New Guinea. The authorities were adamant, and my beautiful golden plumes now grace the museum in Port Moresby.

I solved the dog problem by acquiring a silky terrier here. He bears the auspicious name of Happy. I got him on New Year's Day, so he's a Happy New Year dog. I plan to take him home to perpetuate his breed in the United States. In fact, silkies have become my chief export. I have sent half a dozen home to various friends, and I am glad to report that they are making a good adjustment as immigrants. I noted that a silky won "'Best in Show" at a large dog show in America recently. And, because they are such charming pets, I predict that soon they will be one of our very popular breeds. Zsa Zsa Gabor is a silky owner.

Lastly, the quality that makes serving in Australia so delightful is the absence of hostile attitudes—nobody treats us like "Ugly Americans." I am told that in many places the natives ape American ways, even some of our less attractive customs like tight blue jeans and chewing gum, but nonetheless hiss and spit and jeer us. Australians certainly appear to like us. However, I must say now that your standards of manners and courtesy are so high that we would never guess if you did not. I have never encountered a bit of rudeness or lack of consideration anywhere in your country.

On our last trip from the United States, we changed to a Qantas flight in Honolulu. I was immediately struck by the charm, courtesy, and thoughtfulness of all the Qantas people. You should be very proud of them, for they are truly ambassadors of good will.

I stayed in the United States for two months. It was my private holiday away from official activities, parties, and dinners. I visited with my mother. She will be 91 on December 3 and is extremely alert and physically active. She still sews on the sewing machine, gardens enthusiastically, and goes to church twice a week.

My daughter—who is the light of our lives—has four children. The girls are nine, ten, and eleven years old; and the boy—she calls him her "little miracle in the crib"—is one year old. He was born during the President's visit to Australia.

I planted pomegranates and iris at my little house in East Texas, and a gum tree. We harvested the first pecan nuts from the pecan trees while I was there and gathered pine cones for kindling next winter's fires.

The season was lovely. It was glorious autumn in the Virginia countryside around Washington. The leaves were turning yellow and red. In East Texas, where I have my little house, we don't see as much change in seasons, because the trees are all pines. In fact, my husband frequently says he is not a rancher, but a "tree farmer." We harvest the pines regularly, every few years, sometimes for pulp wood to manufacture paper and sometimes for sawtimber.

The dogwood trees make particularly beautiful red leaves. It is one of my little jokes that in Australia the dogwood is the American national flower and Thanksgiving is our national holiday. Were I there now one of my duties would be to decorate the church for Thanksgiving—it's a harvest festival and we load the altar with the fruit of the field: pumpkins and squash and persimmons and apples and corn and grapes, which we later distribute to needy families. My first year in Australia I received a letter from my altar guild asking me to send something from Australia for the decoration. The only thing that could travel was a box of your beautiful dried flowers, the ever-lastings in heather and flannel flower, which blended with the fruits and vegetables. They were sensational—I received a number of letters about them and many friends took the trouble to make snapshots and slides to send me.

In the northern part of the United States they sometimes have snow, but in my region—the South—a crisp cool day for the football games is the most we can hope for. One of my friends says it is her favorite holiday— she doesn't have to buy anybody a present—or even a new hat for herself— just cook dinner. Mine would be a mid-day meal—served early for the football fans' convenience. If we don't go, we want to at least watch it on television. Because of an expandable company we no longer spread the table with damask; we have a buffet—with turkey and ham, sweet potatoes with marshmallows and brandy, corn bread stuffing for the turkey, squash or turnips, grapefruit salad with poppy-seed dressing, inevitably cranberry sauce and perhaps peach pickle too, and hot rolls, and for dessert maybe ambrosia—a combination of oranges, pineapple, and coconut—or brownies. The day after Thanksgiving we start Christmas shopping and by the first week in December we have a wreath on the door. All too soon, my quiet little family time was over.

Of course, when my husband, the Ambassador, arrived for two weeks, pandemonium broke. We spent a family evening at the White House with the President and Mrs. Johnson. Lynda and her fiance, Chuck, were there, and we were able to personally present her with the white kangaroo coat that we had had made especially for her wedding present. She loved it. Chuck is a wholesome young American and Lynda's parents are thoroughly pleased with her choice. We had corn muffins and peach preserves from the Ranch for dinner.

When Mrs. Johnson came to Texas the following week to receive an honorary degree from *my* husband's old college—Southwestern University at Georgetown, Texas—and I must say there was not a demonstrator or a peace-nik visible—I saw Luci and her young husband, Pat, and their fat blonde cherub, whom the President says looks just like Winston Churchill. My husband opened the Mertz Collection of Australian Art at The University of Texas—five hundred invited guests showed up at four o'clock on a mid-week afternoon and the Chancellor of the University said that earlier in the day two thousand students had trooped through the galleries to see it. Such is the impact that Australia is having in the United States. Say the word and you can get up a crowd.

The University of Texas enrollment is now in excess of thirty thousand students. It has grown tremendously in my absence. It is the sixth largest campus in the United States. I guess there must be some of those horrible people around that I read of in the papers, but in the several weeks that I was on campus daily, I never saw a one. The boys had neatly trimmed hair and the girls were adorably shiny and fresh.

I've talked a lot and I certainly haven't said anything very profound—but I am no official spokesman. I didn't think you invited me to talk about all the grim problems that fill the newspapers and magazines today, so my theme has been just feminine chatter about the two countries we join in loving. It is obvious that I don't find much wrong with either of them.

To the complainers and critics of either of my beloved countries, I hurl in their teeth the all-comprehensive phrase that I've learned here in Australia —"Oh, she'll be right!"

Farewell Toast to Mrs. Edward Clark by Betty Smith
on Behalf of the Embassy Wives at a Farewell Dinner
for Ambassador and Mrs. Clark, Noah's Restaurant, Canberra
December 29, 1967

Several months ago some of us experienced the departure of a diplomat's wife—not in our embassy, thank goodness—who was frankly and almost deliriously happy to leave Canberra. Her outspoken joy and positive GLEE embarrassed many of us who were her close friends. Now we know that Anne Clark is one of the happiest people in Canberra as she awaits her return to home and family. But what a difference! We have nothing but deep PRIDE in the way she is making HER departure. She has given so generously of herself at ALL times to know and to love Australia and its people, and they love her in return.

It is sometimes said that the Residence is the swingingest place in Canberra, and it certainly is the envy of all our colleagues. We all know how generous Mrs. Clark has been in opening the Residence as a venue for those functions, the Australian-American Association among many to be very much in her debt. She will certainly never forget those sometimes mad occasions when the cook and staff stood aside in awe and consternation as an army of women moved into that sanctum—the kitchen—with literally bathtubs of cole slaw, chicken salad, and small mountains of scones and brownies.

But large organizations are not the only ones that have benefited—let us not forget that our children have played cops and robbers in the Embassy grounds, have dropped hamburgers and ice cream on the drawing-room rugs—making interesting patterns with the cigarette burns, the latter made by yet some other hundreds of groups that have enjoyed embassy hospitality Texas Anne and Ed style.

In all of this Mrs. Clark has set us an example of very hard work and intense interest in everything that was going on—although all too frequently she was seemingly involved in what MUST have been a double schedule!

She has unique concern for people and especially their personal interests. There always seems to be time to dispatch a clipping on *art nouveau* or modern liturgy, or a new recipe for her now-famous pot pourri or even for eggs Benedict. AND how can we ever thank her for discovering the now ubiquitous Southern Cross brooch!

One of the most vivid memories of our arrival in Schlich Street will always be a conversation with our gardener. In a "getting to know you" session he asked me quite candidly if it weren't true that all embassy wives received salaries, too? He very sympathetically said he had never seen such a hard-working group of women in his entire life! I had great amusement and a difficult time, too, persuading him that this certainly wasn't the case—but I thought it a smashing idea!

So, with our very hard-working Ambassador's wife returning to Washington, I should like to propose, girls, that we appoint Mrs. Clark our No. 1 lobbyist for the FSWS—Foreign Service Wives' Salaries. Who better could continue to serve us—the POOR, ignored, overworked, but Better Half of the Foreign Service—than one whose own devotion and hard work have been above ALL PRICE!

II

Presentation to His Excellency the Administrator of
Letters of Credence by Mr. Edward Clark
Ambassador Designate of the United States of America
at Government House, Canberra
Monday, 23rd August, 1965

(1) 10.39 a.m. Mr. K. Douglas-Scott, Chief of Protocol, Department of External Affairs, and Mr. G. Pretyman arrive at the State Entrance of Government House.

(2) 10.42 a.m. Mr. Douglas-Scott and Mr. Pretyman leave Government House in Rolls Royce No. 2 with Police Motor Cycle Escort for the United States Embassy, State Circle, Yarralumla.

(3) 10.47 a.m. Mr. Douglas-Scott and Mr. Pretyman present themselves to the Ambassador Designate and invite him and his Staff to accompany them to Government House.

(4) 10.50 a.m. The Honourable Paul Hasluck, Minister for External Affairs, arrives at the Private Entrance to Government House where he is met by Flight Lieutenant D.W. Owens, RAAF, who conducts the Minister to the Administrator's study.

(5) 10.52 a.m. The Ambassador Designate, accompanied by his Staff, Mr. Douglas-Scott and Mr. Pretyman, leave the United States Embassy, State Circle, Yarralumla, with Police Motor Cycle Escort.

(6) 10.57 a.m. The Ambassador Designate arrives at the State Entrance of Government House and alights left hand side to be met by Captain R.M. Keep, A.M.F.

The remainder of the cars stop short of the portico and the Staff and Mr. Pretyman alight right hand side and stand facing the Guard of Honour.

The Rolls Royce moves clear of the portico.

(7)   The Ambassador Designate moves to a position in the

centre of the portico facing the Guard of Honour as follows :—

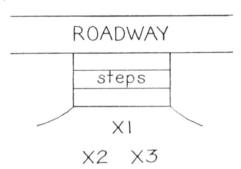

1. The Ambassador Designate
2. Mr. Douglas-Scott
3. Captain Keep

(8)   The Guard of Honour is provided by the Royal Australian
Navy (Guard Commander Lieutenant Elliott, R.A.N.).

The Band is provided by the Royal Military College,
Duntroon.

(9)   When all are in position, the Guard Commander orders
"National Salute Slope Arms".

The Band plays the National Anthem of the United States
of America.

(10) 10.58 a.m. On completion of the playing of the National Anthem,
the Ambassador Designate, accompanied by his Staff and
attended by Mr. Douglas-Scott, Mr. Pretyman and Captain
Keep, enters Government House where the Ambassador
Designate is met by Lieutenant-Commander K.A. Doolan,
R.A.N., Military Secretary, who presents the following
members of the Personal Staff :—

Mr. M.L. Tyrrell, Official Secretary; Lieutenant-Colonel
T.A. Rodriguez, Comptroller; Flight Lieutenant D.W.
Owens, RAAF, Aide-de-Camp Air

(11)   Lieutenant-Commander Doolan conducts the Ambassador
Designate and his Staff to the western end of the drawing
room (curtains drawn).

(12) 10.59 a.m. Captain Keep informs the Administrator of the arrival of the Ambassador Designate and conducts His Excellency and the Minister to the eastern end of the drawing room.

(13) 11.00 a.m. The Ambassador Designate is informed by Lieutenant-Commander Doolan that the Administrator will be pleased to receive him.

The curtains are opened by two Footmen (to be nominated by Colonel Rodriguez) and the Ambassador Designate, his Staff, Mr. Douglas-Scott and Mr. Pretyman are conducted to the eastern end of the drawing room . . .

Schedule for the Official Visit to Hobart, Tasmania, October 1965

GOVERNMENT HOUSE
HOBART
TASMANIA

His Excellency the Administrator	)
The Honourable Sir Stanley Burbury, K.B.E.	) not in
and Lady Burbury	) residence
	)
The Honourable Lady Gairdner	in residence

Personal Staff
Official Secretary   E. E. O'Farrell, M.V.O.

Aide-de-Camp   Captain the Hon. H.D. Hotham
                                              Grenadier Guards.

Honorary Aides-de-Camp   Lt. B. D. Knight, R.A.N.V.R.
                                              Lt. W.J.E. Cox, R.A.A.
                                              Flt.-Lt. L.V. Lovegrove, R.A.A.F.

Personal Secretary
to Lady Gairdner   Miss Joyce Walpole

Domestic Staff Butler   Mr. R. Saunders
                      Head Cook   Mrs. A. Orpan
                      Head Housemaid   Mrs. D. Long
                      Footmen   Mr. Brian Snee
                                              Mr. Barry Conlan

Parlourmaid	Miss Dianne O'Connor
Housemaids	Miss Maisie Nillson
	Miss Margaret White
Lady Gairdner's Personal Maid	Mrs. W. Gardner
Garage	Mr. F. Webb
	Mr. H. Childs

GOVERNMENT HOUSE
HOBART
TASMANIA

M A I L

Mail is delivered to Government House at 9.00a.m. Mondays to Saturday, and at 2.00p.m. Monday to Friday.

Guests incoming mail will be placed on the Hall table.

Outgoing mail is taken to the G.P.O. at 1.30p.m. and at 5.00p.m., Mondays to Friday.

Guests outgoing mail should be handed to the Aide-de-Camp or left on the Hall table.

The Messenger will deliver letters within Hobart, or carry out any messages at 11.00a.m., 1.30p.m. and 3.00p.m.

M E A L S

Breakfast—Weekdays	8.30a.m.—9.00a.m.
Sundays	9.00a.m.—9.30a.m.
	(by arrangement)
Lunch	1.00p.m.
Tea	4.30p.m.
Dinner	7.30p.m.
Sunday Supper	7.00p.m.
	(unless alternative times
	indicated on Daily Programme).

T E L E P H O N E

A telephone is located at the bottom end of the Upstairs Hall, and in the Library. Outside calls may be made by pressing down either of the red buttons at the top, and dialing the number required. If a buzzing noise occurs when you press the red button, the line is engaged. In the event of difficulty, or trunk line calls, please contact the Aide-de-Camp.

Vice-Regal Engagements for the Week Ending
Sunday 10th October, 1965

Monday 4th October.

9.50 a.m.   His Excellency the Ambassador for the United States of Amer-
(approx.)   ica departs Government House to call on the Premier. (Out to
               Luncheon).

                                                    Commonwealth Vehicle.

12.35 p.m.   Mrs. E. A. Clark departs Government House for Luncheon at
(approx.)   the Wrest Point Hotel. (Out to Luncheon).

                                                    Bentley and afterwards
                                                    to Parliament House.

1.00 p.m.   Luncheon for 3 at Government House.

7.15 p.m.   Dinner for 5.

8.20 p.m.   His Excellency the Ambassador and Mrs. Clark depart Govern-
(approx.)   ment House for a Reception given by the Australian-American
               Association at the Naval, Military and Air Force Club.

                                                    Commonwealth Vehicle.

8.30 p.m.   His Excellency arrives at the Town Hall for the Annual Gen-
               eral Meeting of the Tasmanian Branch of the Australian Boy
               Scouts Association.

               Lieutenant Cox   Princess from Rosetta
               (Dark Suit.)   7.48 p.m.
               His Excellency will be met by the Chief Commissioner and
               State President.
               Details on Separate Brief.

Tuesday 5th October.

9.30 a.m.   His Excellency arrives at Franklin Square to preside over a
               meeting of the Executive Council.
               Captain Hotham   Princess 9.23 a.m.

10.40 a.m.   His Excellency the Ambassador and Mrs. Clark depart Govern-
(approx.)   ment House for a Civic Reception.

                                                    Commonwealth Vehicle.

12.30 p.m.   The following Guests arrive for Luncheon :—
                     The Honourable the Premier and Mrs. E. E. Reece
                     Mr. R. Hutchison and Mrs. Hutchison
                     Mr. A. L. Ellis and Mrs. Ellis
                     Mr. J. W. Hutchinson and Mrs. Hutchinson
                     Mr. H. M. Murray and Mrs. Murray
                     Mr. G. T. Wilkinson and Mrs. Wilkinson
                     Mr. R. W. Henry and Mrs. Henry
                     Mr. T. A. Frankcomb and Mrs. Frankcomb
                     Mrs. P. Wilson

1.00 p.m.   Luncheon for 30.

4.30 p.m.   His Excellency the Ambassador and Mrs. Clark depart Llan-
                     herne on A.N.A. Flight Number 156.

                     Captain Hotham   Bentley Luggage 3.45 p.m.
                                                                        Princess 4.05 p.m.

Wednesday 6th October.

9.30 a.m.   His Excellency receives Mr. P. Fletcher.

10.00 p.m.   Lady Burbury, accompanied by Mrs. E. E. O'Farrell, departs
                     from Rosetta for Launceston.

                                                                        Bentley from Rossbank
                                                                        9.50 a.m.

12.30 p.m.   Lady Burbury and Mrs. O'Farrell arrive at the St. James Hotel.
(approx.)

                     (Programme to follow but provisionally, 1.00 p.m. Luncheon
                     at the St. James Hotel; 3.15 p.m. Lady Burbury opens the
                     Women's Section of the Show; 8.00 p.m. Lady Burbury will
                     attend the Womens' Show Judge's Meeting and Supper Party.)

Thursday 7th October.

                     Programme to follow but provisionally :—

9.00 a.m.   His Excellency departs Rosetta for Launceston.

                     Captain Hotham   Princess from Government
                                                                        House 8.45 a.m.

11.30 a.m.   Arrive at the St. James Hotel.

11.45 a.m.   Luncheon.

1.55 p.m.   His Excellency, accompanied by Lady Burbury, opens the Launceston Show.

6.30 p.m.   His Excellency and Lady Burbury attend Launceston Club an-
(approx.)   nual Showday Party.

Friday 8th October.
    PROVISIONAL:
a.m.   His Excellency presides over a Winston Churchill Fellow-Ship Selection Committee Meeting.

p.m.   His Excellency and Lady Burbury return to Government House.

Saturday 9th October.
2.20 p.m.   His Excellency and Lady Burbury arrive at Waterman's Dock (far side) to board the Marine Board launch Egeria.

               Captain Hotham   Princess from Rosetta
               (Dark Suit)   2.05 p.m.

               His Excellency and Lady Burbury will be met by the Deputy Master Warden of the Marine Board, Mr. Wells and the Harbour Master, Captain Copeland, who will conduct His Excellency and Lady Burbury aboard.

               The following will be present.

               Mr. Neil Batt of the Royal Yacht Club of Tasmania and Wardens of the Hobart Marine Board and their wives.

               The Egeria will move to a position off Castray Esplanade where she will be moored.

               The Sail Past will take place—His Excellency will take the salute and will be invited to choose the best dinghy.

               The Egeria will move to a suitable position for afternoon tea.

               The three Commodores, Commodore Geeves, R.Y.C.T., Commodore Blackwood, D.S.S. and Commodore O'May, B.Y.C. will come aboard to pay their respects to His Excellency.

4.30 p.m.   His Excellency and Lady Burbury return to Waterman's Dock.
(approx.)

Sunday 10th October.
9.40 a.m.   His Excellency arrives at the Cenotaph for the Navy Week wreath laying ceremony.

Captain Hotham   Princess from Rosetta
                                                  9.18 p.m.

His Excellency will be met by Commander J. G. B. Campbell and the President of the Naval Association, Mr. Don Arnold.

His Excellency will move to the Saluting Point.

Royal Salute.

His Excellency inspects a Guard of Honour of Sea Scouts.

His Excellency moves to position in line of Wreath Layers.

His Excellency places wreath (on easel) and returns to the line.

Last Post.

Reveille.

His Excellency departs.

9.55 a.m.   (or later if necessary to allow officials at Wreath placing cere-
             mony to arrive first).

             His Excellency arrives at St. George's, Battery Point to attend
             the 31st Annual Mariners Service.

             His Excellency will be met by the Reverend A. George Rey-
             nolds and will be conducted to the Right hand front pew.
             Through a Guard of Honour consisting of men of the parish
             and representatives of shipping companies and yachting Clubs.
             The flags will be trooped in.

             His Excellency will read the 2nd Lesson, St. Mark Chapter
             4 v. 35—end.

             During the last hymn after singing the National Anthem the
             flags will be trooped out.

12.05 P.M.   His Excellency* will depart.
(approx.)

    * This "His Excellency" refers to Sir Stanley Burbury, Acting Governor of
Tasmania. His schedule was also in our room to keep us informed of his move-
ments. Sir Charles Gairdner was in England, but Lady Gairdner was in residence. To avoid protocol problems, Lady Gairdner and Lady Burbury never
appeared together.

A Guide to Events in and around Adelaide
during the Next Fortnight

ADELAIDE FESTIVAL OF ARTS EDITION
10th–26th March [1966]

WEDNESDAY 23rd MARCH
(Adelaide's National Flower Day)

PICCADILLY THEATRE	10.00 a.m.	MARIONETTES, Tintookies.
VICTORIA SQUARE	10.00 a.m.	OFFICIAL OPENING OF FLOWER DAY by the Premier, Hon. Frank Walsh.
	10.20 a.m.	CROWNING OF THE QUEEN OF FLOWERS by Mrs. Walsh.
	10.45 a.m.	FLOWER DAY PROCESSION.
PENNINGTON HALL	11.00 a.m.	MUSIC, Music and Manners No. 5 (Great Britain).
MYER EMPORIUM	11.30 a.m.	WINE TASTINGS, a selec-
(8th Floor)	1.30 p.m.	tion of 75 of South Austra-
	3.30 p.m.	lia's choicest wines.
WAY HALL	12.10 p.m.	THEATRE, The Masquerade
	1.10 p.m.	Mime Theatre.
MEAD HALL	12.10 p.m.	INTIMATE OPERA GROUP
	1.10 p.m.	INTIMATE OPERA GROUP
ARTS THEATRE	1.10 p.m.	THEATRE, Shaw on Love and War.
ADELAIDE TEACHERS COLLEGE THEATRE	2.00 p.m.	THEATRE, The Athens Drama Company, Lysistrata.
PICCADILLY THEATRE	2.00 p.m.	MARIONETTES, Tintookies.
NORWOOD TOWN HALL	2.00 p.m.	FOLK OPERA, Porgy and Bess.
HER MAJESTY'S THEATRE	2.00 p.m.	BALLET, Australian Ballet.

ELDER HALL	3.00 p.m.	RECITAL, International Society of Contemporary Music (Sydney).
ARKABA	3.00 p.m.	MUSIC, The Engel Family.

THURSDAY 24th MARCH

CENTENNIAL HALL	10.00 a.m.	MUSIC, Australian Youth Orchestra.
PENNINGTON HALL	11.00 a.m.	MUSIC, The Age of Monteverdi.
CENTENNIAL HALL	11.30 a.m.	MUSIC, Australian Youth Orchestra.
MYER EMPORIUM (8th Floor)	11.30 a.m. 1.30 p.m. 3.30 p.m.	WINE TASTINGS, a selection of 75 of South Australia's choicest wines.
WAY HALL	12.10 p.m. 1.10 p.m.	THEATRE, The Masquerade Mime Theatre.
MEAD HALL	12.10 p.m. 1.10 p.m.	INTIMATE OPERA GROUP INTIMATE OPERA GROUP
VICTORIA SQUARE	2.30 p.m.	BAND, S. A. Police Band.
ELDER HALL	1.00 p.m.	RECITAL, John Kennedy (cello), Clemens Leske (piano).
ARTS THEATRE	1.10 p.m.	THEATRE, Shaw on Love and War.
PICCADILLY THEATRE	2.00 p.m.	MARIONETTES, Tintookies.
CENTENNIAL HALL	2.00 p.m.	MUSIC, Australian Youth Orchestra.
ELDER HALL	3.00 p.m.	RECITAL, Dr. J. V. Peters (organ).
GOVERNMENT HOUSE	3.10 p.m.	QUEEN MOTHER departs to attend Garden Party at Pinky Flat. Returning 4.15 p.m.

LORD MAYORAL GARDEN PARTY
for the Queen Mother
Pinky Flat, Thursday, 24th March, 1966

DETAILED ARRANGEMENTS

1.30 p.m.   All Corporation Inspectors will take up duty positions as detailed.

2.15 p.m.   The Lord Mayor and the Lady Mayoress will arrive at Pinky Flat.

2.30 p.m.   The Lord Mayor and the Lady Mayoress, accompanied by the Town Clerk and Mrs. Arland, standing on the dais, will commence the receiving of guests, who will be formed into a line by Corporation Inspectors and file along the bitumen roadway past the dais.

2.50 p.m.   The receiving of guests will cease, and the roadway from Gate No. 4 will be cleared by Corporation Inspectors.

In a position on the western side of the dais, Aldermen and their ladies, with Councillors Bridgland and Cook and their escorts, will be in readiness to act as hosts to Ambassadors.

The carpet runner from the front steps of the dais will be laid out across the roadway for a distance of some 10 feet, and tacked down.

2.55 p.m.   *Ambassadors will commence arriving in their motor vehicles, which will enter via Gate No. 4 and draw up in front of the dais. The Ambassadors will ascend to the dais by the front steps and be received by the Lord Mayor and the Lady Mayoress.*

Corporation Inspectors will act as door-openers.

Immediately after being received by the Lord Mayor, Aldermen and the two Councillors will act as hosts to these Ambassadors, as follows:—

Alderman and Mrs. Gerald will act as hosts to His Excellency Dr. J. F. Ritter, K.C.V.O., Ambassador for Germany, and Mrs. Ritter;

> Alderman and Mrs. Nicholls will act as hosts to His Excellency Mr. W. Van Cauwenberg, Ambassador for Belgium, and Mme. Van Cauwenberg;
>
> Alderman and Mrs. Porter will act as hosts to His Excellency Mr. J. Luke Hazlett, High Commissioner for New Zealand, and Mrs. Hazlett.
>
> Councillor Mrs. E. and Mr. Cook will act as hosts to His Excellency Mr. E. Clark, Ambassador for the United States of America, and Mrs. Clark;
>
> Councillor and Mrs. Bridgland will act as hosts to His Excellency Mr. D. S. Tesher, Ambassador for Israel, and Mrs. Tesher.

It is suggested that the Aldermen and their ladies and the two Councillors with their escorts, should ascend to the dais by the steps on the western side, greet the Ambassadors and then escort the latter from the dais by the steps on the eastern side.

The order in which the Ambassadors will be received cannot be forecast, as it is not known in which order their vehicles will arrive, but Mr. John Williams will be in the vicinity of the dais, and will assist the Aldermen and the two Councillors in identifying their special guests.

3.00 p.m.   Six Army and six Air Force Officers will assemble and prepare to form up prior to moving to position in front of the dais.

The Police trumpeters will take up position.

3.05 p.m.   The Hon. the Premier and Mrs. Walsh will arrive, and be received.

Alderman and Mrs. Hargrave will act as hosts.

3.10 p.m.   His Honour the Chief Justice will arrive, and be received.

Alderman and Mrs. Glover will act as hosts.

Mrs. Arland will leave the dais escorted by Mr. Williams.

3.11 p.m.   The bands will cease playing. If necessary, the carpet will be brushed to remove dust. The Army and Air Force Officers will march to positions on the northern side of the bitumen road opposite the dais, as marked by steel studs in the roadway. They will be joined by four Corporation Inspectors, two of whom will take up position on the eastern end of the line formed by the Army Officers, and two on the western end. The two Corporation Inspectors near the dais will remain near the dais.

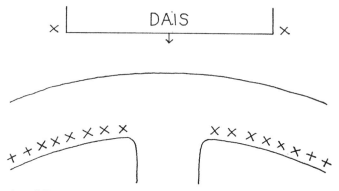

A public announcement will be made on behalf of the Lord Mayor.

The Lord Mayor, the Lady Mayoress and the Town Clerk will move to the front of the dais to receive Her Majesty.

Members of the Council and their ladies will assemble in rear of the dais.

3.14 p.m.   Her Majesty Queen Elizabeth The Queen Mother will arrive via Gate No. 4. There will be some 6 or 7 vehicles in the convoy and, as Her Majesty's vehicle turns into the gateway, the trumpeters will commence playing a fanfare, which will cease
3.15 p.m.   as Her Majesty's vehicle halts opposite the dais.

Police Cadets will act as door-openers to four vehicles in the convoy.

Her Majesty will alight and be received by the Lord Mayor and the Lady Mayoress.

Her Majesty's Standard will be broken by Army personnel.

The vehicles forming the convoy will move in an easterly direction along the bitumen road, and will enter the special area reserved for them.

Her Majesty will be escorted to the dais by the Lord Mayor and the Lady Mayoress, accompanied by the Town Clerk.

Positions as shown hereunder, will be indicated by thumb tacks on the dais carpet:—

Equerry ×	Lady-in-Waiting ×	Town Clerk ×
Lady Mayoress ×	Queen Mother ×	Lord Mayor ×

↓

When Her Majesty has taken up her position facing front on the dais, Central Command Band will play the National Anthem.

3.17–
3.20 p.m.

Her Majesty, accompanied by the Lord Mayor, the Lady Mayoress, the Town Clerk, the Lady-in-Waiting and an Equerry, will descend from the dais, and traverse a route tending towards the Lake.

To make way for Her Majesty's party, four Corporation Inspectors (two from the western end of the line and two from the dais) will form the point of a diamond, to be completed by the twelve Army and Air Force Officers, which will surround the party, with two Corporation Inspectors at the rear. This diamond formation will be formed by the six Army Officers from the east taking up position on Her Majesty's right, and the six Air Force Officers taking up position of the left as shown:—

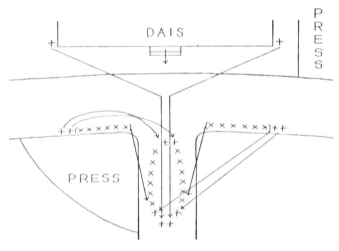

Lengths of white rope with snap hooks at one end and eyes at the other will be issued to Army and Air Force Officers and, if the guests appear likely to press in upon Her Majesty, the ropes will be joined and passed along each row of Officers. This rope will be held about waist high, except when it is raised above head height to facilitate the entry of guests to be presented on the perambulation. Having been presented, guests will leave the roped enclosure via the opening between the two rear Corporation Inspectors.

This formation will be maintained throughout the route taken to the marquee, the hollow centre containing Her Majesty, the Lord Mayor, the Lady Mayoress, the Town Clerk, the Lady-in-Waiting, the Equerry, and some Aides-de-Camp, who will assist in selecting guests to be presented to Her Majesty.

The approximate route to be followed will be plotted and shown to the Officers concerned, so that they may lead the party back to the "Special Guests" marquee at approximately 3.55 p.m.

3.45 p.m.   Members of the Council and their ladies will proceed to the vicinity of Marquee A, preparatory to Her Majesty's entrance and in anticipation of being presented. Mr. John Williams will take up position at the appropriate site, and will assist Members to form up in order of presentation.

3.50–
3.55 p.m.   The four leading Corporation Inspectors from the escort, when a few yards from the "Special Guests" area, will leave the escort, and take up position outside the entrance to the "Special Guests" marquee roped area, and will form portion of the guard of honour.

Her Majesty, under escort, will arrive at the "Special Guests" marquee where Members and their ladies will be presented. Those presented will be ready to move forward shortly after Her Majesty reaches the marquee. The route for presentation will be:—

In the northern end of the Special Marquee, the formation for presentation of guests will be:—

As the presentation is to commence, Mr. John Williams will take up position at the entrance to the Special Marquee, and will indicate to Members and their ladies the appropriate time to enter the marquee. Having been presented, Members and their ladies will move to the other end of the marquee.

All presentations having been made, Her Majesty may then take afternoon tea with the Lord Mayor, the Lady Mayoress and selected guests. The caterer will provide tables, chairs etc. as arranged, in anticipation of Her Majesty taking afternoon tea.

The South Australian Ladies Highland Pipe Band will play for a specified time. Mr. Williams will signal when the presentation has ceased.

4.12 p.m.   The vehicles forming Her Majesty's convoy will move from their parking area and take up position facing north on the roadway adjacent to the "Special Guests" marquee.

4.15 p.m.   The Lord Mayor and the Lady Mayoress, with the Town Clerk and Mrs. Arland, will escort Her Majesty to a point near her vehicle.

Police Cadets will again act as door-openers.

Her Majesty will then be farewelled, and, with her suite, enter their vehicles, which will move off through Gate No. 4 to War Memorial Drive, en route to Government House.

The National Anthem will be played by Central Command Band as the Royal Car moves off.

STATE VISIT TO NEW SOUTH WALES

by

THE HONOURABLE LYNDON B. JOHNSON

President of the United States of America

and Mrs. JOHNSON

Saturday, 22nd October, 1966

PROGRAMME

Arrival at Sydney Airport

11.00 a.m. The President's aircraft arrives at Sydney Airport.

The President and Mrs. Johnson alight from the aircraft by the front steps and are received by:

His Excellency the Governor of New South Wales and Lady Cutler.

The Premier of New South Wales and Mrs. Askin.

The American Consul General and Mrs. Capella.

standing in line facing the aircraft.

The American Flag is broken as the President emerges from the aircraft.

While greetings are taking place the Prime Minister and Mrs.

Holt and the American Ambassador and Mrs. Clark leave the aircraft by the front steps.

Other members of the President's party leave the aircraft by the rear steps.

The President with the Governor on his right and the Premier on his left, walk to a dais.

The Premier welcomes the President.

The President speaks.

The Vice-Regal car moves forward.

The Governor and Lady Cutler enter the Vice-Regal Car and depart for Government House.

The President's car and Mrs. Johnson's car move forward.

The Prime Minister, the Premier and the American Ambassador enter the President's car.

Mrs. Holt, Mrs. Askin and Mrs. Clark are escorted to Mrs. Johnson's car.

The President and Mrs. Johnson may walk to the barrier.

The President and Mrs. Johnson enter their cars.

Other members of the President's party enter their vehicles.

11.15 a.m.   The journey to the Art Gallery commences.

The American flag is struck as the President's car moves off.

Route: O'Riordan Street,
       King Street,
       Florence Street,
       Gardeners Road,
       Anzac Parade,
       Flinders Street,
       Oxford Street,
       Liverpool Street,
       George Street,
       King Street,
       Queen's Square,
       Prince Albert Road,
       Art Gallery Road.
                  Distance 9.1 M.

Order of motorcade—notified separately.

Joint Commonwealth and
State Reception

12.15 p.m.   The President and Mrs. Johnson, the Prime Minister and Mrs. Holt, the Premier and Mrs. Askin and the American Ambassador and Mrs. Clark arrive at the Art Gallery of New South Wales.

The American flag is broken as the President steps from his car.

The President, accompanied by the Prime Minister and the Premier, and Mrs. Johnson, accompanied by Mrs. Holt, and Mrs. Askin, may inspect a display of Australian trees and plants and animals at the entrance to the Art Gallery.

The Premier makes a presentation to the President of a pair of white kangaroos.

They then enter the building.

In the vestibule the Premier presents to the President—

Sir Edward Hallstrom, Executive Director of the Taronga Zoological Park.

The party then moves into the North-Western Gallery and the President and Mrs. Johnson continue into the Board Room.

The President and Mrs. Johnson return from the Board Room and are conducted by the Premier to a position where the Premier, standing on the right of the President, presents—

The Hon. Sir Kenneth Street, K.C.M.G., K.St.J., Lieutenant-Governor of New South Wales and Lady Street.

The Hon. Sir Leslie Herron, K.B.E., C.M.G., Chief Justice of New South Wales and Lady Herron.

The Hon. C. B. Cutler, E.D., M.L.A., Deputy Premier and Minister for Education and Science and Mrs. Culter.

The Hon. E. A. Willis, B.A., M.L.A., Minister for Labour and Industry, Chief Secretary and Minister for Tourist Activities and Mrs. Willis.

The Hon. A. D. Bridges, M.L.C., Minister for Child Welfare and Social Welfare, Advisory Minister for Transport and Vice-President of the Executive Council and Mrs. Bridges.

The Hon. W. A. Chaffey, M.L.A., Minister for Agriculture and Mrs. Chaffey.

The Hon. K. M. McCaw, M.L.A., Attorney General and Mrs. D. Rothwell.

The Hon. P. H. Morton, M.L.A., Minister for Local Government and Highways and Mrs. Morton.

The Hon. Davis Hughes, M.L.A., Minister for Public Works and Mrs. Hughes.

The Hon. J. B. M. Fuller, M.L.C., Minister for Decentralisation and Development and Mrs. Fuller.

The Hon. T. L. Lewis, M.L.A., Minister for Lands and Mines and Mrs. Lewis.

The Hon. J. G. Beale, M.E., M.L.A., Minister for Conservation and Mrs. Beale.

The Hon. S. T. Stephens, M.L.A., Minister for Housing and Co-operative Societies and Mrs. Stephens.

The Hon. J. C. Maddison, B.A., LL.B., M.L.A., Minister of Justice and Mrs. Maddison.

The Hon. A. H. Jago, M.L.A., Minister for Health and Mrs. Jago.

The Hon. W. C. Fife, M.L.A., Assistant Minister for Education and Mrs. Fife.

The Most Rev. M. L. Loane, M.A., D.D., Anglican Archbishop of Sydney and Mrs. Loane.

The Most Rev. James Carroll, D.D., D.C.L., Roman Catholic Auxiliary Archbishop of Sydney.

The Hon. H. V. Budd, M.L.C., President of the Legislative Council and Mrs. Budd.

The Hon. Kevin Ellis, L.L.B., B.Ec., M.L.A., Speaker of the Legislative Assembly and Mrs. Ellis.

Mr. J. B. Renshaw, M.L.A., Leader of the New South Wales Opposition and Mrs. Renshaw.

The Rt. Hon. the Lord Mayor of Sydney, (Alderman the Hon. J. A. Armstrong) and the Lady Mayoress.

Guests proceed to the Main Hall after being presented.

The President returns to the Board Room where he meets—

Sir Frank Packer, C.B.E., Chairman of Directors, Australian Consolidated Press Ltd.

Mr. Warwick O. Fairfax, Chairman of Directors, John Fairfax and Sons Ltd.

Mr. K. R. Murdoch, Chairman of Directors and Managing Director, Mirror Newspapers Ltd.

Mrs. Johnson remains with the Prime Minister and Mrs. Holt, the Premier and Mrs. Askin who are joined by Lady Packer and Mrs. Fairfax.

When the President returns to the Gallery he is accompanied by the Prime Minister and the Premier and Mrs. Johnson is accompanied by Mrs. Holt and Mrs. Askin to a low dais in the Main Hall.

Positions on dais—

	Prime Minister	Mrs. Holt
Front	President	Mrs. Johnson
	Premier	Mrs. Askin

The American Ambassador and Mrs. Clark and other members of the President's party remain on the right of the dais.

The Prime Minister and the Premier in turn welcome the President and Mrs. Johnson.

The President responds.

The President, accompanied by the Prime Minister and the Premier, and Mrs. Johnson, accompanied by Mrs. Holt and Mrs. Askin, then proceed through the Main Hall and the Central Gallery meeting guests informally.

The American Ambassador and Mrs. Clark follow.

12.55 p.m.   The President and Mrs. Johnson, the Prime Minister and Mrs. Holt, the Premier and Mrs. Askin and the American Ambassador and Mrs. Clark walk to the vestibule and leave the Art Gallery.

The President, the Prime Minister, the Premier and the American Ambassador enter the President's car.

Mrs. Johnson, Mrs. Holt, Mrs. Askin and Mrs. Clark enter Mrs. Johnson's car.

Other members of the party enter their vehicles.

1.00 p.m.   The journey to Circular Quay West commences.

The American flag is struck as the President's car moves.

Route: Art Gallery Road,
          Queen's Square,
          Macquarie Street,
          Bridge Street,
          Loftus Street,
          Circular Quay.
                    Distance 1.3 M.

Harbour Cruise

1.15 p.m.   The President and Mrs. Johnson, the Prime Minister and Mrs. Holt, the Premier and Mrs. Askin, the American Ambassador and Mrs. Clark arrive at Circular Quay West.

In an open space near the President's car, Rhonda Elliott, an 11-year old girl (daughter of a deceased serviceman) is presented to the President by the Premier.

She hands to the President a scroll containing a message from the children of Sydney and a book bound by technical college students.

Near the steps the Premier presents Mr. W. H. Brotherson, President of the Maritime Services Board and Mrs. Brotherson.

Mr. Brotherson presents the Master and crew of the launch "Captain Phillip."

The President and Mrs. Johnson, the Prime Minister and Mrs. Holt, the Premier and Mrs. Askin and the American Ambassador and Mrs. Clark join the Governor and Lady Cutler aboard the launch.

Four assigned members of the President's party embark on the launch.

"Captain Phillip" departs for a cruise of Sydney Harbour.

After moving from the Quay the launch travels past a line of decorated boats in Farm Cove.

The photographers who have travelled in "Captain Phillip" are disembarked.

Lunch is served on board.

2.15 p.m.   The launch returns to Circular Quay West.

The party disembarks.

The Governor and Lady Cutler enter the Vice-Regal car and depart for Sydney Airport.

The President, the Prime Minister, the Premier and the American Ambassador enter the President's car.

Mrs. Johnson, Mrs. Holt, Mrs. Askin and Mrs. Clark enter Mrs. Johnson's car.

Other members of the party join their vehicles.

The journey to Sydney Airport commences.

Route: George Street,
Park Street,
College Street,
Oxford Street,
Flinders Street,
Anzac Parade,
Gardeners Road,
Florence Avenue,
King Street,
O'Riordan Street.
Distance 8.8 M.

Departure from Sydney Airport

2.50 p.m.   The President and Mrs. Johnson, the Prime Minister and Mrs. Holt, the Premier and Mrs. Askin and the American Ambassador and Mrs. Clark arrive at Sydney Airport.

The American flag is broken.

The President and Mrs. Johnson are met by the Governor and Lady Cutler.

Prior to boarding the aircraft the President and Mrs. Johnson are farewelled by—

The American Consul General and Mrs. Capella.
The Premier and Mrs. Askin.
His Excellency the Governor and Lady Cutler.

During the farewells the Prime Minister and Mrs. Holt and the American Ambassador and Mrs. Clark board the aircraft by the front steps.

Other members of the party board the aircraft by the rear steps.

2.53 p.m.   The President and Mrs. Johnson enter the aircraft by the front steps.

The American flag is struck.

3.00 p.m.   The President's aircraft departs for Canberra.

INDEX